Fuel Rights Handbook

21st edition

Alan Murdie, Asma Mohyuddin, Carri Swann and
Energy Action Scotland

Child Poverty Action Group

Child Poverty Action Group works on behalf of the more than one in four children in the UK growing up in poverty. It does not have to be like this. We use our understanding of what causes poverty and the impact it has on children's lives to campaign for policies that will prevent and solve poverty – for good. We provide training, advice and information to make sure hard-up families get the financial support they need. We also carry out high-profile legal work to establish and protect families' rights. If you are not already supporting us, please consider making a donation, or ask for details of our membership schemes, training courses and publications.

Published by Child Poverty Action Group
30 Micawber Street
London N1 7TB
Tel: 020 7837 7979
staff@cpag.org.uk
www.cpag.org.uk

A CIP record for this book is available from the British Library

ISBN: 978 1 915324 08 5

Child Poverty Action Group is a charity registered in England and Wales (registration number 294841) and in Scotland (registration number SC039339), and is a company limited by guarantee, registered in England (registration number 1993854). VAT number: 690 808117

Cover design by Colorido Studios
Typeset by DLXML, a division of RefineCatch Limited, Bungay, Suffolk
Printed in the UK by Partridges UK Ltd, NN14 2WD

The authors

Energy Action Scotland is the national charity working for an end to fuel poverty and to promote warm, dry homes for all in Scotland.

Asma Mohyuddin is a debt and civil litigation solicitor at the Mary Ward Legal Centre in London.

Alan Murdie LL.B Barrister is a lawyer and is the chairman of Nucleus Legal Advice in London.

Carri Swann is a welfare rights worker at CPAG.

Acknowledgements

The authors would like to thank everyone who has contributed to this book. In particular, thanks are due to Chantal German, Joanne Porter and the team at Energy Action Scotland for their invaluable comments and assistance. Thanks too to the previous authors for their contribution to the book.

We would also like to thank Nicola Johnston for editing and managing the production of the book, Anne Ketley for the index and Louise Heath for proofreading the text.

The law covered in this book was correct on 1 October 2024 and includes regulations laid up to this date.

Contents

Abbreviations

ADP	adult disability payment
AFIP	armed forces independence payment
CA	carer's allowance
CDP	child disability payment
CSP	carer support payment
CTC	child tax credit
DAP	debt assignment protocol
DLA	disability living allowance
DNO	distribution network operator
DWP	Department for Work and Pensions
ECO	Energy Company Obligation
EHU	Extra Help Unit
EPC	energy performance certificate
EPG	energy price guarantee
ESA	employment and support allowance
EST	Energy Saving Trust
FCA	Financial Conduct Authority
FITs	feed-in tariffs
HB	housing benefit
HEEPS	Home Energy Efficiency Programmes for Scotland
IHD	in-home display
IS	income support
JSA	jobseeker's allowance
PC	pension credit
PIP	pesonal independence payment
PV	photovoltaic
RHI	Renewable Heat Incentive
SEG	Smart Export Guarantee
SLC	Standard Licence Condition
SVT	standard variable tariff
UC	universal credit
WHD	Warm Home Discount

Chapter 1

Introduction

This chapter covers:
1. Sources for your rights (below)
2. The structure of the industry (p2)
3. How to use this book (p6)

1. **Sources for your rights**

The sources to refer to for your rights in respect of the supply of gas and electricity are as follows.

- Primary legislation – principally Acts of Parliament, the Gas Acts 1986 and 1995, the Electricity Act 1989, the Competition and Services (Utilities) Act 1992, the Utilities Act 2000, the Energy Act 2010, the Energy Act 2011, the Energy Act 2013, the Consumer Rights Act 2015, the Energy Prices Act 2022 and the Energy Act 2023. The legislation specific to Wales and Scotland is also passed by the devolved governments.
- Statutory instruments – regulations made under legislation – eg, the Electricity (Standards of Performance) Regulations 2015 No.699 and the Gas and Electricity (Consumer Complaints Handling Standards) Regulations 2008 No.1898.
- Law reports and court decisions of judgments and rulings by the higher courts which clarify the scope and meaning of words and phrases used in legislation. These are especially important in determining whether a contract has been offered, made or rejected.
- Licences – the electricity and gas supply licences set out the conditions that all energy suppliers must adhere to to supply energy to consumers – these are known as the 'Standard Licence Conditions'. Ofgem (the Office of Gas and Electricity Markets) issues, and monitors compliance with, licences. Ofgem acts on behalf of the Gas and Electricity Markets Authority (GEMA). GEMA has a duty to protect consumer interests, promoting effective competition wherever possible, and has powers under the Competition Act 1998.
- Your contract with your supplier – if you get your fuel from one of the licensed gas or electricity suppliers, the rules governing your relationship with that

supplier are in the legislation, in statutory instruments or arise from the contract. The standard terms and conditions for your contract must be freely available from the supplier.

- Codes of practice – each supplier publishes its code of practice or statement of policy for various processes, such as complaint handling, marketing or billing and the installation of smart meters. The codes are not legally binding by themselves, but they do indicate how a supplier should and usually will behave in certain situations. You may be able to get a remedy against a supplier's practice or action simply because it breaches one of the relevant codes of practice. Copies of the complaint handling code of practice should be made available to any person who requests it and should also be published on the supplier's website. Advisers should have the relevant codes for the main suppliers in their locality. The codes may also be referred to in legal proceedings.[1] They are periodically revised and modified with set dates for reviews and changes in codes.[2]
- The gas and electricity minimum standards of performance regulations (see p5). These set minimum standards for the performance of gas and electricity supply companies and distributors for various situations.
- Decisions of the Energy Ombudsman – although not binding, these indicate the standards expected and can help assess the adequacy of responses to complaints.
- Objectives for tackling fuel poverty are set by the Energy Act 2013. A fuel poverty indicator for England was adopted[3] and the Scottish government's Fuel Poverty (Target, Definition and Strategy) (Scotland) Act was passed in 2019.
- Regulations and directives previously issued by the European Union. These provide a framework within which much of the law governing energy is constructed. Existing provisions continue to apply for the time being, and some measures ensuring consistencies in billing have been adopted and incorporated into electricity supply licence terms and conditions.[4]

2. **The structure of the industry**

Since 1999, all gas and electricity customers in Great Britain have been able to choose the company from which they buy their fuel supplies.

Gas

The gas industry is split into three parts: shippers, transporters and suppliers. Each is required to be licensed. Shippers buy gas and put it into the pipes, transporters convey it to your meter and suppliers sell the gas to you (shipping and supplying is normally done by different parts of the same company).

The main effect for you is that the supplier who sends the gas bill does not actually handle the gas itself – that is the role of the transporter. If there is a gas leak, for example, you should contact the transporter, not the supplier. The main gas transportation network is split up into four companies:

- Cadent Gas covers areas of England: the North West, North London, the East of England, South Yorkshire and the West Midlands;
- Northern Gas Networks covers the North of England;
- SGN covers Scotland and southern England (including South London);
- Wales and West Utilities covers Wales and South West England.

There are also a number of independent gas transporters that have various smaller networks throughout Britain.

Electricity

Private companies involved in the generation, transmission, distribution and supply of electricity are required to be licensed. There are no longer regional monopolies.

National Grid owns the electricity transmission system in England and Wales. Local distribution is still done by one of the 14 former public electricity companies. The supply of electricity is entirely commercial and therefore (in theory) competitive, and you can select the supplier from whom you buy your electricity and switch from one to another.[5] In most cases, this is a choice between one of six major suppliers and a number of smaller licensed energy companies, unless you are able to access a smaller supply or establish some degree of independent generation of energy. Companies are obliged to make available a written statement giving a summary of your rights as a customer and the expected standards of performance in law when supplying you with power.[6]

Contracts

Your gas and electricity are supplied under a contract or deemed contract from the supplier/s of your choice. 'Dual-fuel' contract suppliers can supply both gas and electricity under contract.

In theory, contracts are reached by negotiation and agreement. In practice, most terms and conditions are presented to consumers on a 'take it or leave it' basis. The use of contracts means that finding out about your rights is now far more complicated than it was before privatisation of the energy industry.

You need to look particularly at the contract given to you by your supplier. There will be important differences in the terms of the contract when compared with those of other suppliers. Basic principles of contract law are governed by common law relying on definitions established in judicial decisions from the courts over many years. These operate within the wider framework of regulatory law.

Ofgem: the industry regulator

Ofgem, the Office of Gas and Electricity Markets, was set up in March 2000 to replace the separate regulatory bodies for the gas and electricity industries and unify their functions. The main aims of Ofgem are promoting competition in all parts of the gas and electricity industries and regulating them. Its principal objective is to protect the interests of existing and future electricity and gas consumers. The Secretary of State for Energy Security and Net Zero has powers to establish electricity and gas price reduction schemes in Great Britain under the Energy Prices Act 2022.

Ofgem's regulatory functions include granting licences, monitoring performance, regulating the areas where competition is not so effective (such as the monopoly on pipes and wires) and determining the strategy for the fuel industry.

The Domestic Gas and Electricity (Tariff Cap) Act 2018 introduced a price cap which came into force on 19 July 2018. The act's primary focus is to protect consumers on default tariffs. Ofgem is required regularly to review the level of the cap and, towards the end of the initial period, to review market conditions more widely. The Energy Prices Act 2022 enables the government to reduce the prices charged by suppliers of electricity and gas, with a requirement that the benefit will be passed on to the end user – ie, the final customer.[7] Details are set out in regulations.[8]

Ofgem has the power to fine energy companies for regulatory breaches. Those requirements are principally set out in the Electricity Act 1989, Gas Act 1986 and regulated company licenses, and include rules on sales practices and complaint handling.

If an energy supply company becomes insolvent, Ofgem has authority to protect the interests of consumers facing a loss of supply. Ofgem will appoint a new supplier – known as the supplier of last resort – for the affected customers as quickly as possible to ensure minimum disruption.

Consumer protection

Since privatisation, a series of official bodies have been responsible for consumer protection including Consumer Focus, Energywatch and the National Consumer Council. Since April 2014, this role has been carried out by Citizens Advice and Citizens Advice Scotland – known as Citizens Advice consumer service. In addition to providing dedicated telephone lines providing advice on consumer protection, these bodies also run campaigns to promote awareness of energy saving measures and ways of reducing bills.

Consumer Scotland is the advocacy and advice body for gas and electricity in Scotland.

Unfair terms in supply contracts can be made subject to enforcement activity by a range of authorities including the Competition and Markets Authority, Ofgem and local authorities' trading standards departments (see Chapter 14).

Companies can voluntarily choose to compensate consumers who lose out as a result of their wrongdoing. The Energy Ombudsman can also order suppliers to pay consumers up to £10,000 if it deems complaints about sales, bills, supply or switching supplier to be legitimate.

Consumers also have the right to bring their own private legal actions as individuals. You may also seek redress for some aspects of wrongdoing, such as breach of contract, through the civil courts.

Minimum standards of performance

Minimum standards of performance for energy suppliers and distributors are set out in regulations. The Electricity (Standards of Performance) Regulations 2015, the Gas (Standards of Performance) Regulations 2005 and the Electricity and Gas (Standards of Performance) (Suppliers) Regulations 2015 set out minimum standards of service for consumers.[9] If a supplier or distributor fails to meet these standards, compensation is payable to the consumer. Section 13 of the Supply of Goods and Services Act 1982, as amended by the Consumer Rights Act 2015,[10] provides that a term requiring that a service to a consumer is undertaken with reasonable competence and skill must be included in every consumer contract. Standards of performance may also be applied by regulation to heat networks or district heating system.[11]

Debtor protection ('breathing space' scheme)

The debt respite scheme ('breathing space') gives certain legal protections to consumers with debts.[12] There are two types of breathing space.
- A standard breathing space is available to anyone with problem debt who engages with a debt adviser. It gives them legal protections from creditor action for up to 60 days. The protections include pausing most enforcement action and contact from creditors, and freezing most interest and charges on their debts.
- A mental health crisis breathing space is available to someone who is receiving mental health crisis treatment. It has stronger protections, lasting as long as the person's mental health crisis treatment, plus 30 days. Protections, prescribed in legislation, include a restriction on enforcement procedures in respect of the fitting of prepayment meters.[13]

The scheme is set to be reviewed by the Treasury with a report published by 4 May 2026.[14]

---

3. **How to use this book**

Unless specified, everything in this book applies to both gas and electricity. The main legislation applies to Great Britain (England, Wales and Scotland) only. Northern Ireland is not covered. Where the law in Scotland differs, this is noted.

Use this book principally for help in tackling fuel poverty. That has always been this *Handbook's* main purpose. It does not aim to cover policy issues or examine background information in detail, but to act as a guide to the rights of consumers and the actual problems that consumers face in practice.

This *Handbook* consists of two parts:

- chapters dealing with various topics. Look at the contents at the beginning of each chapter and consult the index to find the topic you are seeking. References at the end of each chapter give the sources of information so that you can use them as an authority for actions; chapters 13 and 14 also give a number of key legal sources where further information can be found;
- appendices, which contain supplementary material and information.

There are references in the text to other CPAG handbooks which provide more detail on specific topics, such as benefits and dealing with debt. Where detailed information is required, such as eligibility criteria for benefits, consult the specialist handbook.

Abbreviations are used in the text to save space. The abbreviated term is explained in full the first time it is used in a section and on pviii there is a list of all the abbreviations used.

The references in the text and notes to Standard Licence Conditions refer to the versions which were consolidated on 5 January 2024 (available on the Ofgem website). Generally, the numbering for gas and electricity is the same, but where it differs, both numbers are shown.

Notes

1. **Sources for your rights**
   1 *Laverty and others v British Gas Trading* [2014] EWHC 2721 (Ch)
   2 Ofgem, *Code Modifications/Modification Proposals with Ofgem*, 15 October 2021
   3 DECC, *Fuel Poverty: a framework for future action*, Cm 8673, July 2013
   4 The Electricity and Gas (Internal Markets) (No.2) Regulations 2020 No.1401 implementing EC Directive 2019/944

2. The structure of the industry

5 For a good summary of the position, see the review in *R (on the application of Peak Gen Top Co Ltd and others) v Gas and Electricity Markets Authority* [2018] All ER (D) 123 (Jun)

6 Reg 22 E(SP) Regs; reg 10 EG(SP)S Regs

7 s19 EPA 2022

8 The Energy Bill Relief Scheme Regulations 2022 No.1100

9 E(SP) Regs; G(SP) Regs; EG(SP)S Regs

10 s60 and Sch 1 paras 37 and 38 (c) CRA 2015

11 Sch 18 Part 11 para 62 EA 2023

12 DRS Regs

13 Reg 7(h) and (i) DRS Regs

14 Reg 40 DRS Regs

Chapter 2

. . . .

Choosing a supplier

This chapter covers:
1. Suppliers and switching (below)
2. Marketing and sales (p13)
3. Contracts (p16)

---

1. **Suppliers and switching**

Six major suppliers provide approximately 78 per cent of consumer supply. They are British Gas/Scottish Gas, E.ON Next (incorporating npower), ScottishPower, SSE/OVO Energy, EDF and Octopus Energy (incorporating Bulb and Shell).

Some customers take both gas and electricity from the same company – this is known as 'dual-fuel supply' (see p18).

Switching suppliers

To get the best price, many people switch to a different supplier. If you are on a standard variable rate tariff, you could save money if you move on to a fixed rate deal with your existing supplier or another supplier. **Note:** at the time of writing, energy companies had fewer fixed-rate tariffs available.

Switching supplier is normally fairly simple. During a 14-day cooling-off period you can change your mind about switching. Suppliers are responsible for managing the switch. To protect consumers when switching, there are guaranteed standards of performance set in law.[1] If suppliers fail to meet these standards, they must pay you compensation. The standards related to switching are:[2]

- a switch must be completed within five working days of the new supplier receiving sufficient information to proceed with the switch. The compensation is £30;
- an erroneous transfer payment can be made if a switch is made in error by a supplier. The amount you get, and which supplier pays it, depends on the circumstances. There is a template letter to help with erroneous transfers on the Citizens Advice website;[3]

- your old supplier must issue a final bill, subject to you providing a meter reading as required, within six weeks of no longer having the responsibility to supply you.[4] The compensation is £30;
- if you have any outstanding credit, your old supplier must refund you within 10 working days of the final bill. The compensation is £30.

How do you change supplier?

1. Gather information about your current tariff, payment method and usage over the last year – you can find this on your fuel bill or on your annual statement from your supplier. Use this information to compare suppliers. You can scan the QR code on your bill using a smart phone or tablet. This contains all the information you need to compare and switch supplier.

2. When you have found the best deal for you, agree a contract with a new supplier. The new supplier will write to you within seven working days to confirm the details. The new supplier will contact your current supplier for you.

See the sections below on price, comparing prices and other issues to consider before making a decision.

3. The new supplier will request a meter reading from you so that your old supplier can issue your final bill and your new supplier has the correct figure for your new bill. The new supplier will inform you of the date when your supply will be switched.

4. Check your final bill from your old supplier.

On your gas or electricity bill there is a gas meter point reference number (known as an 'Mpan number') or an electricity supply number which is unique to your address. Once you have signed a contract which bears this number with the new supplier, the switch can take place – this should be sorted out between the new and old suppliers, although you can help by providing the M number or the supply number. Your present supplier may object to the transfer if you are in debt, but you are still entitled to switch where you have a prepayment meter and your debt is below £500 per fuel. For credit customers, if your debt is above £100, a new supplier has discretion whether to take you as a customer and may do so if you have previously been a customer with a good credit history. The new supplier may not accept you if your debt is older than 28 days. In such cases, it may be difficult to switch until that debt is cleared.

It is also possible to stay with your current supplier and switch to a different tariff that is better for you.

Ofgem has a principle to help consumers make informed choices about which tariff they choose. There are specific principles on tariffs[5] which say that tariffs must be clear and easily comprehensible, easily distinguished from each other and easily compared with other tariffs from the same supplier.

The following sections look at what to consider when deciding whether to switch and which supplier to choose. The Citizens Advice website also has information pages on how to switch suppliers, a customer performance rating of suppliers and a price comparison tool.[6]

Price

Price is often the most important factor in deciding which supplier to use. See Chapter 4 for the types of meters and payment methods available.

When considering what suppliers are offering, look at the following.

- **Standing and unit charges** – suppliers are currently only allowed to have one structure for tariffs: a unit rate (or unit rates for time of use tariffs) and a standing charge (which can be zero). Complex tiered tariffs are banned. A 'standing charge' is a fixed monthly/daily amount you pay the supplier for maintenance and other costs, such as maintaining the connection to the power network. 'Unit charges' are the monetary amount chargeable for each unit of electricity or gas consumed and may vary considerably between suppliers, payment methods or product types.
- **Payment methods** – be careful when looking at figures provided by suppliers. Some advertised savings are calculated based on you switching supplier and changing to a different method of payment – eg, from quarterly cash payments to monthly direct debit. You might get the same benefit that switching would give you with your existing supplier by switching to a different payment method. Any difference in charges for different payments must genuinely reflect the cost of the differences to the supplier.[7]
- **Penalty on default** – suppliers do have the power to penalise customers who do not pay their bills by disconnecting them, but typically they attempt to switch customers to prepayment (see Chapter 8). If you have difficulty paying all your bills on time, avoid such terms if possible. See the section on unfair terms on p19.
- **Supplier flexibility** – you might want to change your payment method or some other aspect of your supply. For example, if you are on a prepayment meter, your current supplier might not allow you to change to a credit meter, whereas a new supplier might be more flexible. Ask different suppliers for this information.

Some suppliers offer dual-fuel supply deals (see p18) when you take both gas and electricity from them. Consider whether this would be the best for you. In particular, the convenience of a single supplier might outweigh any price disadvantages for some people.

When deciding whether to switch to a new fuel supplier, it is best to have all the information on prices, terms and conditions so you can compare them and find the deal that best suits you. All suppliers must publish their standard terms and conditions. Citizens Advice publishes the customer performance standards of energy suppliers, which you should refer to before switching.[8]

Note that suppliers are not allowed to enter contracts through agents who require advance payments – you do not need an agent to get you a new contract and you should not use one.

Comparing prices

To make a meaningful price comparison, you need to collect information about your current supplier, payment method, annual usage and bills for the last 12 months, and then use the 'ready reckoner' comparison tables which provide a broad overview. Several services exist that allow you to compare prices.

The potential savings depend on where you live (as prices vary in different parts of the country), whether you want to switch gas or electricity supplier or both, the payment method and whether you have time of use or 'off-peak' tariffs. Not all suppliers operate in all parts of the country.

There are many websites that compare gas and electricity prices. It is not possible to compare all available tariffs on comparison websites, as some tariffs are unavailable online, such as dynamic teleswitched or various time of use tariffs. **Note:** the 'radio teleswitch', which affects customers with meters and tariffs dependent on this, is due to end by the end of June 2025, although this is likely to be extended due to the low rate of smart meter installations. Websites must state that they cannot compare all tariffs,[9] as they should be transparent about the market coverage they offer to energy customers. It is important to remember that there are more websites out there. Check that any website you use has the Ofgem Confidence Code logo. The Confidence Code sets out the minimum requirements that a provider of an internet domestic gas and electricity price comparison service (service provider) must meet to be, and remain, accredited by Ofgem. The prices quoted for energy deals on the accredited websites, and the information given about the offers, must be shown in a fair and unbiased way. For an up-to-date list, check Ofgem's website.[10]

The Confidence Code requires the service provider to be independent of any gas or electricity supplier. It must be a company which runs its own website and uses its own tariff database and calculating system, not merely hosting those of another service provider, and must try to include price comparisons for all available domestic tariffs. The service provider may take commission from energy suppliers, but this must not influence the information given.

Are there other issues to consider before switching supplier?

Although the price offered by a new supplier may suit you, the other terms and conditions may not so check them carefully (see p18 for other terms and conditions to consider).

Before switching supplier, consider the performance and complaint-handling record of the new company. Energy companies must publish regular, detailed complaints data in a common format so that companies can be compared.

You may be entitled to a Warm Home Discount (see p47). Before switching, check that your new supplier offers the discount, and that you are eligible under its criteria.

Switching supplier with existing debts

If you have owed any money for less than 28 days (eg, you have not yet paid a recent bill), you are normally able to change supplier in the usual way, and the debt is transferred to the new supplier.

Switching supplier while in debt after 28 days is subject to a protocol agreed between Ofgem and energy suppliers. If you have a credit account and a debt, your supplier can stop you from moving to a new supplier until you pay off your debt – this is referred to as 'debt-blocking'. If your current supplier blocks your request to switch, it must advise you on the best tariff for you, managing your debt and energy efficiency.[11]

If you have a prepayment meter, you should be able to switch supplier and transfer a debt of up to £500 per fuel.[12] This happens under a debt assignment protocol (see p124).

You may be able to get help to clear energy debts by using funds and grants (see Chapter 12).

Switching supplier with a smart meter

Having a smart meter does not affect your right to switch supplier. If your new supplier uses the same meter as your old supplier, you should be able to carry on using it. If you have an in-home display (IHD), it shows near real-time information about your energy use. Your new supplier will need to reprogram your meter with your new tariff before the IHD can show what you are spending.

There are problems with first generation (SMETS1) smart meters losing meter functionality on change of supplier. Suppliers must inform you of this risk. If you have a SMETS1 meter, it may lose some smart functionality depending on which energy supplier you switch to, although the IHD should still work and show real-time information about your energy use.

SMETS1 meters were expected to be upgraded and enrolled into the collection system by end of December 2023. At the time of writing, this has not happened and there is actually an increasing number of smart meters not operating in smart mode. There is no update on this from Ofgem.

Second generation smart meters (SMETS2) – installed from 2018 onwards – can be operated by all suppliers. The widespread adoption of these meters is expected to result in greater consumer engagement and stronger competition between energy suppliers due to the increased ease of switching. The roll-out of smart meters has been slower than originally anticipated and a 'full' roll-out is not expected until the end of 2025.

Smart Metering Equipment Technical Specifications (SMETS)

SMETS is the standard for the minimum common functionality of smart meters. SMETS1 meters use two-way communications between suppliers and their customers to provide smart services. SMETS1 meters contain a SIM card that connects to the supplier over the cellular network. However, suppliers have implemented different communications technologies meaning that these meters often lose their smart capabilities when customers switch supplier. In such circumstances, the SMETS1 meter can no longer benefit from two-way communications, effectively rendering it a 'dumb' meter.

The second generation of meters (SMETS2) operate using national data and communications infrastructure and aim to operate consistently for all consumers with SMETS2 meters, regardless of their supplier. This means that there is no loss of communication when a SMETS2 meter switches to a new supplier.

Switching supplier when your supplier goes out of business

If your supplier goes out of business, Ofgem will move you to a new supplier through the 'supplier of last resort' process. The new supplier will contact you with details of your new tariff. Once with that new supplier, you can switch to another supplier or to a different tariff in the usual way. You do not have to pay an exit fee/termination penalty. Ofgem's advice is not to switch until the new supplier has contacted you. This makes the process smoother and makes it easier to get any credit balance you may have refunded.[13]

2. Marketing and sales

Marketing standards

Standard Licence Condition (SLC) 25 of the gas and electricity supply licences regulates face-to-face and telephone marketing and sales activities of licensed suppliers and their representatives. If a supplier fails to meet SLC 25, Ofgem can act (see Chapter 14).

SLC 25 has a principle relating to sales activities. Suppliers and their representatives must not mislead or use inappropriate tactics, including high-pressure sales techniques, when selling or marketing to customers. SLC 0 requires suppliers (and their representatives) to take all reasonable steps to treat consumers fairly.

These broad principles relate to how suppliers behave, provide information and carry out customer service processes. They also relate to how suppliers identify vulnerable customers and respond to their needs. These standards apply to all dealings between you and your supplier.

The standards of conduct cover four broad areas.[14]

- **Behaviour towards consumers:** suppliers must behave and carry out any actions in a fair, honest, transparent, appropriate and professional manner.
- **Providing customers with information:** suppliers must provide information (whether in writing or orally) which:
  - is complete, accurate and not misleading (in terms of the information provided or omitted);
  - is communicated in plain and intelligible language, with more important information being given appropriate prominence;
  - is related to products or services that are appropriate to the customer to whom it is directed;
  - in terms of its content and how it is presented, does not create a material imbalance in the rights, obligations or interests of the supplier and customers in favour of the supplier;
  - is sufficient to enable customers to make informed choices about their supply of energy by the supplier.
- **Process:** the supplier must:
  - make it easy for you to contact it;
  - act promptly and courteously to put things right when it makes a mistake;
  - ensure that customer service arrangements and processes are complete, thorough, fit for purpose and transparent.
- **For customers in vulnerable situations:** the supplier must:
  - try to identify the customer in a vulnerable situation, in a manner which is effective and appropriate;
  - apply the standards of conduct in a manner that considers any vulnerable situation.

Information on charges

The supplier or its representative must provide you with an estimate of the annual charges for the supply of fuel under the offered contract. A written copy must be supplied for your own records if you subsequently enter the contract.

Compensation for mis-selling

Compensation may be payable in some cases of mis-selling; however, there is no statutory requirement within the current SLCs for suppliers to award compensation for mis-selling and Ofgem does not currently have the same statutory powers as other regulators (eg, the Financial Conduct Authority) to seek redress on your behalf. However, Ofgem does protect consumers by monitoring the energy market and acting where there is evidence that companies have breached their obligations to consumers. Large penalties have been issued and, where possible, redress has been achieved for consumers.

The Energy Act 2013 makes provision for consumer redress orders which may be used in the future to provide an alternative to lengthy and expensive litigation.[15] The government has agreed to consider the possibility of giving Ofgem stronger and more clearly defined powers of redress in mis-selling cases.

The safest way to switch without the risk of mis-selling is to use an Ofgem-accredited switching service (see p11). See Chapter 14 for the remedies available if any of your rights have been breached. To complain about a possible breach of a licence condition or a code of practice, complain first to the supplier, preferably in writing. There is a letter template on the Citizens Advice website to help you make a complaint.[16]

If you need to, you can then take it further with Citizens Advice consumer service or your local authority trading standards department.

Cancelling a contract

The normal rule in contract law is that if you sign a contract you are bound by the terms and conditions, even if you have not read it.[17] Ofgem regulations ensure a 14-day cooling-off period, from the date of signing a contract, during which you have the right to cancel your contract.

If a contract for electricity supply also includes providing goods or services (eg, energy efficiency measures), the charges for each must be separately identified.[18]

Misrepresentation

A signed contract may be set aside for misrepresentation at common law. This means that where you are led to enter a contract because of a false statement of fact (not opinion or law), you are entitled to have the contract set aside (the legal term for this is 'rescinded'). A mis-statement of fact may be deliberate, negligent or innocent, but if the statement is untrue and induces you to enter a contract, then a legal remedy will exist. A court can order that a contract is rescinded and may also award damages where there has been financial loss. In practice, a supplier may be prepared to cancel a contract if there has been a misrepresentation rather than face legal proceedings. In most cases, the sums involved are £10,000 or below, the level for the small claims court procedure (see Chapter 14).

A similar rule applies to written contracts where the terms of the contract are false or misleading. If a signature is obtained from you because the nature or contents of the agreement are wrongly described, it is not considered binding.

Regulations also ban traders in all sectors from using unfair commercial practices towards you that prevent you from making free and properly informed buying decisions. The Consumer Protection from Unfair Trading Regulations 2008 apply to electricity and gas sales.[19] These prohibit misleading actions whereby traders supply false information or omit to provide certain information. False information includes statements which are untrue or where the overall presentation of information in any way deceives or is likely to deceive the average consumer.

Liability can also attach where the commercial practice omits material information, hides information or provides information in a manner that is unclear, unintelligible, ambiguous or untimely, or fails to identify its commercial intent.

The test is whether, because of the misleading information or omission, the commercial practice 'is likely to cause the average consumer to take a transactional decision s/he would not have taken otherwise' – eg, you are misled into deciding to purchase the product or service.[20]

Offences under the regulations may be prosecuted by trading standards departments and liability may attach to both energy suppliers and subsidiary companies that act on their behalf when selling energy products.[21]

Forging of signatures

Forging of signatures is a criminal offence.[22] Compensation is payable in a case where forgery can be shown. The police or trading standards could act in a case of forgery.

3. **Contracts**

Electricity

Supply contracts

A '**supply contract**' is an agreement for the supply of electricity to domestic premises. A supplier must not supply electricity to such premises except under a supply contract. Electricity suppliers' licences place conditions on what they are allowed to put in supply contracts (eg, terms regarding security deposits) – these are dealt with where appropriate throughout this book. This means that, when offering you a contract and supplying you with electricity, a supplier must conform to its licence conditions or face action from Ofgem (see Chapter 14).

Supply contracts are governed by Standard Licence Conditions (SLCs) 22 and 23. Contracts must be in a standard form, although there can be different forms for different areas, cases and circumstances. They must set out all the terms and conditions on which the supplier relies. If the contract is for goods and services as well as the supply of electricity, the charges for each must be separately identified. Copies of each kind of supply contract used by a supplier must be published in a manner to secure adequate publicity. Copies must be sent to Ofgem and be available on request.[23] The contract should be provided 'within a reasonable period after receiving the request'. You should also be able to get information from the supplier summarising the terms of its supply contracts, with details of anything likely to influence you when deciding whether to take up a contract.

Gas

Supply contracts

Gas suppliers supply domestic customers with gas under the terms of a contract or a 'deemed contract' (see below).[24] Suppliers must have a 'scheme' setting out the principal terms of contracts. The principal terms include details of the prices to be charged for gas and state if there may be any fluctuation in the amount of the bill due to variations in the amount charged by transporters to suppliers for transporting gas to your premises.

Details of the principal terms must be published in a way that will likely bring them to the attention of the customers concerned.[25] Ofgem must be kept informed of the suppliers' principal terms and any variation. You are entitled to a copy of the principal terms on request, and the supplier must send one within a reasonable time of receiving a request.[26] Supply contracts must be in writing.[27]

The terms of contracts may vary between different types of customer, and between different areas, but not so there is undue preference or discrimination between customers.[28] Any difference in terms and conditions offered to customers on different payment methods must reflect actual cost differences.[29] Suppliers increasingly set prices nationally with less local variation than with electricity. Ofgem and the industry openly discuss the need for 'cost-reflective pricing'.

A contract may be for an indefinite period, known as an 'evergreen contract', or for a fixed term. When a contract is due to end, the supplier must offer you a new contract and inform you of the terms of the 'deemed contract' that would apply if no new contract is agreed. A supplier may not enter a contract with you if another person has a contract with a different supplier for gas supply to the same premises,[30] unless that contract will have expired, or have been breached or terminated before you require a supply.

Contracts for other services

Gas suppliers can offer contracts for gas supply together with other services – eg, service pipes or energy efficiency goods or services. Such contracts must clearly and separately identify the charges made for the supply of gas and the other services. These contracts may have different terms and conditions to contracts offered under published 'principal terms'.

Deemed contracts for gas and electricity supply

A '**deemed contract**' is a contract where a customer takes a supply of electricity or gas or both in a manner other than under a contract that has been expressly entered into with a supplier. A deemed contract may arise where a contract has ended without being formally renewed or where there are new occupiers who do not formally arrange a new supply contract. Deemed contracts for electricity and gas are governed by Schedule 4 paragraph 3 of the Utilities Act 2000, Schedule 6 of the Electricity Act 1989, Schedule 2B of the Gas Act 1986 and SLCs 7 and 23 and apply to situations where the supply of electricity and gas continues but the original contract is no longer in force. In such cases, you remain obligated to pay, and the supplier is expected to behave reasonably with respect to terms and conditions and charges. Suppliers are also under a duty to use 'reasonable endeavours' to inform you of the terms and act reasonably towards you and must not impose onerous terms.

A deemed contract continues until such time as a new contract is agreed between you and the supplier or you end the contract by leaving the premises. Schedule 6 paragraph 3(1) of the Electricity Act 1989 and Schedule 4 paragraph 3 of the Utilities Act 2000 also state:

> Where an electricity supplier supplies electricity to any premises otherwise than in pursuance of a contract, the supplier shall be deemed to have contracted with the occupier (or the owner if the premises are unoccupied) for the supply of electricity as from the time…when he began to supply electricity.

Dual-fuel supply contracts

Some suppliers offer both gas and electricity – this is called 'dual-fuel' supply. There are obvious potential advantages of convenience for you if you take a dual supply. Sometimes, there may also be discounts for taking a dual supply. But check whether you will actually get a discount or other advantages – eg, you may have to deal with separate arms of the same company for your gas and electricity, which might feel little different from being supplied by two different companies. Apart from convenience, there are no other automatic benefits of having a dual supply, and you should check the terms of your contract in the same way as for any other fuel contract. Dual-fuel supply contracts must comply with both sets of provisions for gas and electricity.

If you are paying one company a single amount for both your gas and electricity, be aware of how your payment is treated. Normally, the charges for gas and electricity should be separately specified in a bill. If you make only one payment towards the cost of both gas and electricity and do not specify which fuel you are paying for, the supplier can decide which to put the payment towards. For example, if you owe £10 for gas and another £10 for electricity and then pay £10 to the supplier, the supplier can choose whether to put this towards paying off your gas or electricity bill. On the other hand, if you state clearly before you pay that you are paying the £10 specifically for, say, gas, the supplier is normally bound by your decision. If you have a dispute over this, contact your supplier in the first instance, or contact Citizens Advice consumer service. Discounts available on dual-fuel supply contracts should normally be applied directly to a unit rate or a standing charge in clear monetary terms.[31]

Contractual terms

- **Period.** A contract is either for a fixed term of weeks, months or years or it is indefinite. The latter is known as a 'rolling contract' or an 'evergreen contract'.

All contracts can be terminated on 28 days' notice, but there may be a financial penalty if you terminate a fixed-term contract early. Check with the supplier whether there would be a penalty for early termination and how much it would be. In some cases, a supplier may be prepared to exercise its discretion and drop a penalty which might otherwise be imposed for early termination. Early termination is covered by SLC 24.

- **Special services.** Some contracts may be offered together with other services, such as improving the energy efficiency of your home. The costs of the supply and the services should be listed separately, including any credit element, so you can compare prices with other suppliers.
- **New products.** Some electricity suppliers offer special products. Some suppliers guarantee to buy enough electricity from environmentally renewable sources or from coal-generated sources to supply your needs. Other suppliers may offer a variety of combined deals. You need to do careful research and detailed calculations to ensure that a decision to switch supplier is based on your circumstances, usage, location and payment method.

Unfair terms

Compared with most other businesses, gas and electricity are heavily regulated (see Chapter 14). Therefore, there should be less chance of contracts containing unfair terms. If you come across a term which might be unfair, you can initially complain to Citizens Advice consumer service.

However, regulation is not a guarantee. You may still need to assert your rights against unfair terms. Even better, you can try to avoid unfair terms by checking over a contract before signing it. All terms are approved by the Department for Energy Security and Net Zero and reviewed by Ofgem.

An '**unfair term**' causes a significant imbalance in the parties' rights and obligations under the contract to the detriment of the consumer – ie, if a contractual term goes too far in favour of the supplier, it is unfair. An unfair term is not binding on you.[32] Unfair terms are governed by the Consumer Rights Act 2015 (see p255).

Contractual terms must be written in plain, intelligible language.[33] If there is any doubt about the meaning of a particular term, the interpretation most favourable to you should be used.[34]

The courts consider that a doctrine of good faith applies in examining any term and whether it is unfair. In *Director General of Fair Trading v First National Bank plc* [2001], Lord Bingham stated:[35]

The requirement of good faith in this context is one of fair and open dealing. Openness requires that the terms should be expressed fully, clearly and legibly, containing no concealed pitfalls or traps. Appropriate prominence should be given to terms which might operate disadvantageously to the customer. Fair dealing requires that a supplier should not, whether deliberately or unconsciously, take advantage of the consumer's necessity, indigence, lack of experience, unfamiliarity with the subject matter of the contract, weak bargaining position...It looks to good standards of commercial morality and practice.

If you come across possibly unfair terms or unintelligible language, you can refer the contract to the Competition and Markets Authority or Ofgem (see Chapter 14). The civil courts can also grant a remedy known as a 'declaration' to establish a term's legal effect or meaning. Compensation, including for inconvenience and distress, may be awarded.[36]

Terminating a contract

Some gas and electricity contracts can be terminated on 28 days' notice. If you feel you made a mistake in switching to a particular supplier, you can give 28 days' notice and either return to your original supplier or sign a contract with a new one. However, always check your contract – if it was for a fixed period, there may be a penalty for early termination. Some suppliers also offer long-term contracts that provide a 'reasonable' termination payment.

Penalties for terminating a contract

In some cases, a supplier demands payment of a fee or penalty for early termination of a contract, but several restrictions are placed on any power to impose such penalties.

SLC 24 provides that a termination fee shall not be demanded in the case of a contract of indefinite length (ie, a rolling contract, not a fixed-term contract) or where you have notified the supplier of an intention to terminate where the supplier has unilaterally changed or intends to change the contract. Other situations where a supplier may not impose a fee or penalty include where a property is sold, you move out or where a contract of supply is for more than 12 months or is for an initial fixed-term period, followed by a period of indefinite length.

A supplier may be prepared to waive a penalty in certain circumstances at its discretion – eg, where a contract must be ended because you have gone into care. The supplier may also accept a lesser sum in full and final settlement of any claim for the penalty as a way of settling legal proceedings (see p122).

There may also be an argument that a supplier is under a duty to mitigate its loss (ie, take steps to reduce any loss) from early termination of the contract. The duty to mitigate is imposed at common law in a case of breach of contract. A supplier cannot just demand any sum in compensation or damages it sees fit simply because you have broken the contract in some way. The duty to mitigate losses should be referred to in correspondence to settle such a dispute.

Notes

1. Suppliers and switching
1 EG(SP)S Regs as amended
2 Regs 6ZA and 6ZB EG(SP)S Regs
3 citizensadvice.org.uk/consumer/
   template-letters/letters/energy/letter-
   to-complain-to-energy-supplier-about-
   transfer-without-consent
4 Regs 6CA EG(SP)S Regs
5 Condition 25 SLC; EA 1989; GA 1986
6 England and Wales:
   citizensadvice.org.uk/consumer/
   energy/energy-supply/get-a-better-
   energy-deal/switching-energy-supplier
   Scotland: citizensadvice.org.uk/
   scotland/consumer/energy/energy-
   supply/get-a-better-energy-deal/
   switching-energy-supplier
7 Condition 27.2A SLC
8 citizensadvice.org.uk/consumer/your-
   energy/get-a-better-energy-deal/
   compare-domestic-energy-suppliers-
   customer-service
9 Ofgem, *Decision on Implementing the
   CMA's Recommendation to Remove the
   Whole of Market Requirement*, July 2018
10 ofgem.gov.uk/consumers/household-
   gas-and-electricity-guide/how-switch-
   energy-supplier-and-shop-better-deal/
   compare-gas-and-electricity-tariffs-
   ofgem-accredited-price-comparison-
   sites
11 Condition 14.9 SLC
12 Ofgem debt assignment protocol for
   prepayment meter customers letter, 12
   May 2015, ofgem.gov.uk/publications-
   and-updates/decision-make-
   modifications-gas-and-electricity-
   supply-licences-reform-switching-
   process-indebted-prepayment-meter-
   customers-debt-assignment-protocol
13 ofgem.gov.uk/information-consumers/
   energy-advice-households/what-
   happens-if-your-energy-supplier-goes-
   bust

2. Marketing and sales
14 Condition 0 SLC
15 s144 and Sch 14 EA 2013

16 citizensadvice.org.uk/consumer/
   template-letters/letters/energy/letter-
   to-complain-about-energy-mis-selling
17 See *L'Estrange v Graucob* [1934] 2 KB
   394
18 Condition 22.4 SLC
19 Reg 2 CPUT Regs
20 Regs 5(2)(b) and 6(1)(a) CPUT Regs
21 *R (on the application of Surrey Trading
   Standards) v Scottish and Southern Energy
   plc* [2012] EWCA Crim 539
22 Forgery and Counterfeiting Act 1981

3. Contracts
23 Condition 22.8 SLC
24 Condition 22.1 SLC
25 Condition 23.1 SLC
26 Condition 22.8 SLC
27 Condition 22.4 SLC
28 Condition 0 SLC
29 Condition 27.2A SLC
30 Condition 14 SLC
31 Condition 1.2 SLC
32 s62(2) CRA 2015
33 s68 CRA 2015
34 s69(1) CRA 2015
35 [2001] UKHL 52, [2002] 1 AC
36 *West and Another v Ian Finlay &
   Associates (a firm)* [2014] EWCA Civ 316

Chapter 3

· ·

The right to a supply

This chapter covers:
1. Who is entitled to a supply (below)
2. Getting your electricity supply connected (see p29)
3. Getting your gas supply connected (p33)
4. Security deposits (p37)
5. Disruption of supply (p41)

This chapter assumes you are legally responsible ('liable') for your fuel supply. Check Chapter 5 to ensure that you are in fact responsible for the supply.

· ·

Has your supplier gone out of business?
If your energy supplier goes into administration, your supply is protected. Ofgem will move you to a new supplier. Your supply should be preserved and the tariff and price plan will not change. Any credit balance should be preserved. You may switch supplier (if you want to) once a new supplier is appointed.

· ·

1. **Who is entitled to a supply**

Electricity

Contract suppliers have a duty to offer a contract when they receive a 'request from a domestic customer'[1] and will supply electricity if the contract is accepted. Usually, it is quite clear that you are requesting a supply but, to ensure it is treated as valid, your request should include:
- details of the premises to be supplied; *and*
- the day on which the supply should commence; *and*
- maximum power to be supplied, if this differs from that normally required by an ordinary domestic customer; *and*
- the minimum period for supply; *and*
- any reference to a continuing supply already established at the premises (where relevant).

Under Standard Licence Condition (SLC) 22, the supplier must offer to enter into a domestic supply contract with you as soon as is reasonably practical. The duty to provide a supply is only enforceable by Ofgem because it is contained in the supplier's licence, not in the Electricity Act 1989 (see Chapter 14). The contract must be in a standard form containing all the terms and conditions, including the price and your right to terminate the contract. Suppliers must behave in a 'fair, honest, transparent, appropriate and professional manner' and provide you with complete and accurate information.[2]

If you accept the offer of a contract, the supplier must provide, and continue to provide, a supply of electricity until the contract is properly terminated, subject to certain exceptions detailed below. If the supplier fails to fulfil its obligations in the contract, this is a breach of contract that may give rise to legal remedies, including a right to compensation.

It is worth noting that the SLCs for contract suppliers make no mention of 'occupier' or anything else connected with your right to occupy the place where you want a supply of electricity. The term **'occupier'** is not defined in the SLCs but covers any person who occupies any premises legally, whether paying rent or some other charge, or paying nothing or persons remaining in premises where the tenant has gone into care or has died (see p28 for squatters).[3]

A small minority of customers are covered by **tariff suppliers** that have different legal provisions. Tariff suppliers' duties to supply are set out in the Electricity Act 1989, whereas contract suppliers' duties with their individual tariffs are set out in the licence granted to them by Ofgem. Tariff suppliers have a statutory duty to supply you if:[4]

• you are an owner or occupier of the premises; *and*
• you request a supply by giving notice in writing.

Under the regulations, a customer is also defined as any person acting on behalf of the person in need of a supply and any person needing a supply at more than one premises.[5] Relatively few customers are still subject to former tariff arrangements. There is, however, provision for an alternative status for these old tariff customers. This is known as a 'special agreement' under section 22 of the Electricity Act 1989. The terms and conditions which bind both you and the tariff supplier are the terms of the agreement rather than those under the Act. Under a tariff supplier's licence, a special agreement is referred to as a 'contract', so that a special agreement must be a designated supply contract and must conform to the licence conditions covering the form and content of designated supply contracts (see p30).

There are two circumstances in which the question of a special agreement might arise.

• A supplier has the discretion to grant you a special agreement if you ask for one when you give notice requiring a supply.

- You could be required to enter into a special agreement by the supplier if it is 'reasonable in all the circumstances'.

A notice is deemed effective from the day it was given unless it was given after 5pm (in which case it takes effect from the next day).[6] In practice, most domestic supplies are now by way of contract and reference may be made to the SLCs.

Guaranteed standards of performance

Electricity distribution companies are subject to guaranteed standards under the Electricity (Connection Standards of Performance) Regulations 2015.[7] They set out the amounts that electricity distributors must pay you in compensation for failure to meet specified standards of performance in respect of the connection services. The amount differs between standards.

If the distributor fails to meet the standards of connection, you are entitled to receive a payment. The amount depends on the situation and the length of delay.[8] For example, if a quotation for a connection is not provided within five working days, the supplier is liable to pay you £15 for each subsequent day, including the day on which the quotation is provided.[9] (Various sums may become payable where a supplier fails to provide a schedule of works and starting times for different types of connection, within various time periods.[10]) From 1 April 2024, the prescribed sums for each financial year beginning with 1 April 2024 are calculated by:

- adjusting the sums specified in column three of Schedule 1 of the Electricity (Connection Standards of Performance) Regulations by the percentage increase or decrease in the CPIH (consumer prices index) published for the January preceding the financial year for which the adjustment is made in comparison to the CPIH published for January 2023; *and*
- rounding the resulting figure to the nearest £5.

These payments can be made direct to you or via your electricity supplier.

Disputes about whether compensation is payable may be referred by Citizens Advice consumer service to Ofgem.[11] Ofgem must determine the dispute within 80 days, unless satisfied that special reasons apply for extending the period.[12] Ofgem must issue a timetable and the list of documents received for determining the dispute and may also hold an oral hearing.[13] In Scotland, Consumer Scotland may take up this role.[14]

Exceptions to the minimum standards of performance

In a number of situations the minimum standards of performance do not apply.[15] These include where:

- you inform the supplier or operator that you do not wish any action to be taken or you agree another course of action;

- you give information at the wrong address or outside the hours that the supplier or operator has specified;
- it is not reasonably practicable for the supplier or operator to act in a prescribed time owing to severe weather conditions, an industrial dispute or the action of a third party;
- the supplier or operator has been unable to gain access to premises;
- you have failed to pay the relevant charge after receiving a notice or where you have committed a criminal offence;
- there are exceptional circumstances beyond the control of the supplier or operator.

Liability for danger and harm arising from interruptions in supply

Suppliers, distributors, meter operators and smart meter communication providers are bound by the Electricity Safety, Quality and Continuity Regulations 2002[16] which lay down a duty to prevent danger from any works or equipment used in supplying electricity. Meter operators and smart meter communication providers are also bound by the regulations for the purposes of sharing and supplying information as appropriate.[17]

'**Danger**' includes danger to health or danger from electric shock, burn, injury or mechanical movement, or from fire or explosion, as a consequence of the generation, transmission, transformation, distribution or use of energy. It covers dangers to both humans and domestic and farm animals.[18] Generators, distributors and meter operators are placed under a wide duty to ensure that all electrical equipment is sufficient for the purposes and the circumstances in which it is used and that it is constructed, installed, used and maintained so 'as to prevent danger, interference with or interruption of supply' so far as is reasonably practicable.[19] A special duty is imposed on equipment such as a meter situated in your home.[20] A duty of co-operation between generators, distributors and suppliers is also imposed under the regulations.[21]

A distributor may also be liable for acts and omissions that amount to negligence, though technical and expert evidence may be needed to establish this – eg, in the case of a fire. Mere breaches of the regulations applying to distributors do not give rise to action for breach of statutory duty,[22] but where harm results from negligence an action for damages may be available. The Divisional Court ruled:[23]

> ...where there has been a breach of the Regulations by a given distributor, that does not mean that it was culpably negligent; however, such a breach may point to a breach of the duty of care although in practice evidence which goes beyond the mere breach may well be required to establish negligence. A simple failure consistently to perform or discharge a statutory duty with no reasonable explanation or justification therefore may provide grounds for a claim in negligence.

However, it is still necessary to prove that the breach of the regulations actually caused the harm or damage and is directly linked. If the harm would have occurred even if the duty had been carried out, there is no sustainable claim.

Gas

You have the right to be connected to the gas network by a gas transporter (see Chapter 1). Gas mains and service pipes are owned by gas transporters. There are a number of gas transporters, but National Grid Gas is the main one. A gas transporter has a statutory duty to connect your premises to the gas mains if:
• you are the owner or occupier (an 'occupier' is a person who occupies any premises legally, whether or not they pay rent or some other charge); *and*
• the premises are within 23 metres of the nearest gas main.

Where there is an existing domestic supply, you obtain a contract by contacting the gas supplier. Under SLC 22, a gas supplier must offer to enter into a gas supply contract with you after receiving a request. The offer must be made 'within a reasonable time' of receiving the request.

A domestic supply contract or a deemed contract must include:[24]
• the identity and address of the supplier; *and*
• the services provided (including any maintenance services) and any service quality levels to be met; *and*
• if a connection is required, when that connection will take place; *and*
• the means by which up-to-date information on all applicable tariffs and any maintenance charges may be obtained; *and*
• any conditions for renewal of the contract.

If there is no existing supply, you must inform the transporter in writing that you require a supply of gas at the premises concerned (there will normally be a standard form). You are charged for the costs of connecting your premises to the network (see p34) unless you choose to have independent contractors do the work for you (see p31).[25]

All gas suppliers are under an obligation to supply gas under a contract to new customers (ie, owners or occupiers who request a supply) whose premises are already connected to the gas mains either directly or by a service pipe. The 'obligation to supply' is a condition of each supplier's licence. You cannot enforce the obligation to supply without the help of Ofgem because it is contained in the supplier's licence rather than in legislation. All gas suppliers must publish the principal terms of the contracts available from them and bring them to the attention of customers.[26] These cover notifications and the terms and conditions under which gas is supplied and are regulated by conditions within the supplier's licence, which is regulated by Ofgem.

If you have been supplied under the terms of a contract initially, the supplier must continue to supply you until either the contract comes to an end or it is terminated. A gas supplier continues to supply gas under the terms of a deemed contract if your contract has come to an end (see p17).[27] A deemed contract must not:

- have a fixed-term period for the contract to run or have a termination fee;[28] *or*
- require you to give notice before you are able to switch supplier, except where there is a change in ownership of the premises. The supplier must invite you to enter into a further contract to run immediately following the expiry or termination of your existing contract.

The obligation on a gas supplier to supply you with gas under the terms of a deemed contract could also arise if a supplier is ordered to do so by Ofgem. Ofgem has the power to suspend or revoke a supplier's licence. If this happens, or if a supplier is unable to continue to supply gas (eg, if it goes into liquidation), Ofgem can order an alternative supplier to supply you instead.

There are minimum standards for supply, distribution and reconnection of gas, under the Gas (Standards of Performance) Regulations 2005[29] and the Electricity and Gas (Standards of Performance) (Suppliers) Regulations 2015. Such an order is treated as the equivalent of a judgment in the county court in England and Wales or as if it were an extract registered decree arbitral bearing a warrant for execution issued by the sheriff court.[30]

There are minimum guaranteed standards of performance for the service provided by gas transporters, and prescribed sums payable to a customer for compensation for failure to meet those standards for any disruption without seven days' notice.

From 2021, there are extra guaranteed standards of performance including:[31]

- reducing the reinstatement period where there is a planned gas supply interruption;
- an obligation to provide hot meals and access to hot water during interruptions that last longer than 48 hours where more than 250 homes are affected together with the payment of a prescribed sum for failure to comply;
- an obligation to include disconnection in the standards on responses to land enquiries;
- setting prescribed periods under which the transporter must meet the minimum standards, except where notice is given;
- automatic compensation for customers affected;
- uncapped payments under the standard for supply restoration following unplanned interruptions.

Exceptions

There are situations where a supplier/transporter does not have a duty to supply or continue to supply. A supplier/transporter is entitled to refuse to connect a supply or to disconnect a supply which has already been given in certain circumstances – see p31 for electricity and p35 for gas.

Squatters

Squatting in residential buildings is a criminal offence.[32] Suppliers are entitled to refuse to supply fuel to anyone committing an offence. Furthermore, an arrangement of a supply by a trespasser might be taken as evidence that an offence under the Act is being committed by demonstrating an intention to live in the building.

However, the offence is only committed where a person is deemed to be 'living' in the residential building and does not affect squatted premises which involve non-residential activities – eg, where a residential building is used other than for living purposes, such as storage, commercial purposes or cultural purposes such as exhibitions. Nor does it apply to occupancy of non-domestic dwellings such as former shops or pubs.

The legislation considers 'living' as meaning residing for any period of time, but much will depend upon how courts approach cases on their facts, as living at an address is not simply determined by the amount of time spent at a property.[33]

The precise scope of law has yet to be clarified on such matters as temporary occupation in cases where a person may have a settled home elsewhere or cases of mistake.

There may be other situations where a supply is possible without involving a person living in the building – eg, where a trespasser occupies a garden or yard or is living in a non-domestic part of a building such as a garage.

People who had a temporary previous lease or licence are specifically excluded from the offence of squatting[34] and remain entitled to a fuel supply. If an electricity or gas supply is disconnected without lawful authority while a temporary resident or lawful occupier is in place, either by a landlord or energy supplier, an injunction may be sought to restore the supply (see Chapter 14).

Travellers

Local authorities are provided with guidance on practical aspects of site provision and management.[35] The guidance contains the standards for the supply of electricity, gas and water to sites. Standards vary according to the type of site provided. Failure to have regard to the guidance by a local authority may be challenged by judicial review (see Chapter 14).

The local council as landlord is responsible for the supply and is entitled to resell electricity, although its charges cannot exceed the maximum resale price for electricity (see p221).

Mobile home and caravan sites

Sites for mobile homes are licensed by local councils under the Caravan Sites and Control of Development Act 1960. Model standards for the provision of electricity and water are issued to local councils. Local authorities can decide what conditions, if any, to attach to caravan site licences. Guidance to local councils is in very broad terms and suggests that sites should be provided with an electricity supply sufficient to meet all reasonable demands of the caravans situated on them. There is no guidance for the supply of gas.

Always look at the provisions in the caravan site licence to determine if your site owner is obliged to provide a supply of electricity to your site. Site owners may resell electricity to you, but cannot charge more than the maximum resale price (see p221).

If there is no provision for electricity on your site, there is nothing to stop you from applying for a supply to be connected if you are the owner or occupier of a mobile home or caravan. However, note the possibility of significant connection charges.

Contact the National Association of Caravan Owners (nacoservices.com) for further advice.

2. Getting your electricity supply connected

Notice

To obtain a supply of electricity you must contact the supplier with your request. You can do this online, by completing the supplier's standard application form or by writing a letter. However, most suppliers do not always require written notice and will connect your supply if you telephone to request a supply or if you call into a customer service centre. You may wish to safeguard your rights by making your request in writing or by following up your telephone request in writing. Keep a copy in case a dispute arises.

Most application forms contain all the necessary details. If you are writing a letter or email but are not sure what maximum power is required, it should be sufficient to make clear that you want an ordinary domestic supply. If you have a preference, also specify what type of meter you would like and how you wish to pay for your supply (see Chapter 4).

If you choose not to give information about yourself (eg, about your previous address or creditworthiness), you may be asked for a security deposit (see p37). You do not have to give information about other people living in your home, but note that liability for the bill may be decided on who signs the application form or letter (see Chapter 5).

If your requirements on the application form are acceptable (ie, if the supplier is prepared to supply you on your choice of meter, method of payment or other terms and conditions), a contract supplier will offer you a contract that you can accept or reject.

When your supply is connected

If your home has been previously supplied with electricity, you should be given an appointment within two working days for your supply to be connected and a meter installed. If the appointment is not made within the specified time, you are entitled to automatic compensation of £65.[36] If the appointment is made and not kept, you are entitled to automatic compensation of £65.

If your home has never previously had a supply of electricity, and you make a written request for an estimate of the charges of connection, this should be sent within five working days if the work is simple, or within 10 working days if the work is complicated. You are entitled to a compensation payment if the estimate is not sent within these time limits.[37] For a contract supplier, connection times depend on how quickly you respond to its offer of a contract.

If you experience unreasonable delays in getting your supply connected, contact Citizens Advice consumer service.

Conditions of supply

Standard Licence Conditions (SLCs) apply to all suppliers of electricity. A supplier is under a duty to offer you a contract containing standard terms and conditions that comply with its licence conditions – eg, SLC 22.3 provides that fuel will not be supplied unless it is done so under a domestic supply contract or a deemed contract. Once you sign a contract, you are legally bound by its terms, but if you think any are unfair or unreasonable, Ofgem has the power to stop a supplier enforcing any term incompatible with its licence conditions. See p16 for contractual terms and p255 for details about unfair terms.

Charges for connecting a supply

Connecting an electricity supply is carried out by a distribution network operator (DNO), which is licensed to distribute electricity through cables and provide connections to premises. Distributors are not responsible for meter readings or billing – your energy supplier does this.

You may be charged for the connection of a supply. Details of connection charges are available from the DNO's website.

To obtain a connection, you need to notify the DNO, within a reasonable time, of the details of the premises to be connected, the time the connection is required and (to the best of your knowledge) the maximum power to be supplied.

A DNO should provide you with a quotation for connection to its distribution system, but does not normally fit a meter until instructed to do so by your chosen electricity supplier. When providing a quotation, the DNO normally specifies that you need to nominate a supplier before connection takes place, and preferably before accepting the quotation. It is advisable to appoint and sign a contract with an electricity supplier at least 28 days before the date you want the electricity to flow.

Getting your supply connected

When accepting a connection from the DNO, you or your supplier are obliged to enter into a connection agreement. A '**connection agreement**' outlines the rights and obligations associated with the connection.

On connection, the DNO is obliged to maintain the connection for as long as required and to repair or replace any electrical lines or plants when necessary (except when you may be responsible for any damage to the equipment).

If you are dissatisfied with any aspects of connection, complain in the first instance to the company concerned (see Chapter 14).

Independent electrical engineers may be employed for certain electrical connection work. A list of independent electrical engineering companies can be obtained from a local DNO. The National Electricity Registration Scheme lists companies registered as competent for electrical connection work at lrqa.com/en/utilities/national-electricity-registration-scheme-ners.

Cables and wires running between your meter to your electrical appliances are not covered by any connection agreement with the DNO and the electricity supplier – a qualified electrician would have to install them for you. Customer protection equipment such as fuse boxes and switches are also not covered by the connection agreement.

When you can be refused a supply

Electricity suppliers may refuse to supply electricity, refuse to connect a supply to new premises, disconnect an existing supply, or refuse to reconnect a supply which has been disconnected. Disconnection for arrears is dealt with in Chapter 8.

You may be refused a supply for a number of reasons. Some of these reasons applying to tariff suppliers were set out in the Electricity Act 1989, but grounds for refusal are now set out in the SLCs for contract suppliers. All of the following reasons apply.

- You refuse to take a supply on the terms offered.
- You have not paid your bill for any electricity supplied, standing charges, meters and any connection charges within 28 working days of the date of the bill (see p97). You are entitled to two working days' notice of disconnection. Your supply may only be disconnected to the premises where the debt arose.[38] Every supplier is required to have a code of practice on payment of bills, including procedures to deal with customers who have difficulty paying (see p100).[39] The terms of your supplier's code could protect you from disconnection by setting out alternatives. A list of codes and links with them for suppliers is published on the Ofgem website or they are available on request from your supplier.
- You did not pay your bill for any of the above charges at your previous address. The supplier may refuse to connect a supply at your new address. The supplier

is not entitled to payment of your arrears from the next occupier of your previous address. Similarly, you cannot be held liable for debts left by previous occupiers of your new address.

- You have not paid a security deposit within seven days of being sent a notice requiring you to do so and the requirement of a security deposit is reasonable in the circumstances.[40]
- You refuse to accept a supply under a 'special agreement' under the Electricity Act 1989.
- Your premises are already being supplied by another electricity supplier under arrangements which have not expired or been terminated.
- Supplying you with electricity would, or might be, unsafe – eg, because the wiring is in a dangerous condition.
- You refuse to take your supply through a meter.
- There has been damage or tampering to a meter and the matter has not been remedied (see Chapter 9).
- The supplier is prevented from supplying you by circumstances outside its control – eg, if it has been prevented from laying cables because of extreme weather conditions.
- It is not reasonable in all the circumstances. This is a 'catch-all' provision. Most disconnections or refusals to supply will be on one or more of the grounds above, but this provision might be used if those grounds no longer apply – eg, you are no longer in arrears but the supplier is insisting that you can only be supplied through a prepayment meter for future consumption. If you refuse to accept a prepayment meter, the supplier must demonstrate that disconnection is the only reasonable alternative. The supplier cannot use this catch-all provision unless it first gives you seven days' notice of the intention to disconnect.

Where you have a prepayment meter, in addition to providing you with information about its alternative cheapest tariff, the supplier must inform you that, as a domestic customer with outstanding charges, you may be able to switch supplier by agreeing with a new supplier to have the outstanding charges 'assigned' – ie, transferred. Sums under £500 should be capable of such assignment.[41]

Note: suppliers are not entitled to disconnect for alleged non-payment if the amount is genuinely in dispute. **'Genuine dispute'** means a genuine dispute between you and the licensee as to whether you are liable to pay certain charges which have been demanded by the licensee. This should be evidenced in writing, which can include emails or hard copy letters or communications which should be signed and dated.[42] A dispute may be referred to Ofgem for determination by you or by Citizens Advice consumer service.[43]

3. **Getting your gas supply connected**

If you move into a home which is not physically connected to the gas mains network, you will need to arrange a supply. There are three ways to get connected to a gas supply.

- Using a gas transporter that is licensed to supply gas through pipes and is under a duty to provide a gas connection where it is economical to do so. You are charged for the connection costs (see p30). There is also a charge if you ask the transporter to lay any pipes which are needed. In addition, you may be asked to pay a security deposit to the transporter.
- Through a licensed gas supplier that can arrange for pipes to be laid by either the local gas transporter or an independent contractor. The gas supplier can pass on the charge for providing the connection and the pipework. This charge may include an arrangement fee.
- Through a qualified independent engineer installing pipes between a meter and a gas appliance. Once your home is physically connected to the supply network, the gas transporter becomes responsible for the maintenance of the pipe. Ownership of the pipe concerned is transferred to the transporter.

If your home is already connected to the gas mains network, you need to enter into a contract with a gas supplier for your supply of gas. You do not have to use the supplier that previously supplied the premises, although you may be deemed to have a contract with it if you do nothing about it (see Chapter 5). If you do not know who the current supplier is, you can find out through findmysupplier.energy or by calling 0870 608 1524. Usually, the shipper and the supplier are the same company. If not, you are referred to the shipper, who can tell you who the supplier is. See also Chapter 2 for details of contracts for the supply of gas.

When your supply is connected

In practice, the gas supply often remains connected after the previous occupier moves out, so there is often no interruption to the supply. If the supply of gas has been disconnected, the gas supplier you have chosen arranges a date to reconnect. It must do this as soon as reasonably practicable. If the meter has been removed, the supplier arranges with the transporter for a meter to be installed or may itself provide you with a meter. If there is already a meter in place, the supplier will make arrangements with the owner of the meter (usually National Grid) for the existing meter to remain in place. This does not apply when the meter in place is not suitable.

The relevant key standards state that when you request a gas supply:

- if a survey visit is required, contact is made within two working days to arrange an appointment which will be within three working days, or later if you requested;

- following such a visit, a quotation for providing a supply is sent within five working days of the visit if the property is adjacent to a public highway in which there is a suitable gas main, or otherwise within 20 working days;
- if no visit is required, a quotation is sent within five working days of receipt of the enquiry.

If the supply can be monitored remotely via a smart meter, the supplier must offer to provide or make available accurate monthly billing information based on consumption.[44]

In the event of an unreasonable delay, take the matter up with Ofgem.

The Gas Industry Registration Scheme lists companies registered as competent for gas connection work. It can be found at lrqa.com/en/utilities/gas-industry-registration-scheme-girs.

Charges for connecting a supply

You should not normally be charged for the connection of a gas supply when you are taking over the supply at premises that are already connected to the gas network. An exception is where the connection has been capped for over 12 months and a new connection is needed.

A gas transporter charges for connecting your premises to the gas network for the first time. You may be charged for all work done on your home and land and for any pipe which has to be laid, although the first 10 metres of the pipe that is not on your property is covered by the gas transporter. For domestic premises within 23 metres of a relevant gas main, a transporter is obliged to connect premises and provide and install the necessary assets for connecting the premises.[45] For premises further than 23 metres from a main or consuming more than 2,196,000 kWh, the gas transporter quotes a price for connection. All work to connect this type of premises is chargeable.

Potential customers may face high connection charges, particularly if a new supply is required some distance away from the gas mains network or if costs cannot be shared between a number of new customers. Information and quotations can be obtained from National Grid. Any charges should be checked closely to see if the expenditure is reasonably incurred; it may be possible to contest some charges.

Charges are based on National Grid recovering the cost of laying new mains within a five-year period, less a discount reflecting the anticipated revenue from the new customers. You may be charged if your gas main is less than five years old at the time that you ask for a gas supply. You may be asked to finish paying for the costs of having the supply put in, but the extra charge only applies if:

- the amount of the charge is no more than anyone previously supplied from the main has been charged; *and*
- the transporter has not yet recovered the full cost of the main; *and*

- the transporter has supplied you with any information you reasonably requested concerning the cost of the main, the date it was laid and how much has been paid by previous consumers.

This charge does not apply if you are an owner or occupier who has paid contractors to connect the supply.

Ofgem has a duty to resolve disputes about connection charges.

When you can be refused a supply

A gas supplier may refuse to connect a gas supply to a new address, may cut off an existing supply or refuse to reconnect a supply which has been disconnected. A gas transporter may refuse to connect your premises to the gas supply network and may also disconnect your supply in a number of circumstances. Disconnection for arrears is dealt with in Chapter 8.

A **gas supplier** may cut off your supply in the following circumstances.
- You do not pay your bill within the 28 days following the date of the bill (see p97). You are entitled to a minimum of seven days' notice of the supplier's intention to disconnect. **Note:** there is no right to disconnect when the bill is genuinely in dispute. You may be protected from disconnection by conditions in your supplier's licence.[46]
- You switch supplier and you owe money to your previous supplier, in which case the previous supplier can assign some of your debt to your new supplier.[47] The new supplier cannot refuse debt assignment and will collect the debt through a prepayment meter. However, the new supplier is unlikely to cut off the supply. What is termed '**debt blocking**' – the refusal to take on a debtor with a prepayment meter as a customer by a new supplier – should not take place if a debt is £500 or less, following the debt assignment protocol (see p124).[48] **Note:** there is no right to disconnect when the bill is genuinely in dispute. You may be protected from disconnection by conditions in your supplier's licence.
- You do not pay a reasonable security deposit or agree to accept a prepayment meter within the seven days following the supplier's request for a deposit. A supplier's right to request a security deposit is a condition of the supplier's licence.[49]
- You fail to take your supply through a meter.
- You fail to keep a meter belonging to you or to someone other than the gas supplier or transporter in proper order.
- You intentionally damage or interfere with gas fittings, service pipes or meters (see Chapter 9).
- You do not/no longer require a supply of gas.
- You do not/no longer require the use of meters or other gas fittings belonging to the supplier/transporter. You are entitled to 24 hours' notice.

- Your supply has been reconnected without the consent of the supplier.
- Supplying you with gas would, or might, involve danger to the public.
- A gas transporter or another gas supplier has disconnected your supply and is under no obligation to reconnect your supply.
- A gas shipper has prevented the transfer of gas to your premises.
- A supplier's ability to supply its customers would be significantly prejudiced if it were to offer you a supply.
- There are circumstances beyond the supplier's control.[50]

A **gas transporter** may refuse to connect your premises to, or may disconnect your premises from, the gas supply network in the following circumstances.
- Your premises are not within the transporter's authorised area.
- Your premises are not close enough to a gas main – ie, the premises are not within 23 metres of the transporter's gas main or could not be connected by a service pipe to a transporter's gas main.
- A transporter asks you to install a meter as near as possible to its main and you refuse. This applies when:
    – gas was not previously supplied to your premises by the transporter; *or*
    – a new/substituted pipe is required; *or*
    – the meter is to be moved.
    Note that the transporter may permit you to install a meter in alternative accommodation or in an external meter house, but this discretion lies with the transporter.
- You use gas improperly or deal with gas so as to interfere with the efficient conveyance of gas.
- The transporter is concerned to prevent the escape of gas or it suspects there may be an escape of gas.
- You fail to take your supply through a meter.
- You do not pay a reasonable security deposit. A gas transporter can request reasonable security for the initial connection of the supply.[51]
- You fail to keep a meter belonging to you or to someone other than the gas supplier or transporter in proper order.
- You intentionally damage or interfere with gas fittings, service pipes or meters (see Chapter 9).
- You do not/no longer require a gas supply. You are entitled to 24 hours' notice.
- You do not/no longer require the use of meters or other gas fittings belonging to the transporter. You are entitled to 24 hours' notice.
- The transporter is prevented from connecting you or maintaining your connection by circumstances not within its control.
- Supplying you with gas would, or might, endanger the public.
- A pipe laid by the owner or occupier of the premises is not fit for purpose.

4. **Security deposits**

What is a security deposit

A 'security deposit' is money requested by electricity or gas suppliers as a condition of providing a supply. Gas transporters can also ask for a security deposit as a condition of connecting your premises to the mains network.

Deposits may be cash deposits, or a secure method of payment such as a direct debit or a prepayment meter. Conditions in the supplier's licence will limit the circumstances and amounts of deposits that may be requested. Suppliers cannot ask for a security deposit if you agree to a prepayment meter, unless your conduct makes it reasonable to ask for a deposit.[52]

A security deposit must not exceed a reasonable amount.[53]

Deposits are held separately from your normal account and are used to offset costs for the supply of electricity or gas, usually following a disconnection. See p40 for the return of a deposit.

When you can be asked to pay a security deposit

Electricity

Rules for security deposits are set out in Standard Licence Condition (SLC) 27.
Electricity suppliers may ask for a security deposit if:

- you refuse to take a supply through a prepayment meter; *or*
- it is not practicable to install a prepayment meter; *and*
- it is reasonable in all the circumstances to do so (a tariff supplier's power is expressed as the right to ask for reasonable security, which amounts to the same thing).

When a contract supplier asks for a security deposit, it must inform you of when it will be returned (see p40) and of the power of Ofgem to determine any dispute about the deposit. As an alternative, action through the county court (or sheriff court in Scotland) can be used to recover a deposit which is owed to you and which a supplier refuses to refund (see Chapter 14).

If you are a new customer, you may be routinely asked for a security deposit by electricity suppliers, particularly if:

- you refuse to provide information about previous addresses, or you cannot demonstrate a satisfactory payment history at a previous address and you do not otherwise provide sufficient information about your creditworthiness; *or*
- you have been assessed as having a poor credit rating; *or*
- you are in short-term accommodation. You should not be treated as being in short-term accommodation if you are a secure or assured tenant.

Suppliers cannot insist on both a prepayment meter and a security deposit (see p40).

Your supplier's code of practice on the payment of bills should include a statement of its policies on security against the non-payment of future bills. The code should also state if and how policy differs for new and existing customers and what, if any, credit-vetting procedures are used. It should indicate the steps you need to take to improve your creditworthiness or to ensure that security is no longer needed.

Security deposits may also be required from existing customers if:

- your payment plan has broken down. You will almost always be able to have a prepayment meter as an alternative. Remember that the requirement for a security deposit must be reasonable. If the reason your payment plan broke down was that you could not afford it, you may be able to negotiate another payment plan instead of either having to pay a security deposit or having a prepayment meter installed (see Chapter 7); *or*
- theft, tampering or damage to meters/equipment has occurred (see Chapter 9).

It is unlawful for a supplier to discriminate unduly in how it supplies customers, including in respect of security deposits – eg, if people who live on a particular estate are asked for a security deposit. Contracts are individual agreements and a supplier should avoid discriminating against any particular class of customer. A complaint about this may be made to the supplier and also to the Energy Ombudsman. Details of the codes may be referred to in court if a case leads to legal action.[54]

Gas

Gas suppliers can, under the terms of their licence, incorporate demands for security deposits in their contracts and 'deemed contracts' (see p17). Deposits may be cash deposits, or a secure method of payment such as a direct debit or a prepayment meter. Conditions in the supplier's licence will limit the circumstances and amounts of deposits that may be requested. Suppliers cannot ask for a security deposit if you agree to a prepayment meter, unless your conduct makes it reasonable to ask for a deposit.

A gas supplier must not require payment of a deposit where 'it is unreasonable in all the circumstances of the case to require that customer to pay a security deposit.[55] The wording indicates that the supplier is required to consider the individual circumstances of a customer and cannot apply a blanket policy of imposing deposits upon particular classes of customers or certain areas. The deposit must not exceed a reasonable amount.[56]

Your supplier's code of practice on the payment of bills will provide a statement of its policies. All suppliers are subject to the same obligations in respect of security deposits. If you do not provide the security requested, the supplier may refuse to connect your supply, if you are a new customer, or disconnect your supply, if you are an existing customer. Security can mean:

- you pay a cash deposit; *or*
- you join a gas payment plan; *or*
- a prepayment meter is fitted or your smart meter is switched to prepayment mode.

Suppliers may ask for security if:
- you live in short-term accommodation. You should not be treated as being in short-term accommodation if you are a secure or assured tenant; *or*
- you have a poor payment record at your present or last address; *or*
- you are a new customer and you do not give proof of your identity or your last address.

A gas transporter is also entitled to ask for a security deposit if connecting premises to the gas pipe network where the premises are no more than 23 metres from the gas main and it will be laying the pipes needed for the connection. The transporter may refuse to supply and lay the pipe if you fail to pay the security requested.

Amount of deposit

The amount of a deposit must not exceed a reasonable amount.[57] The amounts actually requested vary between suppliers.

If you consider the amount unreasonable, the amount should be referred to Ofgem. What is reasonable requires a consideration of all relevant facts, including your income and capital and personal factors such as disability and previous payment record. Previously, it was considered that suppliers should only request a deposit of a maximum of 1.5 times the value expected in quarterly consumption.

Disconnection if you do not pay a security deposit

An electricity supplier, gas supplier or gas transporter may refuse to connect, or may disconnect, your supply if you fail to pay the requested deposit within seven days of being billed. Your supply may remain disconnected for as long as you refuse to pay the amount requested.

If you cannot afford to pay a reasonable security deposit for a gas supply straight away, your supply will only be disconnected as a last resort if a prepayment meter cannot be installed (or is refused) or Fuel Direct is not available to you. See Chapter 8 for more on disconnections.

A gas supplier is not entitled to withhold the supply or threaten to disconnect for any amount of security deposit which is genuinely in dispute. This applies if you dispute the amount of, or the need for, a security deposit.

Ofgem and the Energy Ombudsman may consider and resolve disputes over security deposits. See Chapter 14 for how to resolve a dispute.

Return of security deposits

Electricity

Contract suppliers must repay any deposit:

- within 14 days where, in the previous 12 months, you have paid all charges for electricity within 28 days of each bill being sent to you; *or*
- as soon as reasonably practicable, and in any event within one month, where you have stopped taking a supply from that particular supplier and have paid all outstanding charges.

Where there is a failure to return a deposit, a small claim could be commenced through the civil courts (see p259).

Gas

Security deposits held by a gas supplier under the terms of a contract or deemed contract must be returned to you if, for a continuous period of 12 months, you:

- pay your bills within 28 days of them being issued; *or*
- otherwise comply with the terms in respect of payment under your contract.

The deposit must be returned within two months of this period, unless it is reasonable for the deposit to be retained due to your conduct.

If you have stopped taking a supply within a period of 12 months and paid all dues, check the terms of your contract in relation to the deposit.

Disconnection and reconnection costs

Electricity suppliers may demand the reasonable expenses of both disconnection and reconnection as well as payment of a security deposit prior to reconnecting the supply.

A gas supplier may demand the expenses of disconnection and reconnection if it has disconnected for failure to pay a deposit.

The supplier is not entitled to payment where the amount of a deposit is genuinely in dispute.

Alternatives to security deposits

- Suppliers routinely accept **payment plans** as acceptable alternatives to cash security deposits.[58]
- Some electricity suppliers accept **guarantors** as an alternative to a security deposit. Potential guarantors should be aware that if the bill is not paid, they are liable for the debt and could be pursued for the debt through the courts.
- Suppliers are not entitled to a security deposit if you are prepared to have a **prepayment meter** and it is reasonably practical for the supplier to provide one. Suppliers can take into consideration the risk of loss or damage to a meter in deciding whether a prepayment meter can be offered. You may be asked to

pay a security deposit and have a prepayment meter if this is reasonable as a result of your conduct – eg, if there is evidence that you may damage the meter.

5. **Disruption of supply**

Suppliers may be liable to pay compensation for any disruption in the supply of electricity or gas. Such disruption can arise in many ways such as severe weather, equipment failure and vandalism. Generators and distributors are also under a duty to avoid interferences and interruptions of supply caused by insufficient clearance between overhead lines and trees or other vegetation.[59] Various options are open to you if you suffer a loss of power, including a claim for compensation under the Electricity (Standards of Performance) Regulations 2015 or a civil action for damages through the courts. In many cases, the claim lies against the electricity distribution network operator (DNO).[60]

DNOs have to meet guaranteed standards of performance for restoring supplies to customers. The basic principle is that a payment is paid where a supply to your home is interrupted as a result of a failure or fault in or damage to a distributor's system and not restored within a set time period. Further payments are payable for each subsequent 12-hour period in which power is not restored.

If your electricity supply fails during normal weather conditions because of a problem with the distribution system, the DNO should restore it within 18 hours of becoming aware of the problem. If the DNO fails to do so and you make a valid claim within three months, you are entitled to £75 and a further £35 for each additional 12 hours you are without supply.[61]

A longer period applies for larger scale interruptions of power, affecting large numbers of customers. If the incident involves 5,000 customers or more, the DNO is required to restore supply within 24 hours. If the DNO fails to do so and you make a valid claim, you are entitled to £75 and a further payment of £35 for each additional 12-hour period that you are off supply up to a maximum of £300.[62]

If your electricity supply fails because of a problem on the distribution system due to severe weather, generally, if a supply is not restored within 24 hours, you are entitled to £70 and a further £70 for each additional 12 hours you are without supply up to a maximum payment of £700.[63]

The scheme does not apply to an island where the supply is provided via a line situated on or under the seabed.[64]

Ofgem will look into cases of power cuts.

A claim can be started by writing directly to the supplier with details of the disruption to supply. The letter is the key document to begin the process and should set out details of the dates and times when the loss of power occurred (so far as it can be identified) and any particular consequences it has had on members of the household concerned. A reasonable time limit of 14 days should be given to the supplier to respond. Contact Ofgem about a claim for sums payable under the regulations arising from disruption of supply if the company concerned has already offered a payment, particularly if the payment (known as an ex gratia payment) is lower than the sum suggested by the regulations. Equally, amounts may be higher where there has been special damage which has arisen from the loss of power.

Energy Ombudsman

The Energy Ombudsman can act in claims about supply to your home. It can ask the company to take practical action to resolve a dispute and, in some cases, make a financial award. You must try to resolve the problem with your supplier in the first instance. See Chapter 14 for more details.

Court action

As an alternative to seeking compensation from a supplier, if you have lost either electricity supply or gas under contract, you may bring a claim under contract or negligence through the civil courts (known as 'delict' in Scotland).

Claims may be brought in relation to the terms of the contract or with reference to section 14 of the Supply of Goods and Services Act 1982, which puts an implied term into every consumer contract for services that the service will be provided with a reasonable degree of competence and skill. Where there is a failure in the service, the provider may be liable to pay compensation for breach of this implied term.

Sums awarded by a court for nuisance and inconvenience arising from disruption of supply are likely to reflect those set out in the regulations. In addition, any losses which flow directly from the breach of supply and which are reasonably foreseeable as a result of power loss may also be recoverable. For example, these might include the cost of spoiled food in a freezer where power supply has been lost or where damage has been caused to a computer hard drive by a loss of power.

If a failure to supply power results in serious loss or damage or personal injury, legal advice should be taken on a claim.

It is possible that in extreme weather cases, energy companies will claim the benefit of a common law defence known as 'Act of God'. If such a claim is raised, seek specialist advice.

Liability for damage arising from faulty connection

If damage arises from a faulty connection (or reconnection), the energy company and/or its sub contractor are liable. An energy company is liable for the negligence of its sub contractor under a principle known as 'vicarious liability'. Both the supplier and its sub contractor could be treated as defendants in any claim, pleading the negligence of the sub contractor and negligence on the part of the supplier in selecting an unsuitable sub contractor. Seek legal advice if the claim is substantial or personal injury has been caused.

End of supply with change of ownership or occupation

The supplier must include a term in all supply contracts that it will end supply no later than:[65]

- if you have given notice at least two working days before the date on which you stop owning or occupying the premises, that date; *or*
- if you stop ownership or occupation and have not given notice, whichever one of these next steps happens first:
  - the end of the second working day after you notify the supplier that you have stopped owning or occupying the premises; *or*
  - the date on which any other person begins to own or occupy the premises and takes supply of electricity at those premises.

Notes

1. Who is entitled to a supply
1 Condition 22 SLC
2 Condition 0 SLC
3 *Woodcock v South Western Electricity Board* [1975] 2 All ER 545
4 ss16 and 64 EA 1989
5 Reg 2(3) E(CSP) Regs
6 E(CSP) Regs
7 SI 2015 No.698 as amended by Electricity (Standards of Performance) (Amendment) Regulations 2023 No.887
8 Sch 1 E(CSP) Regs as amended by Electricity (Standards of Performance) (Amendment) Regulations 2023 No.887
9 Reg 5(2) and Sch 1 E(CSP) Regs
10 Sch 1 E(CSP) Regs
11 Sch 2 E(CSP) Regs
12 Sch 2 para 2 E(CSP) Regs
13 Sch 2 paras 2 and 5 E(CSP) Regs
14 Consumer Scotland Act 2020
15 Reg 15 E(CSP) Regs
16 SI 2002 No.2665, as amended by the ESQC Regs

17 Reg 4 as inserted by Electricity and Gas (Smart Meters Licensable Activity) Order 2012 No.2400
18 Reg 1(5) ESQC Regs
19 Reg 3(1) ESQC Regs
20 Reg 24 ESQC Regs
21 Reg 4 ESQC Regs
22 *Morrison Sports Ltd and Others v Scottish Power* [2010] UKSC 37; [2010] 1 WLR 1934; [2011] UKSC 1
23 *Smith and Others v South Eastern Power Networks plc and Others* [2012] EWHC 2541, per Akenhead, J
24 Condition 22.5 SLC; Electricity and Gas (Internal Markets) Regulations 2011 No.2704
25 s10(1)(b) GA 1986; see also condition 4B Gas Transporters SLC
26 Condition 23.1 SLC
27 Conditions 7 and 23.2 SLC
28 Condition 7.6A SLC
29 As amended by The Gas (Standards of Performance) (Amendment) Regulations 2021 No.257
30 s39B (4)(a) and (b) EA 1989

31 G(SP) Regs as amended by The Gas (Standards of Performance) (Amendment) Regulations 2021 No.257

32 s144 Legal Aid, Sentencing and Punishment of Offenders Act 2012

33 *R (on the application of Williams) v Horsham DC* [2004] EWCA 39 J; *Frost (Inspector of Taxes) v Feltham* (1981) 1 WLR

34 s144(2) Legal Aid, Sentencing and Punishment of Offenders Act 2012; *R (on the application of Best) v Chief Land Registrar (Secretary of State for Justice, interested party)* [2014] EWHC 1370

35 Department for Communities and Local Government, *Planning Policy for Traveller Sites*, September 2015; Welsh government, *Designing Gypsy and Traveller Sites*, May 2015; Scottish government, *Improving Gypsy/Traveller Sites – guidance on minimum site standards and site tenants' core rights and responsibilities*, May 2015

2. Getting your electricity supply connected

36 Reg 9(2) and Sch 1 E(CSP) Regs
37 Reg 12(2) and Sch 1 E(CSP) Regs
38 Sch 4 para 2(1) UA 2000
39 Condition 27.5 SLC
40 Condition 22.7(c) SLC
41 Condition 14.6 SLC
42 Condition 14.12 SLC
43 s39B (1)(a) and (b) EA 1989

3. Getting your gas supply connected

44 Condition 21B(5) SLC
45 Condition 4B Gas Transporters SLCs
46 Condition 27.9-11 SLC
47 Condition 14 SLC
48 Condition 14.6 SLC
49 Condition 27.3 SLC
50 Condition 22.5 SLC
51 s11 GA 1986

4. Security deposits

52 Condition 27.3 SLC
53 Condition 27.4 SLC
54 *Laverty and Others v British Gas Trading* [2014] EWHC 2721 (Ch)
55 Condition 27.3(b) SLC
56 Condition 27.4 SLC
57 Condition 27.4 SLC
58 Reg 6(1) (a) and (b) EG(SP)S) Regs

5. Disruption of supply

59 Reg 20A ESQC Regs
60 Regs 4-10 E(SP) Regs

61 Reg 5(2)(a) and (b) and Sch 2 E(SP) Regs
62 Reg 6(2) and Sch 2 E(SP) Regs
63 Reg 7 and Sch 2 E(SP) Regs
64 Reg 9(3) E(SP) Regs
65 Condition 24.1.(a) and (b) SLC

Chapter 4

· ·

Meters and methods of payment

This chapter covers:
1. Standing charges and tariffs (below)
2. Types of meters (p48)
3. Payment methods (p56)
4. Fuel Direct (p58)
5. Choosing how to pay (p58)

For more information on reading your meter, see Appendix 2.

1. Standing charges and tariffs

'Standing charges' are fixed charges which must be paid regardless of how much fuel you use. Suppliers make these charges to cover costs such as billing, meter reading, customer services and servicing meters.

A **'tariff'** is the package of charges and conditions a supplier offers you for providing electricity, gas or both.

All tariffs are structured in the same way and comprise a standing charge and a unit rate (or rates, for time of use tariffs). Note that although the structure of all tariffs is the same, suppliers can choose to offer tariffs where the standing charge is set at zero.

Every tariff has a specific name. It is important to know the name of your tariff, particularly if you want to shop around for a better deal. The name of your tariff is shown on your bill and your annual statement. Your supplier must tell you, via your fuel bill and other communications, whether it has a cheaper tariff available and how much you could save by switching to it.

All suppliers should provide a **'tariff information label'** which details each tariff's key terms and conditions. Suppliers are not permitted to increase prices on, or make other changes to, fixed-term tariffs without your consent, though structured price increases that have been set out in advance and that comply with consumer protection law are allowed. The following exemptions also apply:

- a change in price due to an increase/reduction in VAT;
- your payment method is changed because of your debt and/or failure to comply with contractual terms.

If you are on a fixed-term contract that is coming to an end, your supplier cannot roll you forward on to another fixed-term contract without your consent. Your supplier gives you a six-week period before your contract is due to end to decide about your preferred tariff and supplier. Standard Licence Condition 22C concerns fixed-term contracts.

Price caps

Price caps set the maximum price per kWH suppliers can charge for electricity and gas on standard variable tariffs (SVTs) and default tariffs.[1] This is the unit from which your bill is calculated. Ofgem sets the price cap, using a method set by the Competition and Markets Authority. Regional differences in the cap reflect regional variation in the costs of distribution and supply. To ensure prices reflect changes in the cost of supplying energy, Ofgem reviews the caps quarterly, and these revisions take effect in January, April, August and October.

The price cap does not affect you if you are on a fixed-term tariff or have a standard variable green energy tariff.

Note: being on a price-capped tariff does not protect you from bill increases as price caps are not a limit on the total amount of your bill – how much you pay still depends on how much energy you use, whether you have both gas and electricity, where you live, your current deal and how you pay.

There are two energy price caps: the default price cap and the prepayment meter price cap.

Default price cap

Since 1 January 2019, a price cap has been in place for SVTs and default tariffs. If you have never switched tariff or supplier, or if you took no action when your last fixed deal ended, you are likely to be on one of these tariffs. SVTs or default tariffs are typically substantially more expensive than the cheapest deals on the market. The cap aims to ensure that customers pay a 'fair' price for energy, with any price changes reflecting genuine changes in energy costs experienced by suppliers.

This price cap is for people paying by direct debit or by standard credit. Those on standard credit typically pay 6 per cent more than those paying by direct debit. See p47 if you have a prepayment meter.

If you are on a fixed-term contract, your prices are fixed and are not covered by the cap. However, when your contract ends, you will automatically be moved to a default tariff if you do not have a new contract in place or switch supplier.

Prepayment meter price cap

To prevent prepayment meter customers from being overcharged, Ofgem introduced a price cap in April 2017. The unit charges within the prepayment meter price cap from 1 July 2023 was equalised[2] with those paying by direct debit. The standing charges have traditionally been higher for prepayment meter households, but from April 2024 Ofgem is working towards equalising these changes with those paying by direct debit.[3]

As with the other cap, the level may increase and your bills may go up.

Warm Home Discount

The Warm Home Discount (WHD) is a one-off discount of £150 on your electricity bill. If you are eligible, your supplier allocates the discount to your bill by the end of March. The money is not paid to you. If your supplier provides you with both gas and electricity, you may be able to get the discount on your gas bill instead.[4]
Note: the £150 includes VAT, so the rebate shows on your bill as a credit of £143 – ie, before VAT is applied.

If you have a prepayment meter and qualify for a WHD, ask your supplier how you will receive the discount – eg, it may be paid as a bar-coded top-up voucher or a post office voucher.

If you permanently live in a park (mobile) home and pay for fuel directly to your park site manager, see parkhomeswhd.com for more information.

Which suppliers offer the Warm Home Discount?
By law, energy companies must give a WHD to some of their most vulnerable customers. All suppliers with more than 1,000 customers must participate and suppliers with fewer customers are able to participate voluntarily.[5] See gov.uk/the-warm-home-discount-scheme/energy-suppliers for an up-to-date list of suppliers offering the WHD.

From 2022/23, there are separate WHD schemes for England and Wales and for Scotland. The WHD scheme currently runs to March 2026.[6]

England and Wales

You may be able to get a WHD if your supplier participates in the scheme and you:[7]
- get the guarantee credit element of pension credit (PC) (core group 1); *or*
- have a low income and live in a property with a 'high-energy cost score', determined by the Valuation Office Agency (core group 2).

You must be named on the electricity account or bill of a participating energy supplier and meet the eligibility requirements on the qualifying date (usually in August).

Data sharing between the government and energy suppliers means most eligible households will receive the WHD automatically. Suppliers usually pay out over the winter months and must pay by 31 March. You will receive a letter in November or December if you are due to get the discount. This may invite you to confirm eligibility or to take part in a review.

Further information is available at gov.uk/the-warm-home-discount-scheme.

Scotland

There are two main groups within the WHD scheme.

- **Core group.** Eligibility alters each year but is targeted at customers over PC age. In 2023/24, you were eligible if, on the qualifying date (13 August 2023), you were receiving the guarantee credit element of PC (even if you get the savings credit as well). The DWP data matches its records with participating energy suppliers so, if you are eligible, you should be contacted automatically. The bill must be in your or your partner's name.

- **Broader group.** Participating suppliers have discretion over the eligibility criteria for the broader group, but they are still required to target those in, or at risk of, fuel poverty. The eligibility criteria are subject to approval from Ofgem. There is no data-matching with this group so, if you think you are eligible, contact your supplier. The discount is awarded on a first-come-first-served basis. During 2023/24, if you had a child under the age of five and your income was below £17,005 or you received a means-tested benefit, you may have received support on a first-come-first-served basis until supplier obligation budgets were exhausted.

Check gov.uk/the-warm-home-discount-scheme from October 2024 for the eligibility criteria for winter 2024/25.

2. **Types of meters**

Meters are owned by meter operator companies contracted by suppliers to provide metering services to their customers. In many cases, meters are owned, checked and read by National Grid and the privatised electricity suppliers even if another company supplies the fuel. Metering remains the supplier's responsibility, which is liable for the acts and omissions of its sub-contracting meter operator company.

The main types of meters are standard credit, variable rate credit, prepayment and smart.

Standard credit meter

Fuel is supplied in advance of payment. Credit meters record consumption and your supplier contacts you to ask you to provide a meter reading at least once a year.[8] Estimated bills are sent for the rest of the year, with a customer reading correction facility available by phone or online.

Estimated bills are a frequent source of complaint. A succession of estimates can result in inaccurate billing, with you paying too much or not enough. If you have problems with arrears due to a succession of estimated bills, see p105.

A bill is sent at the end of each billing period, after the meter has either been read, or was due to be read, or estimated. The price per unit of fuel does not vary according to the time of day or night the fuel is used when you use a standard credit meter. Appendix 2 describes how to read your own credit meter.

If you are of pensionable age or disabled, you could use the special meter reading facility under the Priority Services Register (see p98).

Variable rate credit meter

Variable, or off-peak, electricity credit meters record different rates or 'tariffs' at different times of day or night. Night-time off-peak electricity usage is generally cheaper than on-peak day usage. The most common type of variable rate credit meter is known as Economy 7 in England and Wales and sometimes referred to as white meter in Scotland (see below).

Suppliers offer different systems, depending on your supply area, and these may change from time to time. Ask your supplier for information on the type of system it operates.

Economy 7/white meter

Economy 7/white meter charges for electricity at two different rates or 'tariffs'. You need a special meter, usually an Economy 7 credit meter, but in some areas Economy 7 prepayment meters are also available. A white meter is a similar type of meter which preceded Economy 7 meters.

Electricity is charged at two different rates per unit, with a lower rate at night. The daytime rate is charged at a higher rate than the standard rate for credit meters. The standing charge is often higher than for credit meters. The amount of the charges varies from supplier to supplier.

Consider changing to an Economy 7/white meter if you use electricity to heat your home and to heat water overnight. You may also be able to save on your fuel costs if you run electrical appliances (such as washing machines and tumble dryers) overnight, usually by setting a timer to ensure the appliances operate within the optimum time band. If you have an electric vehicle, charging it on an off-peak tariff may be cheaper.

The higher standing charge and higher daytime rate may counterbalance any savings made if your night-time electricity use is not large enough. Look carefully at the amount of electricity you use during the day and night, and at the rates, to establish if an Economy 7/white meter would save you money. Suppliers should have specialist staff to advise you.

Time of use (off-peak) tariffs and meter clocks

There have been problems with time clocks for some meters which have left customers out of pocket. The problem is largely down to the clocks on some meters not changing for GMT or BST at the appropriate time of year (some will change automatically) and, as a result, time-of-use tariffs are not charged correctly. Power cuts may also affect the clocks that control switchover times.

It is the supplier's responsibility to ensure metering equipment is correct so if you suspect there might be a fault, contact your energy company. Suppliers are not required to specifically check meter clocks, but Ofgem rules mean they must take reasonable steps to ensure accuracy in terms of the amount of electricity supplied.[9]

If necessary, the accuracy of the meter can be checked by the Office for Product Safety and Standards.

Prepayment meters

A substantial number of people have a prepayment meter – many were installed to recover a fuel debt.[10] Frequently marketed as a 'pay-as-you-go' budgeting method, there are several types of prepayment meters, including smart, card and key meters. Some electricity prepayment meters can operate with Economy 7 and other variable rate tariffs.

If your supplier has gone out of business, you should not lose supply and can top-up your meter in the normal way. Ofgem will contact you when a new supplier has been appointed. Any arrears you have will normally be transferred to the new supplier. Contact Citizens Advice or Advice Direct Scotland if you have any problems.

Collecting arrears

Prepayment meters can be set to collect a fuel debt. They allow you to pay for your fuel supply, a daily standing charge and extra for any arrears you owe. It is important to note that the settings for these charges operate on a regular, usually weekly, basis. If you are due to spend time away from your home (eg, on holiday or in hospital), ensure your meter is topped-up with enough credit to cover these charges.

If you are paying off a fuel debt via a prepayment meter, your supplier is meant to take into account your ability to pay when determining the weekly arrears recovery amount. If you feel the arrears repayment level is unaffordable, you may be able to negotiate with your supplier (especially if you can be considered vulnerable) to have the arrears recovery level set on a par with Fuel Direct (see p190) – ie, £4.25 a week.

Emergency credit

If your fuel runs low or runs out, you can use an emergency button on the meter to obtain a small amount of credit (typically worth £5). The next time you top up, the credit is used to pay for the emergency fuel – no more fuel is available until this has been paid. Under Standard Licence Condition (SLC) 27A, suppliers must offer:

- **'friendly-hours credit'** – this is emergency credit provided overnight (typically between 6pm and 9am), at weekends and public holidays, when top-up points may be closed and a prepayment meter runs low or runs out; *and*
- **'additional support credit'** – this is provided to customers in vulnerable circumstances who may have exhausted other options.

These credits are repaid at the next top-up, but suppliers should consider your ability to pay and agree an affordable rate. Where it is not technically feasible and/or outside the supplier's control to offer emergency credit and friendly-hours credit, the supplier must take all reasonable steps to provide you with alternative short-term support.[11]

If the emergency credit runs out and you cannot top-up, contact your supplier to discuss an affordable repayment plan.

Some suppliers offer an alert service where you or someone you nominate (eg, a friend or family member) gets a text message or email when your credit is running low.

Self-disconnection

'Self-disconnection' is an interruption to energy supply to prepayment meters because of a lack of credit on the meter or account. With insufficient funds in a prepayment meter, you effectively disconnect yourself, rather than the supplier having to take steps to enforce any debt. Reasons for self-disconnection can include:[12]

- insufficient money available to top-up;
- forgetting to top the meter up in time;
- not realising the meter was low on credit.

Under SLC 27A, suppliers must identify and support customers who self-disconnect and support vulnerable customers who might be self-disconnecting and **'self-rationing'** (deliberately limiting fuel use to save money). Suppliers must take into account your ability to pay when calculating instalments.[13]

Examples
Caroline has a mental health condition which makes her forgetful and she regularly self-disconnects her prepayment meter when she forgets to buy top-ups. Her son contacts her supplier, which offers to replace her prepayment meter with a standard meter and places her on its Priority Services Register.

Ewan and Ben claimed universal credit (UC) and are waiting for their first payment. They do not have enough money to top-up their prepayment meter. They can apply for a short-term advance of UC. They will have to repay the advance by deductions from future payments, but they will not be charged interest.

Ibrahim had a prepayment meter installed to collect arrears. He has an outstanding balance of £182. The prepayment meter deducted a large proportion of all top-ups to repay the debt and the standing charges. During the winter, Ibrahim found this unmanageable and was regularly self-disconnecting. The supplier agreed to reduce the amount deducted from each top-up for arrears.

Maya's employment and support allowance has been stopped and she is appealing the decision. She has no income while the appeal is pending and could not top-up her meter. Her adviser contacts a specialist support organisation. It negotiated with Maya's supplier, which agreed to provide discretionary credit that she will pay back at £4.25 a week. The supplier also awards a Warm Home Discount (WHD).

Help if you are facing self-disconnection

– Contact your supplier and explain your situation. It could help you apply to a trust or grant scheme, offer emergency prepayment support or ensure your energy account is set up to meet your specific needs. If your meter is collecting arrears, the supplier may be able to reduce the proportion of the top-up used for arrears. Suppliers are obliged to set repayments at an affordable level. Draw up a financial statement (see p109) to help you negotiate a reduction in your debt repayments. If your supplier is unhelpful, contact a local advice service which may be able to contact the supplier again on your behalf.
– Check with your supplier whether you are eligible for a WHD (see p47).
– Get help from a local advice agency such as Citizens Advice or a law centre. They might be able to contact energy trusts for help (see p208) or a specialist advice organisation (see p206) on your behalf.
– See if you can get help from your local welfare assistance scheme (see p189).
– If you are waiting for your first payment of UC, you may be able to get a short-term advance. You must repay the advance by deductions from future payments, but you will not be charged interest.
– If you are considered vulnerable or are in a vulnerable situation (see p139), contact a specialist advice organisation.
– If you have been referred to a foodbank or are working with a local energy advice/ housing association or other body, you may be able to get a fuel voucher. This can provide a top-up of two weeks' worth of fuel for prepayment meters. **Note:** this is only available in a limited number of organisations, which changes frequently.
– Check that you are receiving all the benefits you are entitled to.

Advantages of prepayment meters

- They can be useful as a budgeting aid, as they restrict your fuel use according to your means. You are forced to become aware of your fuel consumption. This can be useful if your budget is limited, but you should also consider the risk of self-disconnection. Many customers choose to retain their prepayment meter as a budgeting aid even after arrears have been paid off.
- Ease of adjustment – the smart card or key reads your meter and conveys the information to your supplier. If your supplier agrees to change the setting, there is no need for a visit, as the card/key adjusts the setting of the meter the next time you charge it up and use it. Smart prepayment meters can be adjusted remotely in real time.
- Meters can be reset to pay off arrears as an alternative to disconnection.

Disadvantages of prepayment meters

- These meters should never be installed if you are at risk of leaving appliances turned on after the money has run out, or are incapable of operating the meter or obtaining the top-ups to operate them.
- You cannot spread the cost of large winter bills over the whole year if you pay for your fuel in advance week by week. A payment plan might be preferable if you cannot afford to pay for your heaviest weeks' consumption from your weekly income.
- 'Self-disconnection' is a problem if you cannot afford to top-up your meter. Fuel costs may take up too high a proportion of your income, particularly if you live in a property that is hard to heat or if your income is low.
- Paying back arrears and emergency credit can result in hardship. If a meter is set to collect arrears, a supply of fuel may not be available until the arrears charge has been paid. With some types of meters, if you are away from home or cannot afford to charge the meter for a week, you have to insert two weeks' arrears before you can obtain a supply. With most types of prepayment meter, if you have used your emergency credit, you also have to pay the amount of the emergency credit before obtaining a supply. In some situations (eg, if you come out of hospital), you may be able to persuade the supplier to reset your meter – check first that this will not involve any extra cost.
- Your repayment of arrears may be highest when you can least afford it if you use the crude mechanical gas prepayment meters. These operate by overcharging for each unit of gas used, so the more gas you use, the more you pay towards your arrears. However, this means that there is no problem if you are absent from your home for any period of time – you will always get gas for every top-up.
- Using the meters can be difficult, particularly if you have visual problems or disabilities. Note, however, that meters can often be re-sited free of charge to make them easier to use and some suppliers have accessible in-home display (IHD) units for blind and partially sighted people (see p55).

- There are hidden costs. If you cannot afford to buy much fuel at any one time, you may need to make frequent journeys to the nearest charging point. The extra cost of travel is effectively part of your fuel cost. In this situation, it may save you money to move to a smart prepayment meter which allows you to top-up online or use an app.
- Obtaining top-ups may present problems. Frequent journeys to buy them may present difficulties if you are caring for small children, are disabled or have limited mobility, or are in full-time work. It may be difficult to obtain top-ups outside shopping hours. Vending machines have had problems with jamming, vandalism and becoming full. You should consider the safety aspects of trying to obtain cards out of hours. Be sure to keep your receipts when charging keys/cards so that you have a record of payments.
- Keys can be easily lost or mislaid. If you lose your key, ask the supplier to replace it.
- You may be denied the option of changing to Fuel Direct (see p190) to pay your arrears if you already have a prepayment meter that has been reset to recover arrears.

Smart meters

The smart meter roll-out

The Energy Act 2008 establishes the mandate for installing smart meters. It requires that gas and electricity customers are provided with 'information on actual time of use' as far as is technically feasible.[14] The government's aim was for every household to have a smart meter at no upfront cost by the end of 2020. This target was not met. Energy suppliers were subsequently required to take all reasonable steps to roll out smart meters by the end of December 2021. From January 2022, all suppliers have binding annual installation targets to roll out smart and advanced meters to their remaining non-smart customers by the end of 2025.

The term 'smart meter' relates to the services and benefits obtained from such a meter rather than a specific type of technology. Smart meters measure your exact fuel usage and send the information electronically to your supplier without the need for meter readings to be taken. Smart meters can be set in either credit or prepayment mode.

Smart meters give better budget management tools, such as low credit and high consumption alerts, which may safeguard against self-disconnection.

Fuel companies are responsible for meeting the cost of installing smart metering equipment.[15] This comprises a smart meter, a communications hub, an optional IHD and prepayment interface device. The Smart Meter Installation Code of Practice sets out the rules to be followed by suppliers when installing smart meters.[16]

Second generation smart meters (SMETS2) are currently being installed (see p12). These meters enable easier switching of supplier without losing smart functionality. First-generation smart meters (SMETS1) are in a software upgrade programme that will enable them to match the functionality of SMETS2. These upgrades were expected to be completed by the end of December 2023. This did not happen and, at the time of writing, there is no new required date.

The IHD provides real-time information about your consumption, and shows the amount of energy being used at 30-minute intervals and over various periods (day, month and year), and the cost of this energy in pounds and pence. The information may also be accessible online or via an app to track energy and costs. You can set up email or text message alerts to track unusual consumption patterns.

Smart meters are expected to improve the experience of prepayment meter customers. Potential benefits include:
- more convenience and choice in payment top-up methods;
- greater flexibility and emergency credit arrangements – including low credit alerts;
- the ability to switch remotely between credit and prepayment modes.

Over time, smart meters are expected to result in greater consumer engagement and stronger competition between energy suppliers due to the increased ease of consumer switching, information on true consumption and tariffs. The digital energy infrastructure will enable new technologies and efficiency savings to be integrated into the existing system and respond to outages. The government publication *Smart Meters: a guide for households* is a useful source of information.[17]

Advantages of smart meters
- There is no need for estimated bills, with suppliers able to read meters remotely via two-way communications technology. This should dramatically reduce the number of inaccurate bills issued.
- You have real-time information to help control and manage your energy use, save money and reduce emissions.
- It heralds the end of having to read meters in inaccessible locations in the home, such as under the stairs and in cupboards. The information on your energy use can be provided through the IHD unit, via the internet or through a mobile phone.
- Smart meters provide more detailed, user-friendly information on your energy consumption. The IHD shows you how much energy you are using and roughly how much it costs you in pounds and pence. It is believed that by knowing how much you are using and how much your appliances cost to run, you can reduce your energy consumption and save money.
- Some suppliers offer accessible in-home display (AIHD) units for blind and partially sighted people. AIHD units have accessibility features such as text-to-

speech, large vibrating buttons, coloured LEDs for indicating fuel usage and screens optimised for visual impairment and colour blindness.

- If you have a smart prepayment meter, it should be easier to top-up your meter. Cash payment can always be accepted, but suppliers also offer more convenient ways to top-up, such as over the phone, online or on an app.

Disadvantages of smart meters

- A major disadvantage is remote disconnection of your gas or electricity supply in the event of non-payment, or an error creating an assumption of non-payment. This removes the protection afforded by most suppliers with the previous system – that suppliers could not disconnect your supply in the first instance without being given access to your property to perform the disconnection, or to fit a prepayment meter. With smart meters, entry is not necessary for disconnection. Ofgem has rules to ensure that suppliers treat disconnection as a last resort. Suppliers must ensure that vulnerable households are not disconnected. If you have an energy debt, discuss repayment options with your supplier.
- Suppliers can remotely switch the meter between credit and prepayment modes and do not have to physically visit the property to change meters. Energy UK guidance states that suppliers must first ensure that it is safe and reasonably practical for a customer to use a prepayment meter.[18] Ofgem has a new set of standards expected of suppliers regarding the forced movement from credit to prepayment, which applies to both physical meter change and remote smart switching.
- There can be problems if you live in a rural area with limited connection.
- Some consumer groups are concerned that safeguards are needed to manage the collection of consumers' data uploaded by meters and the right to privacy.

Safeguarding smart meter data

The government publication *Smart Meters: a guide for households* focuses on, among other areas, consumer protections and consumer privacy. You should be able to choose who can access information collected by the meter by opting out of particular types of data management. Energy UK has published a guide that explains what information smart meters can collect, who the information may be passed on to and in what circumstances – eg, other industry parties in connection with supply and distribution issues, or police and law enforcement agencies to prevent and investigate fraud.[19] Restrictions on collecting electricity data are also contained in SLC 47 for electricity.

3. Payment methods

Your choice of payment method depends on the type of meter you have. You may wish to change your meter to allow you to use a particular payment method. If your circumstances change, you may be able to switch to a more suitable payment method.

Each supplier publishes a code of practice on the payment of bills, outlining the various options available. Many also publish additional detailed information about the costs of the different options.

Credit meter payment methods

Payment can be made on receipt of a **quarterly bill** – by posting a cheque, using a credit or debit card or paying directly into the supplier's account at a bank, post office, PayPoint or using online banking. A service charge may be applied if you pay at the post office. Your supplier may have an app through which you can pay. Using a credit card could be an expensive way of obtaining credit because of the interest charged on balances. If you are in financial difficulty, consider the other budget options available.

Paying on receipt of a bill is the most expensive way to pay for gas and electricity. Switching to direct debit will save you money.

Direct debit is the cheapest way to pay for gas and electricity. Your estimated annual costs are spread over 12 monthly payments (or four quarterly payments), which are deducted direct from your bank account. Payments should be enough to cover your annual consumption. If the direct debit payments are set too low, you will accumulate arrears. Suppliers can adjust the direct debit amount but must inform you when this is the case. Setting up an **online account** with your fuel supplier and paying by direct debit attracts a discount. This 'paperless billing' process lets you view your bills online and submit regular meter readings.

Standing order is similar to direct debit, with monthly or quarterly payments deducted direct from your bank account. The main difference is that you must instruct the bank of any changes to the debited amount. You are unlikely to be able to access the savings offered for direct debit associated tariffs if you pay this way.

Remember to consider the extra costs of becoming overdrawn if you are considering standing orders or direct debits.

A range of **budget schemes** allow you to pay for your fuel on a weekly, fortnightly or monthly basis. This gives flexibility and helps you to budget, but is not the cheapest payment method. This is a useful way to pay if you do not have a bank account.

A **flexible payment scheme** enables you to pay any amount at any time, at a bank or by post. The amount paid is credited towards your next bill, which must then be settled each quarter. This is useful if you have a variable income.

PayPoint is a free national bill payment network aimed at households who prefer to pay utility bills in cash on a weekly, fortnightly, monthly or quarterly basis. Locations of PayPoint outlets can be found at paypoint.com.

Prepayment meter payment methods

- **Smart prepayment meters.** Top-up methods vary between suppliers and tariffs. Generally, you get a payment card which can be topped-up at a PayPoint, online, by text, by phone or via apps. As soon as there is credit on the card, it is transferred remotely to your meter.
- **Key meters.** You are provided with a rechargeable 'key' when the meter is installed. The key can only be used in your meter. You need to charge the key by paying at a charging point (eg, at a PayPoint outlet) or you may be able to top-up at home using the internet and a device provided by your supplier. Your key is electronically encoded at the charging point with the amount you have paid. When the key is inserted into the meter, the amount of fuel you have bought is registered and the key is cancelled. A certain amount of emergency credit is usually available on these meters. Your key may be able to read your meter and pass on the reading when you charge it. Key meters do not need to be manually updated after a price rise.
- **Token and card meters.** These have almost all been phased out. Electronically coded payment cards or tokens, usually available in units of £5, can be purchased from local shops. Your account is credited every time you purchase a token/card. When the token or card is inserted into the meter it records the amount of fuel purchased and then automatically cancels the token/card. Token meters need to be manually adjusted after every price rise. Your supplier should give you advance notice of a price increase and should take steps to recalibrate your meter as soon as possible.

4. Fuel Direct

Fuel Direct, the DWP's 'third party deduction system', allows an amount to be deducted from your benefit entitlement and paid directly to your energy supplier. Payment for fuel arrears plus ongoing consumption, or for fuel arrears only (if you have a prepayment meter), is deducted directly from benefit. See p190 for details.

5. Choosing how to pay

The legal provisions affecting your choice are broadly similar for both gas and electricity. An assessment is made of your creditworthiness and of your ability to pay for fuel. If you cannot show creditworthiness in general, provisions relating to the requirement for security come into play. If you cannot show an ability to manage your gas/electricity account, both provisions relating to security and policies for debt management come into play. **Note:** an existing fuel debt is not an automatic bar to switching to a supplier who may offer a different type of payment method (see p59).

A supplier can restrict the choices available to you if it can demonstrate that it is reasonable to regard you as not creditworthy, even though you may not necessarily be in arrears with your gas/electricity bill. If it is reasonable for the supplier to require some form of security from you, your choices are restricted so that you are not allowed to accrue charges in the same way as customers paying quarterly in arrears. Payment to the supplier is required at least monthly, and possibly fortnightly or weekly, under the terms of the various budget schemes available.

If you can show that a request for any kind of security from you is unreasonable (ie, you can prove your identity, show that you are creditworthy and have a good record of paying your gas/electricity bills on time, live in settled accommodation and are not in arrears with your bill), there is no reason for a supplier to attempt to restrict your choice of meter or method of payment. You should be allowed to pay using the method of your choice.

Payment in advance of receiving a supply, or prepayment, is at the other end of the scale. This method of payment is the ultimate security for the suppliers. No money – no fuel.

A prepayment meter may be your only option if the supplier has established a right to disconnect your supply, if you are in arrears and cannot manage a payment plan. Similarly, if the supplier can demonstrate that a requirement for security is reasonable, and you cannot pay a deposit or arrange an alternative form of security, such as direct debit, a prepayment meter is the only alternative to disconnection.

Supplier discretion in switching with a debt

There is nothing to prevent a supplier allowing you to switch if you have arrears. However, you may be required to pay what you owe before you switch (see p12). The decision to take on a customer with an existing debt is at the discretion of the company, and several suppliers appear willing to take on consumers who may have been previous customers and who have had good payment records. Switching supplier may also prevent disconnection from another supplier to whom a debt may be owed.

If you use a prepayment meter and have a debt of less than £500 per fuel, you may be able to switch to another supplier, taking any debt with you (see p124).

Notes

1. Standing charges and tariffs
1 Domestic Gas and Electricity (Tariff Cap) Act 2018
2 UK Government Spring Budget Speech, 15 March 2023, available at gov.uk/government/speeches/spring-budget-2023-speech
3 Ofgem, *Decision on adjusting standing charges for Prepayment Customers*, 23 February 2024
4 **EW** Reg 10(3)(b) WHD(EW) Regs
  S Reg 9(3)(b) WHD(S) Regs
5 **EW** Reg 6 WHD(EW) Regs
  S Reg 6 WHD(S) Regs
6 **EW** Reg 4 WHD(EW) Regs
  S Reg 4(2)(b) WHD(S) Regs
7 Reg 10 WHD(EW) Regs

2. Types of meters
8 Condition 21B.4 SLC
9 Sch 7 EA 1989; SLCs
10 Ofgem, *Vulnerable Consumers in the Energy Market: 2018,* 18 June 2018
11 Condition 27A.3 SLC
12 Citzens Advice, *Switched On: improving support for prepayment consumers who've self disconnected*, April 2018
13 Conditions 27A.1 and 27.8 SLC
14 ss88-91 Energy Act 2008
15 Condition 33A SLC
16 recportal.co.uk/smicop; Condition 41 Electricity SLC and 35 Gas SLC
17 gov.uk/guidance/smart-meters-how-they-work
18 For suppliers' obligations, see energy-uk.org.uk/wp-content/uploads/2023/03/Sept15_EUK_Safety_Net.pdf
19 For suppliers' obligations, see energy-uk.org.uk/wp-content/uploads/2023/03/Sept15_EUK_Safety_Net.pdf

Chapter 5

Responsibility for the bill

This chapter covers:
1. Introduction (below)
2. When you are liable for an electricity bill (p62)
3. When you are liable for a gas bill (p67)
4. Common problems (p72)

1. Introduction

It is always worth checking whether you are legally responsible for a bill, particularly when you are in dispute with a gas or electricity supplier about arrears. It may be that you are not liable for all, or some, of the bill – perhaps because the bill was in the name of a partner who has left, a flat-sharer, a previous occupant, your landlord or someone who has died. Suppliers may attempt to recover these sums from you – but they are not always entitled to do so.

Electricity

Liability for electricity charges is determined by the rules of the law of contract.[1] Generally, the person who signs a contract is the person who is liable to pay under that contract. However, a contract can also be expressed through other means, such as online or verbally over the telephone.

Many suppliers accept you as a customer without you actually having signed a contract. A county court case covering the pre-1989 law suggests that it does not matter if you actually apply in writing, or sign a contract, so long as it is clear who asked for the supply. While this case is helpful in establishing the liability to pay for customers who have requested a supply, whether in writing or not, it does not deal with the situation where nobody has requested a supply. Normally, once you take ownership, control or occupation of a property, you are deemed responsible for any consumption, but only from the date that you received a supply.[2] For this reason, it is essential that you take a meter reading as soon as you move into a new property.

Electricity suppliers – or debt collecting companies assigned the right to collect debts – may attempt to secure payment from people who have used the electricity supplied rather than chase the people actually legally liable. Previous suppliers may also assign the right to recover debts to new suppliers where the consumer has switched supplier. One example is where, on the breakdown of a relationship, if the bill was in the sole name of the partner who has left, the remaining partner is asked to pay the arrears.

Gas

Gas is supplied by gas suppliers under the terms of contracts and 'deemed contracts'[3] – ie, where gas is supplied without any formal express contract being agreed (by either the supplier or the customer). In these circumstances, the supplier is deemed as having contracted with the occupier from the date that the supply began. If the details of contracts are clearly confirmed in writing, disputes about liability are less likely to occur. However, the provision for deemed contracts (see p17) in many situations enables gas suppliers to hold owners or occupiers liable to pay a gas bill where they are the 'person supplied with gas' and in the absence of an express contract. If you are in this situation, consult Citizens Advice consumer service or Advice Direct Scotland. Suppliers may be prepared to reach an agreement and settle an argument over liability by the part-payment of a bill in return for a new, signed or expressed contract being established.

Ultimately, the existence of a contract is open to interpretation by the courts and will depend on each individual case.

2. When you are liable for an electricity bill

In this section, all references to 'the bill' refer only to 'charges due' for the supply of electricity and do not include other charges such as credit sales charges for appliances. See p134 for more information about 'charges due'.

Your liability for the bill depends on how, or even whether, you contacted the supplier to say you required a supply of electricity.

Your liability when you have signed for the supply

You are liable to pay an electricity bill to a contract supplier if you signed a contract. Your liability for the bill begins from the date you stated you wanted the supply to start, providing your supply was actually connected on that date agreed, or from the date you signed the contract.

You are solely liable for the bill if you alone signed for the supply, regardless of whether you live alone or with other adults. You are jointly responsible for the bill if you and one or more others also signed for the supply.

Your liability ends:[4]

- where you give at least two working days' written notice that you will no longer be an owner or occupier of the premises, on the day that you cease to be the owner or leave, as the case may be;
- where you did not give at least two working days' written notice that you were leaving, the earlier of any of the following two events:
  - two working days after you actually give written notice of ceasing to be an owner or occupier; *or*
  - when any subsequent owner or occupier gives notice requiring a supply or signs a contract for a supply to the same premises.

You can also bring your liability to an end by terminating the contract in accordance with any provision for termination contained in the contract. You must give at least 28 days' notice of termination of a contract. You continue to be liable to the original supplier until another supplier takes over the supply to your home or until the supply is cut off altogether.[5]

If you have a fixed-term supply contract, you are not required to provide notice of termination of a contract.[6]

Your liability when you contacted the supplier by telephone

Many electricity suppliers will connect your electricity supply without asking you to sign anything at all to confirm that you require a supply or that you accept liability to pay for any electricity supplied. Many operate a system where you negotiate with them by telephone to obtain your supply. In these situations, it is often clear exactly who is requesting the supply. Usually, payment is requested from the person who made the telephone call.

In the law of contract, in most situations, a verbal contract is as good as a written one. So what matters is not whether you signed a formal document but whether it can be shown that you were the person who asked for the supply and entered into the contract.

There is a danger that someone can contact the supplier over the phone to say that you want the supply to be in your name, but you have no knowledge of this and do not consent to it. In one case, a gas supplier attempted to obtain payment from a tenant. The tenant did not contact the supplier to request the supply in his name and, in fact, paid his landlord for gas with the rent. One bill was paid in the tenant's name, but there was no evidence the tenant had made this payment. It was held that the tenant was not liable to pay for the gas consumed.[7] Although this case relates to gas, the principles apply equally to electricity.

Establishing joint liability for a supply may be problematic if you contact the supplier by phone. In practice, it is straightforward to ask the supplier to include someone else's name on the bill as well as your own, but what if that person denies they had an agreement to be jointly liable with you? It is best in these circumstances if everyone who requires the supply in their name signs for the supply. Your liability to pay starts from the date you ask for the supply to be put in your name. It ends based on the rules on p62. Always arrange a final reading of the meter, and take a reading yourself to check your final bill.

Your liability when you contacted the supplier online

You can get quotes, negotiate and set up an electricity supply account online with most suppliers. This is commonly achieved through registering your details with a supplier and often the contracted terms and conditions are expressly confirmed in a durable medium, such as an email or online account. Access to the express contract and terms and conditions are also often available through the same, or similar, mediums. In these situations, it is often clear exactly who is requesting the supply and about acknowledgment of liability. Usually, payment is requested from the person who registered their details with the supplier.

When a dispute arises, parties should seek to resolve it between themselves. Alternatively, you can raise a formal complaint through the supplier's internal complaints procedure. If this is unsuccessful, the dispute may be referred to the Energy Ombudsman for determination (see p270).

Your liability when no one has contacted the supplier

You may be liable to pay the supplier if:
- there is no tariff customer and no one has a contract; *or*
- the liability of the tariff customer or contract holder has come to an end; *and*
- you have, in practice, been supplied with electricity.

This situation often occurs when people move into new premises where the existing supply is already connected, or where the bill was in the name of another joint occupier but that person has left. There is nothing illegal about continuing to use the supply in another person's name, or where the bill is addressed to 'The Occupier', so long as you intend to pay for it. Anyone who uses fuel without intending to pay could be prosecuted for theft (see Chapter 9). The suppliers could rely on the law relating to 'unjust enrichment' to ensure payment in these circumstances. This applies when someone unjustly obtains benefit at someone else's expense. In England and Wales, the idea of unjust enrichment arises in the law of restitution; in Scotland, the equivalent is found in the law of recompense. However, if it can be shown that the supplier continued to provide fuel despite a request to disconnect or terminate a contract then the doctrine of unjust enrichment and the requirement of restitution do not apply.

Establishing who should pay the bill depends on the facts in each case.

Example
Louisa is a sole occupier and did not ask for a supply because it was already connected when she moved into her flat. She receives bills addressed to 'The Occupier'. Based simply on the facts, Louisa could be held liable for the bill from the date she moved in.

Where there is more than one occupier, establishing who is liable is often more difficult. Facts which might be relevant in establishing who is liable include:

- your status as an occupier;
- the extent of control you have over the use of fuel;
- your actual use of fuel;
- the degree of control you have over income within your household;
- the terms of any tenancy agreement;
- the date you moved in and the date another occupier moved in;
- where the bill was previously in the name of another joint occupier, their status as an occupier and the date they left;
- whether you are registered at the dwelling for council tax or other utility bills.

It is advisable to give the supplier notice that you are leaving, to avoid disputes about the end of your period of liability, and supply an up-to-date meter reading. Keep a record for yourself, such as a note of the reading, a photograph of the meter and the date, in the event that a dispute arises over your final bill.

Your liability when someone else has been responsible for the supply

You are not liable to pay the supplier for the electricity bill if:

- you have not entered into a contract; *and*
- someone else is liable for the supply under contract and that person's liability for the supply has not come to an end (see p62).

You should also not be held liable for the supply when it is clear that someone else took responsibility for it, perhaps as a result of phone contact with the supplier. In one case, the court held that the wife of a deceased man should not be held liable for an electricity bill accrued by him in his name. She was only liable to pay for the supply following his death. The supplier had tried to argue that the woman should be held jointly liable for the debt, as she had benefited from the use of the supply – the 'beneficial user argument'. The judge declined to follow the county court case cited by the supplier in support of its argument.[8]

You are usually liable to pay for a supply of energy even if you did not read the contract before signing it. However, if there has been misrepresentation to induce you into signing, such as by way of fraud or negligence, the contract may be rescinded. Even if a court claim for misrepresentation is successful, you may still have to pay for the energy consumed if you have had the benefit of this.

Sending the bill to another person

Where reasonably practical, suppliers can send the bill to another person to deal with[9] – eg, a friend or relative. You can request this if you:

- are over pension age;

- have a disability or long-term health condition;
- have a hearing or sight condition;
- are pregnant or have children under five;
- have a mental health condition;
- have experienced domestic abuse;
- have another vulnerable characteristic or situation or have requested to be added to the Priority Services Register (see p98).

Suppliers must ensure that they obtain your informed consent before disclosing such information to ensure, among other things, compliance with data protection regulations.[10] This can be achieved by recording a third party's details on the supplier's system or records. You need to ensure that a third party is not erroneously added to the account as an account holder, which may result in the third party being deemed liable by a supplier.

Privity of contract

In some cases, a legal principle known as 'privity of contract' may help establish liability. The principle provides that only the parties who have entered into and established the contract are subject to binding rights and obligations under it. If one party breaches the contract, the other party is the only person(s) entitled to seek a remedy. Liability cannot be imposed on a third party who is a stranger to the contract unless an agreement or guarantee is given. In general, a contract cannot confer or enforce rights or impose obligations (such as claiming compensation or damages) arising under it on any person except the parties subject to it.

Examples

Katy is a student and lives alone. Her father is the guarantor for her energy supply. A bill has gone unpaid. The supplier can approach Katy's father and demand payment.

Ayo is a student and lives in a house with other students. His name is on the energy bill. An energy bill has gone unpaid. The supplier cannot approach Ayo's parents and demand payment of the bill. Ayo's parents are not liable for Ayo's debts, since no contract was made with them.

Rowan moves into a new property where previous occupiers have failed to pay an energy bill. Rowan cannot be held liable for the bills left behind.

The doctrine of privity of contract is of importance where a house is in multiple occupation and residents are transient. In many cases, it is arguable that the long-term occupiers or the landlord are those who are liable under the supply contract, since these are the individuals who have actually reached a binding agreement with the supplier, either in writing, orally or by conduct.

3. When you are liable for a gas bill

In this section, all references to 'the bill' refer only to 'charges due' for the supply of gas and do not include other charges such as credit sales charges for appliances. See p135 for more information about 'charges due'.

Supply of gas to domestic properties must be under a supply contract or deemed contract.[11]

The Gas Act 1995

Since 1 March 1996, gas has been supplied to existing customers of British Gas under the terms of a 'deemed contract'. From this date, new customers who request a supply from any supplier, including British Gas, are supplied under the terms of a 'supply contract'. Any new customers who receive a supply of gas from a gas supplier without first entering into a contract are supplied under the terms of a 'deemed contract' instead (see p8).

You are liable for a gas bill if:

- you were a tariff customer of British Gas on 31 January 1996. You will have had a deemed contract with British Gas from 1 March 1996. You are liable to pay for your supply under the terms of the deemed contract which applies to you;
- you entered into a contract with any supplier from 1 March 1996. You are liable to pay for your supply under the terms of the contract;
- you have a deemed contract with a supplier that started after 1 March 1996.

Former tariff customers under the Gas Act 1986

If you were a tariff customer of British Gas immediately before 1 March 1996, you will have automatically become a customer with a deemed contract.[12] You can be held liable to pay the bill under the terms of a deemed contract if you were the tariff customer under the provisions of the Gas Act 1986, before it was amended by the Gas Act 1995. This can only be decided under the terms of the law that applied at that time.

A '**tariff customer**' was defined as 'a person supplied with gas' under the Gas Act 1986;[13] and should not be confused with customers under special tariff schemes run by suppliers. Each supplier is required by the Gas Act to act in accordance with the 'Gas Code' laid down in Schedule 2B of the Gas Act 1986.[14]

Termination of deemed contracts

The Gas Code does not specify when a deemed contract ends. This means that a deemed contract continues until it is actively terminated. The contract starts from the moment that fuel is supplied to your home other than under a contract. The duration and methods for terminating a deemed contract should be specified, like the other terms, by each supplier in its contract or terms and conditions – ie, the original contract contains renewal provisions. Typical provisions for termination include the customer entering into an express contract, registering with another supplier or disconnection. The liabilities under a deemed contract continue in accordance with the terms of the contract until it is actively brought to an end.[15]

Ofgem has published a statement providing a general, but legally non-binding, interpretation of the deemed contract provisions. Its interpretation of the legislation is that gas and/or electricity must be consumed in order for a deemed contract to arise between a supplier and the occupier and/or owner. It equally accepts that, ultimately, the existence of a deemed contract is open to interpretation by the courts and depends on each individual case.[16]

Customers with contracts

Your liability for the bill

To enter into a contract, you must be the owner or occupier of the property where the gas supply is needed. You must request a supply, though your request need not be in writing.[17]

A supplier cannot enter into a contract with you if someone else has a contract for the supply of gas with another supplier for the same premises, unless that contract will expire or terminate before you require a supply. In practice, you do not have to terminate your existing contract formally before entering a new one – if you sign up to a new contract, the switch should be handled by the two suppliers.

You must agree to the terms of your contract with your supplier. Terms of contracts are not individually negotiated. However, contracts must be in writing and include terms detailing the charges for the supply and termination of the supply.[18] Your supplier has a scheme, approved by Ofgem, setting out the principal terms of the various contracts on offer. Your supplier must take all reasonable steps to communicate the principal terms to you.[19] You can request a copy of the principal terms, which must be sent within a reasonable period.[20]

Contracts may be for an indefinite period (known as a 'rolling contract') or a fixed period. Where a contract is due to come to an end, you have the option of agreeing either a new fixed-term contract or a new rolling contract with your existing supplier. If you do nothing, your supplier must switch you to the relevant cheapest rolling tariff it is able to offer or a further fixed-term default tariff. This switch happens automatically if no new contract is agreed.[21] The terms of contracts are restricted by provisions within a supplier's licence and regulated by Ofgem.

Ending your liability for the bill

You are liable to pay for the supply under the terms of the contract until one of the following applies.

- **Your contract comes to an end.** If a fixed-term contract is due to end, the supplier must provide you with a statement of renewal terms no earlier than 49 days before the term is due to end.[22] This must be separate from any other document such as a bill, statement of account or marketing material.[23]
- **You terminate your contract while you are still an owner/occupier of the premises.** A contract for a fixed period may be ended at any time during that period if you give the supplier notice according to the contract and pay any termination fee referred to in the contract, if liable, unless either of the following conditions apply.[24]
  - **Your contract is of an indefinite length of time.** This also applies where an initial fixed-term contract has expired and you have continued to receive a supply from the company on a rolling contract.[25]
  - **Your supplier has unilaterally varied a term in your contract.** The most obvious example is a price increase. However, any other changes made to your terms which significantly disadvantage you also apply here, such as placing you on a higher tariff.[26]
- **You terminate your contract with your supplier and switch to another supplier.**[27] See Chapter 2 for more information about this process. You do not have to pay a termination fee if you want to switch because your supplier has changed the terms of your contract unilaterally. You must notify your current supplier of your intention to switch on or before the date the variation takes effect to avoid the possibility of you being charged a termination or exit fee. This notification does not have to be in writing. If you notify your supplier orally or online, make a note of the date and the name of the person you spoke to or keep a copy of your email or online account record. You do not have to actually switch supplier or switch within a particular time frame to avoid the termination fees, you simply need to notify your intention to do so.

  If you have arrears with your current supplier, you can still change supplier in theory, but you must clear the arrears within 30 days. A supplier can stop you from switching to another supplier where a debt has not been repaid for 28 days or more. This is known as a 'debt objection'.

  If you have a prepayment meter, your supplier can only block you from switching to another supplier if you owe more than £500.[28] If you switch, you take your debt with you and repay it to your new supplier under a 'debt assignment protocol' (see p125).[29]
- **You no longer occupy the premises.** The supplier must include a term that the supply contract ends two days after you have told the supplier of the date on which you stop owning or occupying the premises.[30]

  Where a contract ends in this way, you remain liable for the supply of gas to the property until the date on which that contract ends.[31]

If you give your supplier a minimum of two working days' notice, or if your supplier agrees to accept a shorter period of notice before you leave, your contract ends on the day you leave.

If you do not give your supplier notice that you are leaving, your contract will not terminate, and you will continue to be liable to pay for the supply of gas until the earlier of:[32]

– two working days after you have told the supplier you have left; *or*
– the date when another person requires a supply at the premises from either the same or a different supplier.

It is always in your interest to inform the supplier that you are leaving or have left. Make sure you arrange for the supplier to take a final meter reading and also read the meter yourself so you can check your final bill in the event that a dispute arises over it. Keep a copy of any correspondence and a photograph of the meter.

- **The supplier varies the terms of your contract.** If your supplier increases the charges made under the terms of your contract or varies other terms of your contract unilaterally and the variations will significantly disadvantage you, the supplier must inform you of the changes made. Suppliers must give you reasonable time and notice in an appropriate form (taking into account your characteristics and preferences)[33] of a price rise or any other change which will leave you worse off.[34] The supplier must also notify you that you have the option to change supplier, that you may financially benefit from doing so[35] or enter into a new contract[36] and provide you with information, tools and services to make informed tariff and consumption choices[37] and avoid any changes before they take effect.[38] This includes switching information, such as the cheapest available tariff, estimated annual costs and information about your existing tariff to enable you to compare tariffs across the retail market.[39] If you decide to terminate your contract after receiving a price increase notice, and switch to another supplier, your old supplier must terminate your contract within 20 working days of receiving confirmation that you now have a contract with your new supplier.[40] Your old supplier cannot apply the price rise to your bill for the remainder of your contract with it.[41]

- **The supplier's licence is revoked by Ofgem.** This can be for reasons including regulatory intervention or the supplier entering administration. If this happens, your contract with that supplier is terminated. Ofgem will require another supplier to continue to supply you with gas under terms directed by Ofgem.[42] You then become liable to pay the new supplier under those terms. If you choose to enter into a contract with the new supplier, the terms of the contract apply from the date you enter into the contract. The same applies if you choose to be supplied by a different supplier.

Customers with deemed contracts

Your liability for the bill

You are supplied with gas under the terms of a deemed contract if you are a consumer at the premises supplied with gas and:[43]

- you are the owner or occupier of the premises supplied with gas, and the liability for the supply of the former customer has come to an end or been terminated; *or*
- you became the new owner or occupier of the premises on or after 1 March 1996 and you have not entered into a contract with a supplier for a supply of gas; *or*
- your contract for the supply of gas has come to an end or been terminated and you continue to receive a supply of gas from the supplier; *or*
- you are being supplied with gas by another supplier because your supplier's licence has been revoked by Ofgem.

The terms and conditions of a deemed contract are determined in accordance with a scheme set up by the supplier.[44] They may include terms and conditions enabling the supplier to determine the amount of gas supplied to you if a meter reading has not been taken at the start of the deemed contract. Your liability is assessed under these terms until the earliest of the following three events:[45]

- the date of the first meter reading; *or*
- the time the supplier ceases to supply you with gas; *or*
- the date you cease to take a supply of gas.

Disputes over the rate of gas consumption

There may be a dispute over the amount of gas consumption, particularly where appliances have broken down or have not been used. In such a case, a supplier providing a gas supply under a deemed contract is required to act reasonably and take into account relevant consumption data for the premises.[46]

For more on high bills, see Chapter 6.

Ending your liability for the bill

Your liability under the terms of a deemed contract continues until one of the following applies.

- **You enter into a contract while you are still an owner or occupier of the premises.** You continue to be liable under the terms of a deemed contract until your new contract takes effect.

  You may terminate a deemed contract at any time by giving the supplier seven days' notice. The notice period may be shorter if the supplier agrees. If you have not arranged to enter into a contract with the same supplier at the end of the notice period, your supply continues under the terms of a further deemed contract.

If you intend to switch supplier, you must give your existing supplier at least 28 days' notice, unless the supplier agrees to accept a shorter notice period.

You may not bring a deemed contract to an end without the agreement of the supplier, if you are being supplied by an alternative supplier because your supplier's licence was revoked by Ofgem.[47] You can only bring such a deemed contract to an end:

– with the agreement of the supplier (which will be given if you accept a contract with that supplier);[48] *or*
– by transferring to another supplier; *or*
– by ceasing to take a supply of gas at the premises.[49]

- **You cease to occupy the premises.** If you give your supplier a minimum of two working days' notice, or if your supplier agrees to accept a shorter period of notice before you leave, your deemed contract ends on the day you leave.

If you do not give your supplier notice that you are leaving, your deemed contract does not terminate and you continue to be liable to pay for the supply of gas until the earliest of:

– 28 days after you inform the supplier you have left;
– the next date the meter is due to be read;
– the date when another person requires a supply at the premises from either the same supplier or a different supplier.

4. **Common problems**

Your liability when your name is on the bill

Electricity

The person named on a bill is not always liable to pay. Sometimes only one person is actually named on a bill, even if several people signed the notice requiring a supply or the contract or no one signed anything. For example, suppliers sometimes ask outgoing occupiers the names of the next occupiers. You may find that your name is on a bill without you ever having had any contact with the supplier. A person who is named on the bill has sole liability for the bill if they alone gave written notice requiring a supply or they alone made a phone request for the supply or other authorised and recognised means to acknowledge liability. Otherwise, the name on the bill is only evidence of who *might* be liable.

Gas

If you have a deemed contract with British Gas (see p67), you need to check that you are liable under the provisions for deciding who becomes a customer with a deemed contract (see p71).

If you have entered into a contract with a gas supplier and your name is on the bill, you are liable under the terms of the contract (see p68).

Who is liable when no one is named on the bill

Electricity

When no one is named on the bill, liability depends on the individual facts.

Gas

If no one is named on the bill, you may be liable for the bill under the terms of a deemed contract (see p71).

Moving in: becoming liable for the supply

When moving to a new address, make a note of the meter reading and preferably agree the reading with the last occupier(s), so that you can use this as evidence of when your liability for supply started. If possible, arrange to have the meter read by the supplier, and inform them that you require a supply. Check your first bill carefully to ensure that the dates used by the supplier are correct and the bill does not include the previous occupiers' charges or arrears. You cannot be held responsible for the previous occupiers' arrears of electricity or gas.

Electricity

If an electricity supplier does not routinely use application forms, consider whether you should request a supply in writing. One person can give notice if that person wants to take responsibility. If you are a joint occupier who wants to share liability, ensure that everyone living in the property signs the application form, letter or contract.

If one joint occupier moves out and you move in to take their place, there is nothing to prevent you from giving notice specifying that you are replacing a joint occupier or arranging a new contract. Liability depends on who signs the new arrangement.

Gas

If you do not inform a supplier that you have moved in, the last supplier to supply gas at the premises is entitled to charge you for any gas you have used under the terms of a deemed contract. To avoid this happening, take proactive steps to contact the supplier to obtain a supply. You are initially liable under the terms of a deemed contract, until you enter directly into a contract with the supplier.

If you do not know the last supplier to supply gas at the premises, call the Meter Point Reference Helpline on 0870 608 1524 or visit findmysupplier.energy for details of your gas supplier and your Meter Point Reference Number.

Moving out: ending liability for the supply

If you are an occupier and you give a supplier proper notice that you are leaving, you should not be held liable for the fuel used after you have left.

You remain liable for six years after the date on which a bill for gas or electricity fell due in England and Wales; five years in Scotland. So, if you change supplier but have an outstanding debt to a previous supplier, the previous supplier has a right to bring legal action against you for up to six years. Thereafter, the debt becomes irrecoverable under the Limitation Act 1980.[50] In Scotland, the limitation period is five years.[51]

Electricity

In the absence of notice, ending liability depends on the terms of your contract with the supplier.

Gas

There are provisions in both the Gas Act 1986, as amended by the Gas Act 1995, and in suppliers' licence conditions that set out when your liability for gas ends under supply contracts (see p69) and deemed contracts (see p71).

Who is liable when the person named on the bill has left

Sole liability

Electricity

A person who is named on the bill has sole liability for the bill if they alone became the customer by giving written notice requiring a supply or entering into a contract. Their liability ends either when they left if they gave notice of leaving or with the passing of time. As a joint occupier, spouse or co-habitee, you cannot be held liable for their bill if you have not given notice requiring a supply or entered into a contract. If you remain in the property after the co-habitee has left, you should request a new supply in your name. This is the point at which your liability for supply commences (see p65).

Gas

If you alone entered into a contract for the supply of gas, your responsibility for that supply ends either on your terminating the contract (see p69) or with the passing of time. One or more remaining occupiers may subsequently have responsibility for the supply under the terms of a deemed contract (see p71).

If you are liable under the terms of a deemed contract, your liability ends either with the termination of that deemed contract or with the passing of time (see p71). The liability of the remaining occupiers is also under the terms of a deemed contract.

Shared liability

Electricity

If the person who left gave written notice or entered into a contract to obtain the electricity supply, their liability ends either when they inform the supplier they are leaving or with the passing of time (see p62). Any remaining occupiers who originally gave notice in writing or entered into the contract are liable for the arrears along with the person who has left.

Where nobody gave notice or signed a contract, liability for the arrears depends on the facts of each case. You could still be held liable for all of the arrears, but may be able to negotiate a compromise with the supplier (look at the supplier's code of practice on payment of bills and treatment of arrears, which may contain an indication of the supplier's attitude or general approach).

As a joint occupier or sharer, you could ask for the amount of the arrears to be apportioned between the people responsible for the bill, particularly if the supplier knows the whereabouts of all the parties. Electricity suppliers are entitled to refuse to supply an occupier who owes arrears[52] and, in any event, could pursue each debtor separately through the courts.[53] If the occupier who left was your partner, and you had little or no control over the income of the household (eg, only your partner had a wage, received state benefits or you were the victim of economic abuse),[54] you could argue that you should not be held responsible for any arrears that accrued while your partner was present and ask the supplier to pursue your partner for the arrears.

Gas

If you were jointly supplied under the terms of a supply contract, the terms of the contract apply. There may be scope for you to argue that any arrears should be apportioned between all the parties to the contract. When the previous joint occupier leaves, make sure you inform the supplier of the meter reading and/or apply for a new contract/deemed contract in your own name so the arrears relating to the joint occupancy are clearly established.

Where a joint deemed contract comes to an end because one of the occupiers has left, inform the supplier and establish any arrears relating to the period of joint occupancy.

The strict application of this legal position on liability for a bill can create problems for many customers with children left with large arrears after a spouse/partner has left. Gas suppliers should, therefore, be urged to treat these situations sympathetically and positively, taking into account the individual circumstances of each case. They should also take into consideration the existence of formal or informal agreements between the parties concerned for responsibility for household expenses, including gas. Get advice if you do not feel your gas supplier is acting reasonably.

Who is liable when the person named on the bill dies

When the person named on the bill dies, the supplier may attempt to secure payment from someone who was living with them. In these circumstances, the situation is as outlined above. Where no one else is liable for the bill, any bills outstanding can be charged to the deceased's estate. This means that outstanding bills must be paid for out of money belonging to the deceased, or out of the proceeds of the sale of any belongings. The cost of the funeral and any costs involved in dealing with the estate take priority over all other debts except 'realised securities' such as a mortgaged property. So, if a consumer dies with an outstanding mortgage and the house is sold to meet this debt, anything left will go first to pay for the funeral and administration costs; any outstanding fuel bills are a lower priority. See CPAG's *Debt Advice Handbook* or *Debt Advice Handbook Scotland* for more details.

If the person left nothing, the bill lapses and the supplier must bear the loss. If you have paid the bill of a person who has died in the mistaken belief that you were responsible for doing so, the supplier can usually be persuaded either to credit your account or refund the money. If the supplier refuses to do so, get legal advice about the options available to you. This can include making a formal complaint with the supplier or recovering the monies through the small claims court.

Assignment of outstanding charges to your new supplier

You might become liable for an old energy bill where the supplier has assigned the outstanding debt to your new supplier. If you fail to pay the old supplier within 28 days of the charges being due, it may assign the debt to your new supplier. If your new supplier agrees, it can take over the debt where:
- it has become due to the first supplier; *and*
- it had been demanded in writing; *and*
- you were notified that the charges might be assigned.

However, it is more likely that the transfer will be blocked by a supplier within the framework laid down by Standard Licence Condition (SLC) 14.

Domestic customer transfer blocking

Under SLC 14, the supplier may prevent a proposed supplier transfer where:[55]
- there are outstanding charges; *or*
- you did not ask for a transfer.

A supply transfer cannot be prevented where gas is supplied by a prepayment meter and you have agreed to pay the existing charges, which should be no greater than £500. Nor can a transfer be stopped where the supplier has increased charges but has not reset the prepayment meter within a reasonable period, and the outstanding charges only relate to the period since a price increase.[56]

The Limitation Act 1980

Energy companies may sometimes attempt to pursue debts more than six years after the sum fell due. A six-year legal recovery limit is placed on sums due under the contract (actual or deemed), after which time it is statute-barred.[57] In Scotland, the limitation period is five years.[58] The Limitation Act 1980 applies to a contract to supply energy in the same way that it applies to other contracts. This means that if you have not acknowledged the debt for six years, the energy company cannot take court action to recover the money claimed. Paying the energy company for the sum claimed would constitute acknowledgement, as would any written correspondence about the debt. It is not usually possible to acknowledge a debt verbally – eg, over the telephone. You should exercise caution about your contact with the energy company if the debt is nearing the six-year limit, as acknowledging the debt can start the clock running again.

Do not ignore any summons from the county court and seek advice about whether you need to defend the claim – eg, because the time limit for taking action has expired. If you do not do this within 14 days of being sent the proceedings, a judgment in default may be entered against you even if there is no valid basis for the claim.

If the supplier has obtained a county court judgment within the relevant limitation period, then in theory there is no limit on the amount of time that the energy company can pursue you for the balance due under the judgment. This is because enforcement action is not subject to a limitation.[59] However, if the judgment is over six years old, the creditor will need to obtain the permission of the court to enforce the debt. The court will consider the supplier's reasons for the delay in enforcement action, why leave should be granted and reasons for enforcement. Caselaw has shown that the court will refuse to grant permission unless there are 'exceptional circumstances'.[60] For more information on court proceedings, see Chapter 14.

Harassment by suppliers and debt collectors

In some cases, a supplier may wrongly attempt to pursue a claim against you long after any supply and any liability have ended. Such acts may constitute harassment if the supplier persists despite you establishing the true position.

In extreme cases, sending demands for payment accompanied by threats of disconnection or referral to credit reference agencies may constitute harassment both in civil and criminal law.[61] Remedies can include reporting the harassment to the police as a criminal offence, seeking a civil injunction in the county court or applying for a breathing space moratorium (see p103).[62]

Suppliers' licences also contain conditions requiring them and any agent/representative to behave and carry out any actions in a fair, honest, transparent, appropriate and professional manner.[63] Referrals and complaints can be made to Ofgem if a breach is suspected. A formal complaint can also be raised against the supplier and ultimately with the Energy Ombudsman.

In other cases, an old debt may be assigned by the energy company to a firm of debt collectors. These companies may contact you frequently by letter and telephone, threatening to take legal action against you. Often they are based far from where you live and have no intention of issuing any sort of legal proceedings or visiting you, despite claims in the letter that they will do so (see Chapter 14).

If you deal with these companies, do so in writing or email, rather than by telephone, bearing in mind the advice above about the limitation period if you have not had any contact with the supplier or its representatives for some time. You should seek advice if possible before responding.

Any such claim should be closely examined to ensure that there has not been a mistake. If contacting a debt collecting company, request copies of all the alleged paperwork on which the claim is based. As fuel debts are based upon contracts, there should be evidence of a valid assignment of the debt between the energy company and the debt collector. An **'assignment'** is a legal document whereby the legal right to claim the debt is transferred from one person to another, including the right of enforcement. The details of any assignment must match precisely the amount being claimed. You should ask the debt collecting company to produce a copy of any assignment from the original supplier.

Debt collectors have no right of entry to your home. If they make threats or commit acts of harassment, contact the Financial Conduct Authority (FCA),[64] which has responsibility for regulating such companies and will investigate incidents of serious misconduct. The FCA's *Consumer Credit Source Book* may be useful here; particularly section 7 which refers to the conduct of external debt collection companies. Although gas and electricity contracts are not regulated agreements, the guidance in section 7 can be used as useful guidance as to what constitutes reasonable behaviour. See handbook.fca.org.uk/handbook/conc.

Under the Consumer Duty, FCA-regulated debt collectors are expected to act to deliver good outcomes for customers and avoid forseeable harm. This could be an additional means by which to change incidents of serious misconduct.[65]

Notes

1. Introduction
1 Condition 22.1 SLC; Sch 6 para 3(1) EA 1989
2 Sch 6 para 3(1) EA 1989
3 Condition 22.1 SLC; Sch 2 para 8(1) GA 1995

2. When you are liable for an electricity bill
4 Condition 24.1 SLC
5 Condition 24 SLC
6 Condition 24.8 SLC
7 *British Gas Plc v Mitchell* (unreported) Pontefract County Court, May 1994
8 *Faulker v Yorkshire Electricity Group Plc* [1994] February 1995, *Legal Action* 23

9 Condition 26.5(b) SLC
10 Condition 26.6 SLC

3. **When you are liable for a gas bill**
11 Condition 22.1 SLC
12 Sch 5 para 19(2) GA 1995
13 s14(5) GA 1986, repealed by GA 1995
14 Sch 2B GA 1986
15 *Laverty and Others v British Gas Trading Ltd* [2014] EWHC 2721
16 Ofgem statement on deemed contracts, 24 June 2010, ofgem.gov.uk/publications/statement-deemed-contracts
17 Condition 22.2 SLC
18 Condition 22.4 SLC
19 Condition 23.1 SLC
20 Condition 22.8 SLC
21 Condition 22C.7 SLC
22 Conditions 24.17 and 31I.1 SLC
23 Conditions 22C.5 and 31I.7 SLC
24 Condition 24.1 SLC
25 Condition 24.3 SLC
26 Conditions 14A.6 and 24.3 SLC
27 Condition 14A.6 SLC
28 Ofgem, The Debt Assignment Protocol; condition 14.6 SLC
29 Ofgem, The Debt Assignment Protocol
30 Condition 21.1(a) SLC
31 Condition 24.2 SLC
32 Condition 24.1(b) SLC
33 Condition 31I.3 SLC
34 Conditions 23.3 and 31I SLC
35 Condition 31F.4 SLC
36 Condition 31I.4 SLC
37 Condition 31F.3 SLC
38 Condition 31I SLC
39 Condition 31F.5 SLC
40 Condition 24.10 SLC
41 Condition 24.11 SLC
42 Condition 8.2(b) SLC
43 Conditions 7 and 22 SLC set out the obligations of a supplier under deemed contracts
44 Sch 2B para 8(8) GA 1986
45 Sch 2B para 8(9) GA 1986
46 Condition 7.9 SLC
47 Condition 7.1 SLC
48 Condition 7.5(c) SLC
49 Condition 7.5(d) SLC

4. **Common problems**
50 Limitation Act 1980
51 Prescription and Limitation (Scotland) Act 1973
52 Condition 22.7 SLC
53 *Laverty and Others v British Gas Trading Ltd* [2014] EWHC 2721

54 s1(3) Domestic Abuse Act 2021
55 Condition 14.4 SLC
56 Conditions 14.5 and 14.6 SLC
57 s24(1) Limitation Act 1980
58 Prescription and Limitation (Scotland) Act 1973
59 *Lowsley v Forbes* [1998] UKHL 34
60 *The Society of Lloyd's v Longtin* [2005] EWHC 2491 (Comm)
61 *Ferguson v British Gas Trading Ltd* [2009] EWCA Civ 46
62 DRS Regs
63 Condition 0.3(a) SLC
64 fca.org.uk
65 fca.org.uk/firms/consumer-duty

Chapter 6

High bills

This chapter covers:
1. Amount of the bill (below)
2. Accuracy of the bill (p83)
3. Accuracy of the meter (p88)
4. Meter faults and faulty appliances (p93)

1. Amount of the bill

This chapter looks at ways of checking whether you are paying the correct amount for your gas and electricity. If your bills are correct, see Chapter 4 for how to pay; Chapters 11 and 12 for financial and other help with paying them; and Chapters 7 and 8 if you are in arrears and/or facing disconnection. Chapter 14 suggests remedies for when a supplier charges you the wrong amount.

Understanding your bill

Your bill must show what you have paid and what you owe, a summary of your energy usage and details of your supplier's cheapest deal.

Suppliers must provide a bill or statement of account at least twice a year, or quarterly if you request a quarterly bill.[1] For smart meters with remote energy monitoring enabled, a supplier must offer to provide or make available accurate monthly billing information based on consumption.[2] Bills should be available 'in plain and intelligible language',[3] in a form you can retain,[4] easily available for reference[5] and free of charge.[6] A supplier cannot charge for providing you with a bill, details of consumption used to calculate the bill or any statement of account. However, your supplier can charge for providing copies of bills that have already been sent to you.[7]

Suppliers must give you reasonable notice, in an appropriate form and frequency (taking into account your characteristics and preferences), of a price rise or any other change to billing which will leave you worse off.[8] Suppliers also have to actively enable you to understand and manage your costs and consumption on an ongoing basis, such as by providing you with information, tools and services to make informed tariff and consumption choices.[9] Standard Licence Condition (SLC) 31H requires that suppliers include in your bill a machine-readable label (such as a QR code) and an 'About Your Tariff' label, providing you with key data and information about your tariff and consumption to enable and encourage you to compare the energy retail market and make more informed decisions about your choice of energy supplier.[10]

If you have a smart meter calibrated to take remote meter readings, your supplier must provide monthly billing information based on actual consumption.[11]

Your supplier must include information about sources of independent and impartial advice.[12]

Duty on suppliers to obtain meter readings

Suppliers must take all reasonable steps to obtain accurate meter readings from customers annually or monthly from a remote transmission reading by a smart meter.[13]

The supplier can fulfil its obligation by accepting a meter reading which you take and supply to the company, which should then be reflected in your next bill.[14] If the supplier does not accept your reading, it must take all reasonable steps to contact you to obtain a further reading[15] or it must obtain its own reading.

Check consumption

If a bill seems too high, first check whether your consumption has actually increased. You can do this by comparing the units consumed with those used during the same period in previous years, by looking at bills for previous years. SLC 31H makes this process relatively straightforward as it requires that your bill should include a comparison of your fuel consumption for the period covered by the bill with your consumption for the same period in the previous year where that is known. It should also include, among other requirements:

- the exact tariff name;
- your annual consumption details;
- your estimated annual costs;
- the relevant and alternative cheapest tariff available to you;
- your chosen payment method.

If you do not receive regular bills (eg, because you have a prepayment meter), your supplier must send you an annual statement which contains the same information.

If you have not kept previous bills, ask the supplier for copies. Some suppliers may charge for these.[16] If the charge seems unreasonably high, contact Citizens Advice consumer service or Advice Direct Scotland for guidance.

Bear in mind that consumption fluctuates seasonally, so you are likely to consume more fuel in cold winter months than you are in the summer.

Consumption: reasons for a high bill

There may be multiple reasons for higher consumption – eg, because of:
- a change in your household, such as a new baby or working from home;
- using appliances and older models that are not energy efficient;
- introducing and using new appliances, such as a tumble dryer;
- higher usage of electronics, such as desktop computers, gaming consoles, set-top boxes and smart home technologies;
- your home being poorly insulated and not energy efficient.

Consumption: exceptional reasons for a high bill

Check whether consumption is higher than usual because of exceptional reasons – eg, because of:
- an emergency, such as a flood;
- a new heating system that you are not used to operating;
- a new heating system that may need a different tariff;
- a defective heating system;
- a period of exceptionally cold winter weather or a hot summer;
- a fault or leak in your supply;
- someone in the household being ill.

If you think the bill is accurate after taking any exceptional circumstances into account, see Chapters 4, 11 and 12 for help on how to pay.

Other charges in the bill

Bills may also be high because they include items other than the cost of fuel and standing charges. Typically, utility bills comprise two parts: a standing charge for the service to be available to you and a variable charge for the usage of the fuel. A supplier may also include charges for disconnection or reconnection, and for replacing meters. Check to see if these have been lawfully charged by reading Chapter 3 on supply and charges for connecting supply, and Chapter 8 on disconnection for arrears.

Other variables and drivers for a high bill, unrelated to your consumption, include:
- supplier increasing the cost of its energy because of wholesale energy market and network price increases;
- supplier regulated investments;
- structure maintenance and improvements;
- energy efficiency infrastructure development;
- low-carbon energy technology investment and climate change reforms;

- government schemes and targets to tackle pollution and reduce emissions;
- changes in government policies to protect consumers from rising costs;
- supplier failure-related costs;
- obligated costs for support for vulnerable households.

2. **Accuracy of the bill**

Always check that the supplier has calculated your bill correctly. If the units consumed are correctly recorded, check that the cost has been correctly calculated.

If disconnection or prepayment meter installation is threatened but you think the bill is inaccurate, tell the supplier immediately. A supplier cannot disconnect or install a prepayment meter for part of a bill that is genuinely in dispute.[17] However, you cannot avoid paying for gas or electricity used simply because of a mistake resulting in an inaccurate bill – the supplier has the legal right to make you pay for what you have used, even if it initially made an error on the bill.[18] In particular, you should take steps to pay for the part of the electricity bill that you do not dispute, or you could be disconnected for that alone. If you cannot afford to pay the amount you agree you owe in full, set up a payment plan to demonstrate you are willing to pay for what you have used (see Chapter 7).

If you experience difficulty dealing with a supplier, particularly if staff at call centres cannot help, be prepared to raise a formal complaint. This usually results in reaching a more senior member of staff to deal with the issue. If you are vulnerable (see p139), request that your account be handled by a specialist team or member of staff. Suppliers have obligations under their standards of conduct that you are treated fairly[19] and that their actions are honest and transparent.[20]

Suppliers are obliged to facilitate and develop your understanding of bills, tariff, cost and energy consumption. Bills and statements of accounts must be provided to you in a suitable form (such as paper, app or online) for you to readily retain or have access to for ease of reference.[21] Suppliers are obliged to provide you with the following billing information at least once a year or at key prompt points, appropriate to your circumstances:[22]

- any charges, fees or payments debited or credited from your account;
- your balance;
- detailed breakdown of charges, fees or payments;
- when and how you must make payment;
- when and how you will have payments deducted, with reasonable time afforded to arrange payment before its due date;
- any expected changes to your product and when they are due;
- whether or not the price is guaranteed until a given date.

Since 1 May 2018, suppliers are prohibited from sending retrospective bills (back-bill), or otherwise recover and reconcile fuel arrears, which date back for more than 12 months.[23] These back-bills result from a supplier's failure to undertake an actual meter reading or problems with a supplier's billing system and only sending you a bill once an accurate meter reading is taken. This is subject to certain exceptions and does not apply if you have been obstructive or unreasonable, such as preventing a supplier from taking or receiving accurate readings, including obstructing access to the meter or tampering with the meter.[24]

You must also be able to show that you have made a reasonable attempt to contact a supplier to make or arrange payment either in full or by instalments.

Where a supplier issues a bill which is contrary to the back-billing licence conditions, it should credit your account with the value of the unbilled energy consumed over 12 months ago, taking into consideration any payments already made by you or credits applied to the account, so that you are not required to pay any additional sums towards this previously unbilled energy consumption. Refusing to do so may suggest non-compliance with Standard Licence Condition (SLC) 21BA and give rise to a regulatory complaint to Ofgem. Initially, a formal complaint should be raised with the supplier upon receipt of an erroneous back-bill. If this does not result in a remedy, you can complain further to the Energy Ombudsman (see Chapter 14).

Billing delays

You may find that the supplier has billed you for a longer period than normal and, when you finally receive the bill, it covers that whole period. A delayed bill can cause a high bill. Suppliers are not obliged to bill you at any particular interval, although they usually send bills every three months or six months. However, they must provide a bill at least twice a year, or quarterly if you request a quarterly bill.[25] If you have a prepayment meter, statements are usually sent to you at least once a year. If you have a smart meter, calibrated to remotely transmit meter readings, your supplier can provide accurate monthly bills based on your consumption.[26]

If regular bills have not been sent, or are late, point out to the supplier that it has directly contributed towards the high level of debt by making it difficult for you to monitor or modify consumption. It should be possible to negotiate time to pay. Suppliers must take into account your ability to pay.

Bills sent after a long time should be examined with care: the charges and tariffs may have changed since the previous bill. The majority of consumers still do not switch providers or indeed tariffs, resulting in them being overcharged, the supplier earning excess profit with little incentive to operate efficiently. Ofgem has found that more than half of energy consumers tend to be on a standard variable or default tariff[27] and in the absence of the statutory default tariff price cap,[28] consumers would be overcharged for the energy they use.

If fuel or energy prices have increased or you have changed your tariff, check to ensure that the supplier has charged accurately and at the correct unit rate and standing charge. If it has not, the bill should be amended and reduced accordingly. Also check that the supplier has complied with the requirement at SLC 31I to give you reasonable notice, in an appropriate form and time, of any changes to the cost of your supply.

There have been cases of bills generated to customers after months or even years. Unless fraud is involved (see Chapter 9), charges cannot be recovered:
- in England and Wales, if you last made a payment or acknowledged the debt more than six years ago;[29] *or*
- in Scotland, if the supplier has not raised legal proceedings against you for the charges and you have not acknowledged the charges for five years.[30]

Otherwise, you must pay for the fuel that was supplied to you (see Chapter 5). With a bill that is very late, much of the bill may be estimated (see p86). The longer the delay, the better the chances of having part or even the entire bill written off, deemed unenforceable or being given time to pay. Be prepared to negotiate and put forward proposals in writing, setting out your circumstances as necessary. Citizens Advice consumer service or Advice Direct Scotland can advise and the Energy Ombudsman could apply pressure on the supplier to settle on a reasonable solution as appropriate (see Chapter 14).

Obtaining information under the data protection law

Your supplier is likely to hold a large amount of information about you electronically. This may include details of previous bills and consumption, credit ratings and prosecutions. If a supplier refuses to provide information voluntarily, you may still be able to get hold of this information by using your rights under data protection laws. This is known as a 'subject access request' (SAR). The UK General Data Protection Regulation (GDPR) and Data Protection Act 2018 provide a right of access to the information held on you by suppliers.

To exercise your rights, contact the supplier's data controller or data processing department. There is no standard form to make a request so long as you make it clear that you are asking for details of your own personal data held by the supplier. The supplier must respond to a SAR 'without undue delay and in any event within one month of receipt of the request'.[31] Generally, the supplier cannot charge a fee to comply with a SAR. However, where a request is manifestly unfounded or excessive (such as if it is repetitive or further copies of the same information are requested), the supplier may charge a 'reasonable fee' for the administrative costs of complying with the request. The Information Commissioner's Office (ICO) website contains a useful guide to doing this and a sample letter.[32] The supplier will then provide the information.

You also have the right to:
- have inaccurate information corrected;
- claim compensation for loss caused by inaccurate information;

- complain to the ICO if the supplier fails to provide the information, to correct inaccuracies or to obtain and process information fairly and lawfully.

Estimates

Check whether the bill has been estimated; another cause of high bills. This is when a bill is calculated based commonly on an algorithm of past energy consumption, seasonal adjustments and the size of your home. Your supplier must clearly indicate on your bill if an estimated reading has been used. The abbreviation 'E' ('estimated') may be next to the meter reading figure. Actual readings (where the meter has been read) are shown by an 'A' ('actual'). Customer readings are shown by a 'C' ('customer'). However, suppliers may also use their own abbreviations, letters or symbols – these should be explained on the bill.

If practical, take your own reading if the bill is based on an estimated reading (see Appendix 2). Do this as soon as possible after receiving the estimated bill and make an allowance for units consumed since the date of the bill so that the comparison is as accurate as possible. You can calculate an average daily rate and deduct that amount for the appropriate number of days.

Alternatively, to decide if an estimate is unreasonable, compare the amount of fuel used over the same period in the previous year with the estimated consumption on the present bill. If a bill covering the same period is not available (eg, because you have recently moved), try making a reasonable estimate using any bill you do have, or by calculating how much would be used by the appliances you have and the frequency with which you use them. Your supplier must provide you with an explanation of how your bill has been derived in plain and intelligible language if you so request.[33]

If you do not think the estimate is accurate, notify the supplier. Call the number on the bill, or record your own meter reading on the back of the bill and ask for a more accurate bill to be reissued later. An accurate bill is not likely to be reissued immediately after you provide your supplier with a meter reading as bills are produced in accordance with your agreed billing schedule with your supplier. However, you can request that your supplier reissue you an accurate bill.

If you have established a discrepancy in the bill and are able to, pay the amount claimed on the bill and the supplier should work out the difference it owes you. Back up a telephone request by email or letter, keeping a copy. If your own reading shows that the bill is an overestimate, the supplier must take all reasonable steps to reflect your meter reading in your new bill – in line with SLC 21B.

However, remember that if a bill has been underestimated, a higher bill will result from any complaint. It is still important to obtain an accurate bill from your supplier which reflects your actual usage so that you can start addressing the bill promptly. If you are worried that receiving a higher bill will cause you financial hardship, see Chapter 7.

Also, be aware of cases where a high bill is the result of a low estimate on a past bill followed by an accurate meter reading later. This is one of the most common reasons for an extraordinarily high bill: several quarters' bills are significantly underestimated, followed by an actual meter reading by the supplier which brings the account back up to date. This results in a large back-bill, consolidating the usage not paid for in the previously low estimated bills. For this reason, it is crucial to give an accurate reading yourself whenever you receive an estimated bill. The points made about billing delays on p84 also apply here.

Errors in reading the meter

Although actual meter readings are likely to be correct, even the supplier's own meter readers can sometimes make mistakes. You can use the same methods discussed above to detect errors, but the supplier might want to take a second reading to check any reading which you have taken. If the supplier has made a mistake, it should obtain new meter readings and the bill should be amended.[34]

Errors in assigning bills

In some instances (eg, where there are properties in multiple occupation or blocks of flats where meters are often grouped together), readings can sometimes be attributed to the wrong meter. Every gas and electricity meter has a unique reference number that effectively links the meter to a specific address. Meter ID numbers identify your supply point (meter) so your supplier can charge you correctly for your energy use. For electricity meters, this is known as the meter point administration number (MPAN). The format of MPAN is standard and consists of 21 digits. For gas, it is known as the meter point reference number (MPRN). The format of MPRN is also fairly standard and consists of between six and 10 digits. Occasionally, these are also referred to simply as 'meter ID numbers' or as 'M' or 'S' (supply) numbers. The reference numbers must be shown on your fuel bills and your annual statement. Your MPAN and MPRN are unique to your property and do not change. Do not confuse your MPAN/MPRN with your supplier account number or the meter serial number printed on your meter. It may be worthwhile checking with your supplier that the MPAN/MPRN on your fuel bill 'belongs' to your address. If the meter ID number does not match the number as recorded on your bill, you may be billed for the incorrect address.

If you cannot locate your MPAN, contact your Distribution Network Operator (DNO). For a full list of DNOs, see energynetworks.org/operating-the-networks/whos-my-network-operator. If you cannot locate your MPRN, call the Meter Point Reference Helpline on 0870 608 1524 or visit findmysupplier.energy.

Smart meters

Smart meters can remove the need for bills to be estimated at all, allowing you to pay only for the fuel you actually use and ending the need to provide your supplier with regular meter readings. Meter operatives also no longer need to attend your home to read your meter. These digital meters are currently being introduced across the UK to replace traditional meters. The government aims to install smart meters in every UK household by 2025 (see p54).

3. **Accuracy of the meter**

Even if the details on the bill appear to be correct, the meter itself may be faulty. Meters must be approved and certified by meter examiners.[35] If, as is the normal situation, the meter belongs to the supplier (or gas transporter), it is responsible for keeping it in proper working order.[36] An electricity meter is deemed to be accurate if it does not vary more than +2.5 per cent to -3.5 per cent from the correct reading. For gas meters, the limits are +2 to -2 per cent.

Note also that if appliances are old and/or have not been serviced recently, they may no longer perform in accordance with their rating.

Prepayment meters

It is important when moving into a new property with a prepayment meter that you ensure the supply is in your name from the date you start living at the property. Otherwise, you may find that what you pay for fuel is not credited to your account or that you are inadvertently paying for a fuel debt accrued by the last occupant.

Contact the supplier at your new address as soon as you move in. Do not use the previous occupants' payment card/key as you may inadvertently make payments to their account. You may also enter into a deemed contract for supply.

Ask your supplier for a new card or key in your name. Some suppliers can reset a key or card remotely but will still require you to provide them with a meter reading from the date that you moved in. In other cases, your supplier may need to visit your property to reset the meter, depending on the age and type of the device. Contact your supplier to establish the procedure for your meter. You should also be able to request a credit meter facility be provided to you, rather than a prepayment meter. You can also request that the meter is changed to a smart meter, although the supplier is not obligated to provide it upon request.

Smart meters

The accuracy and reliability of smart meters come under the Measuring Instruments Directive 2016 (MID).[37] They are certified as accurate by the Office for Product Safety Standards (OPSS) to prove their accuracy upon manufacture only; unlike traditional, analogue meters which are deemed accurate for a certain period of time after manufacture. Smart meters are subject to annual in-service testing by the OPSS and replaced if found to be inaccurate or faulty.

Smart meters contain self-regulation technology and alongside meter readings, they collect and send information about their environment to the supplier. This information is used to diagnose meter reading inaccuracies, unusual energy consumption, meter faults, theft, damage and tampering issues. Suppliers will take any appropriate action, triggered from the information gathered.

If you think there is a fault, you can ask the supplier to investigate. There are a myriad of indicators of a faulty smart meter, including:

- varying and erratic bills;
- high levels of consumption during non-peak times;
- similar or same levels of consumption during different times of day and night;
- high levels of consumption when appliances are switched off;
- energy consumption and bill (cost of unit or tariff) do not align;
- your meter reading not changing or going backwards.

Checking your meter

Gas meters must be installed in a readily accessible position and, if situated in a box or compound, you must be given a key.

If you are disabled, your meter may be repositioned or replaced with a specially adapted one for free[38] – ask your supplier to do this for you. You may also be eligible to reposition your meter if you are on the Priority Services Register and you cannot readily access it. This should be permitted by your energy supplier.

You can check your meter by using the following method.

- Switch off all appliances, including pilot lights.
- Read the meter (see Appendix 2).
- Turn on an appliance with a known rate of consumption and note the time.
- Leave the appliance on for a measured time, preferably in whole hours.
- Switch off the appliance and read the meter again.

If everything is working properly, the following formulae should work.

Electricity
Difference in readings = rating of appliance (kW) x time on (hours).
Example
If your electric fire has a one kilowatt (1kW) rating and is switched on for one hour the figures on each side of the '=' sign should both be '1'.

Where an electricity meter is faulty and its readings are outside the statutory margins of error, you fall within the standards regulations and may be entitled to bring a claim. For electricity, the margin of error is laid down by paragraph 13 of Schedule 7 of the Electricity Act 1989.

Gas

Difference in readings =

$$\text{(hundreds of cubic feet)} \times 3.6 = \frac{\text{appliance rating (kW)} \times \text{time on (hrs)}}{\text{(calorific value* for region)} \times 2.83}$$

*The amount of heat produced by burning a specific amount of gas

Example

The rating for an average gas fire is 2.5 kilowatts (kW), assuming that the fire is on full and all the elements are being used. If it is switched on for one hour in an area where gas has a calorific value of 38.2, then the figures on each side of the '=' sign should both be 0.023 – ie, the reading should be 2.3 cubic feet.

To find out the rating of an appliance, if it is not marked on the appliance, contact the manufacturer, the appliance supplier or the gas supplier. The calorific value for the area will be shown on your gas bill, or you can ask your supplier.

Where a reading falls outside a specified margin of error, there may be the basis of a claim under the Gas Standards Regulations. The relevant standards are those set out in the Gas (Meters) Regulations 1983.

Standards of performance

The Electricity and Gas (Standards of Performance) (Suppliers) Regulations 2015 may apply where you or the supplier considers that a meter may be faulty. The regulations detail performance standards required for suppliers for fixing faulty meters and prepayment meters reconnection after disconnection for unpaid charges. If it fails to meet these standards you are entitled to compensation.

Where the supplier needs to visit your property, it is expected, within a reasonable time, to offer you an appointment during working hours that is no more than four hours long.[39] The supplier must not rearrange an appointment with less than one working days' notice without your agreement.[40]

Standard meters

Once notified, the supplier is normally required, within five working days, to:[41]
- complete an initial assessment; *and*
- take an appropriate action; *and*
- offer to confirm in writing the nature and outcome of that initial assessment, the actions it will take and the timescale within which those actions will occur.

If it does not respond within the five days, you are entitled to a £30 payment, unless there is an exception (see below).[42] If the supplier fails to do that, you are entitled to an additional payment of £30 within 10 days of that failure.[43]

Prepayment meters

Where you notify the supplier of a loss of supply of gas or electricity from the meter, the supplier must restore the supply within three hours on a working day or four hours on any other day.[44] This can be done remotely or by visiting your property. Where you contact the supplier outside normal working hours, the communication is deemed to have been made the next working day. If the supplier does not meet these standards, you are entitled to a £30 payment, unless there is an exception (see below).[45] If the supplier fails to do that, you are entitled to an additional payment of £30 within 10 days of that failure.[46]

Exceptions

Circumstances in which you are not entitled to a £30 payment include:[47]
• you requested the supplier not to attend the premises;
• you requested the supplier not to take any action, or any further action;
• where the prepayment meter is found to be working correctly;
• it not being reasonably practicable for the supplier to meet the individual standard of performance as a result of not obtaining necessary access to the premises, severe weather conditions and other exceptional circumstances beyond its control.

Meter examiners

If you think that a meter is not functioning properly, complain first to the supplier (or gas transporter, as appropriate) who can inspect it. High energy bills may be due to a faulty meter that is incorrectly recording the amount of gas or electricity you are using; however, this is unusual.

Your supplier may try a simple test of the meter without moving it, such as putting a check meter to run alongside your meter for a week or two or undertaking a meter test. If you are still not satisfied, refer the matter to an independent meter examiner. You are legally entitled to request an independent test of your gas or electricity meter to check for inaccuracy or faults. The supplier/ transporter can also make the referral. Although the test is free, you may have to pay your energy supplier for organising it if your meter is found to be performing correctly and accurately recording consumption afterwards.

If a meter seems to be over-registering and inaccurate, you should, if you can afford to, pay the supplier for the amount of fuel you think you have definitely consumed, without waiting for the examiner's decision. This effectively helps neutralise the threat of disconnection and the dispute will be considered a genuine one (see p83).

If the meter is removed, suppliers must install a replacement meter of the same type and leave the supply connected on the same terms as before, unless they are exercising powers to disconnect. There should be no charge for this.

Electricity

The electricity meter examiner's service is contracted out to the OPSS by the Department for Energy Security and Net Zero. An examiner tests the meter and the supply at your home. They discuss your concerns and queries, check the meter for accuracy and whether it was installed correctly. The supplier is invited to send a representative to be present while the examiner tests the meter at your home. Depending on the results, the meter may be removed for further tests at an Ofgem-approved laboratory. Where the meter needs to be removed, a replacement is fitted. Take a note of the reading on the meter and meter serial number before it is removed. The examiner issues you a report, called a 'determination', with their findings. It confirms whether the meter is within or outside prescribed legal limits, accurate and operating correctly. This concludes the meter examination and is final and binding. Copies of the determination are sent to you, the electricity supplier and the owner of the meter. An electricity meter examiner's services are free, but the supplier is likely to charge in cases where no defect or inaccuracy is found.

If the examiner finds meter inaccuracy or fault, the supplier may compensate you for over-billing or prepare a payment plan for you where under-billing has occurred.

If a notice is served by you, the electricity supplier or anyone else interested in the matter, then no one can alter or remove the meter until the dispute is resolved or a meter examiner has finished their examination.

The findings of an electricity meter examiner can be produced in court and are presumed to be correct unless proven otherwise.

Gas

Gas meter examiners are also contracted out to the OPSS. If there is a dispute about meter accuracy, rather than attending your home for an onsite visit, they request that your supplier sends them the meter for examination. Make a note of the reading and meter serial number before it is removed. The meter will be removed, securely packaged and sent to an Ofgem-approved laboratory for testing by an independent examiner. The examiner does performance checks on the meter and ascertains if there are faults that can affect its accuracy and operation. The examiner issues a report, called a 'certificate', with their findings. It confirms if the meter is within or outside prescribed legal limits, accurate, operating correctly as well as if any fault exists causing unreliable meter readings. If your meter is faulty, the certificate says it is a failure and details the fault. This concludes the meter examination and is final and binding. Copies of the certificate are sent to you, your gas supplier and the owner of the meter.

The supplier may charge you for removing the disputed meter, installing a replacement, transporting the disputed meter for testing and reinstalling the meter at your property. This charge will be refunded if the disputed meter is found to be operating inaccurately or faulty. The charges made for meter examining vary – check with your supplier.

Results

If your meter is found not to be working properly, the supplier has to make a refund, compensation or an extra charge to you. The amount of the refund or compensation depends on how long and by how much the meter is thought to have been registering incorrectly.

For electricity, the meter examiner has a duty to give their opinion about how long and by how much the meter has been operating outside the prescribed limits. For gas, the meter is deemed to have been registering incorrectly for the whole period since the last actual meter reading. Argue that this should be resolved in your favour. For example, if the gas meter was over-registering, you should receive the entire extra amount charged, but if the gas meter was under-registering, you should argue that you should only pay that part which exceeds the 2 per cent limit of variation.

It is recognised that older gas meters with leather diaphragms are prone to drift into over-reading after a substantial period of years. Since 1 April 1981, gas suppliers have installed only meters with synthetic diaphragms, which are more reliable. If you have an older meter and you suspect it is recording inaccurately, you can refer it to a meter examiner. New meters may be distinguished from old ones as they have either a yellow label with a large 'S' on the meter casing or a reference number which begins or ends with an 'S'. Often the supplier simply replaces the old meter.

Note that if a meter is removed by the supplier because it has made an allegation that it has been tampered with (see Chapter 9), the meter must be preserved so that it can be inspected after removal. Each supplier sets out in its relevant code of practice how long it will keep a meter in such circumstances before destroying it. Check that the code of practice is being followed.

---

4. Meter faults and faulty appliances

Meter faults

To check whether a meter's circuit or installation is faulty, turn off all appliances (including pilot lights) and see if the meter is still registering. If an electricity meter is still registering, there may be a short circuit or a leak to earth. If a gas meter is still registering, there may be a gas leak. Apart from the effect on the bill, they are both dangerous and should be dealt with immediately. Once everything is turned off and the meter has ceased to register, each appliance can be checked to ensure it is registering a reasonable level of consumption by using the formulae given for checking the meter (see p89 and p90).

In rented accommodation, landlords are nearly always responsible for gas piping and electrical wiring. Your landlord must keep in repair and proper working order installations for space heating, heating water and the supply of gas and electricity.[48] If you have informed your landlord about defects in installations or in wiring/piping, you should ask them to fix the problem and to pay the difference between a high bill and the normal level of the bill, if the difference is due to the defects.

Faulty appliances

If a fairly new appliance is faulty and consumes more fuel than it should, you can claim some of the excessive bill from whoever supplied the appliance by using your rights under the Consumer Rights Act 2015. If you bought your goods on or before 30 September 2015, previous legislation – the Sale of Goods Act 1979 – applies. Under these Acts, there are several promises incorporated into the contract between you and the supplier of the appliance, imposing implied terms and minimum standards to be met by the goods. These include that the appliance is of satisfactory quality, is fit for purpose, matches the description, sample or model and is installed correctly (implied terms).[49] The appliance is of **'satisfactory quality'** if a reasonable person would regard it as such, taking into account how it was described, its price, its fitness for the purpose for which it is normally supplied, its appearance and finish, freedom from minor defects, and safety and durability.[50] During the expected lifespan of the product, you are entitled to the following:

- a right to reject the goods if faulty and a full refund within three days of purchase;
- a right to repair or replacement if faulty within six months of purchase;
- a price reduction or right to reject the goods if faulty and unable to be repaired or replaced within six months of purchase;
- a right to reject the goods up to six years (five years in Scotland) if faulty or the goods do not last a reasonable time subject to fair wear and tear.[51]

Liability for a breach of the Consumer Rights Act 2015 lies with the seller of the goods (ie, who you made the contract with), not with the original manufacturer. The seller is liable for faults which are present at the time of sale, whether they know about them at the time or not. However, manufacturers may also be liable on occasion where a manufacturer's guarantee is included with the sale contract or under the law of negligence where faults in the goods cause damage to either individuals or to property.

The Supply of Goods (Implied Terms) Act 1973 puts similar terms into a hire purchase (HP) agreement – ie, of satisfactory quality, fit for purpose, matches the description, sample or model and lasts a reasonable length of time. This makes the HP company responsible for the quality of the goods supplied.

If an installation (eg, central heating) is installed defectively, you can use your rights under the Consumer Rights Act 2015. These provide that work must be undertaken with a reasonable degree of competence or care and skill, in a reasonable time, for a reasonable charge and that information spoken or written is binding where the consumer relies on it.[52] If it is not, the person providing the service is liable. There are also the Gas Safety (Installation and Use) Regulations 1998 covering the installation of gas fittings (such as meters and pipes) and gas appliances (such as for heating or cooking).[53] Any gas fitting installed must be soundly constructed and not made of lead or lead alloy.[54] No gas appliance can be installed unless it can be used without danger to anyone and this has been checked by the installer.[55]

If goods are bought on HP or credit for £100 or more, and the credit was supplied by a lender associated with the supplier (this includes credit cards), then the lender of the money is liable for faults as well as the supplier under the Consumer Credit Act 1974.[56] Here, it is the finance provider, rather than the supplier, who is legally responsible if there are problems with the goods. This means you can sue (or threaten to sue) the credit card company or other lender. This tactic can be used to put pressure on the supplier to settle any dispute or to get redress if the supplier has gone out of business.

If damage is caused by a faulty appliance, you may be able to claim additional or alternative redress, including a claim for compensation or damages from the manufacturer under the general law of negligence or the Consumer Protection Act 1987. If the damage includes physical injury to someone, seek legal advice.

Notes

1. Amount of the bill
1　Condition 21B.5 SLC
2　Condition 21B.5(a) SLC
3　Condition 21B.7 SLC
4　Condition 31H.3(a) SLC
5　Condition 31H.3(b) SLC
6　Condition 21B.8 SLC
7　Condition 21B.8 SLC
8　Conditions 31H.1 and 31I SLC
9　Conditions 31H.1, 31F.3 and 0.3(b)(v) SLC
10　Condition 31F.4 SLC and 31H.4(d) SLC
11　Condition 21B.5A SLC
12　Condition 31H.5 SLC
13　Condition 21B.4 SLC
14　Condition 21B.4 SLC
15　Condition 21B.2 SLC

16　Condition 21B.8 SLC

2. Accuracy of the bill
17　Sch 6 para 2(1) EA 1989; Sch 2B para 7 GA 1986
18　*Maritime Electric Co Ltd v General Dairies Ltd* [1937] AC 610
19　Condition 0.1 SLC
20　Condition 0.3 SLC
21　Condition 31H.3 SLC
22　Conditions 31H.1 and 31H.12 SLC
23　Condition 21BA.1 SLC
24　Condition 21BA.2 SLC
25　Condition 21B.5 SLC
26　Condition 21B.5A SLC

27 53 per cent of consumers on a default
tariff, not including prepayment meter
tariffs. Ofgem, *State of the Energy Market
2019*, at ofgem.gov.uk/sites/default/
files/docs/2019/11/20191030_state_
of_energy_market_revised.pdf

28 Domestic Gas and Electricity (Tariff Cap)
Act 2018

29 Limitation Act 1980

30 s6 Prescription and Limitation
(Scotland) Act 1973

31 Art 12(3) UK General Data Protection
Regulation; ss45 and 54 Data Protection
Act 2018

32 ico.org.uk/for-the-public/getting-
copies-of-your-information-subject-
access-request

33 Condition 21B.7 SLC

34 Condition 21B.2 SLC

3. Accuracy of the meter

35 Sch 7 EA 1989; s17 GA 1986

36 Sch 7 para 10(2) EA 1989; Sch 2B para
3(3) GA 1986

37 The Measuring Instruments Regulations
2016 No.1153, as amended by the
Product Safety and Metrology etc.
(Amendment etc.) (EU Exit) Regulations
2019 No.696, gov.uk/guidance/mid-
approved-gas-and-electricity-meters

38 Sch 6 para 1 EA 1989; Sch 2B para 6 GA
1986

39 Reg 3(3) EG(SP)S Regs

40 Reg 3(7) EG(SP)S Regs

41 Reg 4(4) EG(SP)S Regs

42 Reg 8(2) and (9) EG(SP)S Regs

43 Reg 8(3) EG(SP)S Regs

44 Reg 5(3) and (4) EG(SP)S Regs

45 Reg 8(2)and (9) EG(SP)S Regs

46 Reg 8(3) EG(SP)S Regs

47 Reg 9 EG(SP)S Regs

4. Meter faults and faulty appliances

48 s11(1)(b) and (c) LTA 1985; Sch 10 para
3(1)(b) H(S)A 1987

49 s9-18 CRA 2015

50 s9(1)-(3) CRA 2015

51 s19-24 CRA 2015

52 s49-52 CRA 2015

53 GS(IU) Regs

54 Reg 5 GS(IU) Regs

55 Regs 26 and 34 GS(IU) Regs

56 s75 Consumer Credit Act 1974

Chapter 7

Arrears

1. What are arrears

You are in '**arrears**' of electricity or gas if you are liable to pay a bill but have not paid it on demand. This is a priority debt. You risk disconnection of your:
- **electricity** supply if you do not pay within 28 working days of receiving your bill;[1]
- **gas** supply if you do not pay within the 28 days following the date of your bill.[2]

The provisions discussed in this chapter only apply to arrears for charges due for the supply of electricity and gas, and not for any other purchases you have made from suppliers, for appliances or other services. Always check that you are liable for the arrears (see Chapter 5). If your bill is high, because of billing delays or incorrect reading of your meter, see Chapter 6.

This chapter looks at the position where charges for the use of gas and electricity have been correctly incurred, but you have been unable to pay within 28 days.

2. **Protection when you are in arrears**

Standard Licence Condition 26: pensioners, the chronically sick, disabled and others evidently vulnerable

Under Standard Licence Condition (SLC) 26, provision is made for customers who are over pension age, have a disability, impairment or long-term medical condition or with other vulnerable characteristics or are in vulnerable situations. If you fall into one of these categories, the following services may be available from suppliers:[3]

- a password may be agreed with you so that you can safely identify any person representing the supplier who visits your home;
- your bill or statement of account can be sent to someone you nominate;
- help with reading a meter each quarter if you need it;
- a prepayment meter may be moved if you have reduced mobility and cannot access it.

If you are blind, partially sighted, deaf or hearing impaired, the supplier must provide information on bills and charges that is accessible to you (eg, braille or video relay service) and provide facilities, free of charge, which enable you to ask or complain about any bill or statement of account.[4]

The Priority Services Register

Suppliers are obliged to establish and maintain a Priority Services Register listing customers who:[5]

- are over pension age;
- have a disability, impairment or long-term health condition;
- have a hearing or sight condition;
- are pregnant or have children under five;
- have a mental health condition;
- have experienced domestic abuse;
- have another vulnerable characteristic or situation;
- have requested to be added to the Priority Services Register.

The definition of a vulnerable 'personal characteristic' or 'vulnerable situation'[6] is wide-ranging and can include, for example, if you have mental health problems, are unable to communicate in English, or where you need extra support for a limited amount of time – eg, during cancer treatment. Suppliers are expected to consider Ofgem's *Consumer Vulnerability Strategy* when identifying vulnerability.[7]

Someone can make a request on your behalf for you to be added to the register. If you are on the register, you could get:

- priority support in an emergency;
- free advice on using gas and electricity;

- a password protection scheme;
- a prepayment meter moved to a more accessible location if it is safe to do so;
- a free quarterly meter reading if you are unable to read your meter;
- bills sent to a friend, relative or carer so they can check them on your behalf;
- extra help if a gas supply is disrupted if all adults living in your property are eligible for the Priority Services Register (such as alternative cooking or heating facilities);
- advance notice if an electricity supply has to be interrupted, where possible;
- meter readings and bills provided in a suitable format: braille, large print, audiotape, textphone or typetalk.

You may be entitled to a free, annual gas safety check of appliances and other gas fittings if you are eligible for the Priority Services Register, own your home, receive an income-based benefit, have not had one in the last 12 months and:[8]
- are of pensionable age, disabled or chronically sick and either:
  - live alone; *or*
  - live with other adults, all of whom are eligible or under 18; *or*
- live with others, at least one of whom is a child aged five or under.

If you are a tenant, this obligation is usually upon your landlord.

Suppliers must 'take all reasonable steps' to identify eligible customers to receive Priority Services Register services and promote its existence. This includes having suitable systems in place to identify such customers.[9] This is strengthened by the 'Standards of Conduct' principles[10] – overarching fairness rules placed upon suppliers to engage with customers, identify any genuine needs, particular circumstances and vulnerabilities they have and provide them with appropriate tailored support and services.[11] Suppliers that are signatories to Energy UK's 'Vulnerability Commitment'[12] also agree to equip staff to identify and support vulnerability and ensure that a culture of understanding of vulnerability is embedded throughout. Most suppliers have extra care or support teams you can seek assistance from if you are facing arrears and have vulnerabilities. These teams provide additional, tailored support and an easier point of contact if you are vulnerable.

Do you have essential electrical medical equipment at home?

If you are medically reliant on your electricity supply to run equipment such as oxygen concentrators, home dialysis, stair lifts, ventilators or nebulisers, contact your supplier to join the Priority Services Register. You will then get advanced notice of planned power cuts – eg, when maintenance and engineering work is planned. If you have a prepayment meter, your supplier may change it to a standard meter so that your electricity supply is uninterrupted.

If you have arrears, your supplier must refrain from involuntary installing a prepayment meter if you require a continuous supply for health reasons (including dependence on powered medical equipment), you have a medical dependency on a warm home or have terminal health conditions. See p115 for more details.

Standard Licence Condition 27: difficulty in paying

SLC 27 requires suppliers to produce and publish codes of practice setting out their procedures for customers who have difficulty in paying. You should obtain an up-to-date copy of your supplier's code of practice, as they vary from one supplier to another. Suppliers must publish their codes of practice on their websites and provide copies on request.

The code of practice represents the stated policy of the supplier. It is not legally enforceable in individual cases, although a departure from the published code at policy level may be a breach of the relevant licence condition. Individual breaches should be reported to Ofgem, Citizens Advice consumer service or Advice Direct Scotland.

The licence conditions state that suppliers must take certain steps when dealing with customers in arrears. In particular, they must protect customers who 'can't pay' due to low income or inability to cope, as opposed to those who 'won't pay'. Further provisions offer protection from disconnection for vulnerable groups such as those over pension age, who should not be disconnected during the winter months, and not being permitted to forcibly install prepayment meters for those over 75 years or under two (see p115). In practice, suppliers typically seek to install prepayment meters instead of disconnecting the supply, although this may result in self-disconnection (see p51).

The supplier must offer services (a range of alternative payment options) when it becomes aware or has reason to believe that you are having *or will have* difficulty paying all or part of the charges for the supply of fuel.[13] The following circumstances could indicate that there is a need for such assistance:

- high consumption (over £1,274 for electricity or £1,304 for gas per year);[14]
- a sudden increase in usage;
- arrears equivalent to more than a quarter of your usual consumption;
- multiple priority debts – eg, rent, council tax or water arrears;
- payment by Fuel Direct or cash (prepayment or budget scheme);
- failed direct debit;
- a history of struggling to pay or self-disconnection;
- an unpaid fuel bill;
- you live in a target area as defined by the fuel poverty index or indices of social deprivation.

Proactive engagement and alternative repayment methods

SLC 27 requires suppliers to take a proactive approach and act before arrears accumulate where they are anticipated. It may be useful to quote these provisions when negotiating with a supplier. They include:[15]

- using Fuel Direct, where available (see Chapter 11);
- accepting payments by regular instalments calculated in accordance with an agreed plan and paid other than by a prepayment meter;
- providing a prepayment meter or smart meter set on prepayment mode calculated in accordance with an agreed plan;
- giving energy efficiency advice.

Ability to pay principle

SLC 27 requires suppliers (or third party representatives)[16] to take into account and understand your 'ability to pay' when setting repayment plans with you and recovering debts.[17]

Ofgem has developed six 'key principles' that suppliers must fulfil to ensure they properly and proactively take into account your ability to pay and comply with SLC 27.[18] These should ensure that realistic repayment rates are set and there is a reduced risk of disconnection. The six key principles are:

- **appropriate credit management policies and guidelines** – suppliers' policies and guidelines should be flexible and deal with debt repayment on a case-by-case basis to ensure suitable repayment rates are set. These should be incentivised on outcomes and not value of repayment rates;
- **proactive contact to establish any payment difficulties** – early intervention by suppliers to identify if you have payment difficulties and provide you with appropriate solutions;
- **understand your individual ability to pay**:
  - suppliers should gather information about your circumstances and make full use of that information when discussing your ability to pay;
  - suppliers should explore all payment methods available with you to find one that best meets your individual needs;
  - suppliers should make use of specialist in-house teams or third party advisers;
- **setting repayment rates reflective of your ability to pay**:
  - suppliers should not insist on lump sum payments before agreeing to a particular repayment method;
  - standard or default repayment rates set by suppliers should be used as a guide and not a rule;
  - your circumstances should be taken into account when deciding upon a particular repayment rate (such as deduction rates from a prepayment meter);
  - suppliers should be prepared to alter repayment rates on prepayment meters to what is affordable, particularly where it has been installed without knowledge of your circumstances;

- ensuring that you understand any arrangement made:
  - suppliers should confirm any arrangement in writing with you;
  - suppliers should confirm the repayment amount with you;
  - suppliers should confirm the repayment period with you;
  - suppliers should make it clear you can contact them if you have a change of circumstances or experience difficulties with any arrangement;
  - for prepayment meters, suppliers should confirm that repayment amounts do not change, regardless of seasonal changes in usage;
- monitoring any arrangement once made:
  - suppliers should generally monitor repayment arrangements, in some cases for the life of the arrangement, to ensure that the method of repayment is appropriate for your needs and is affordable;
  - suppliers should monitor debt repayment arrangements that have been broken by credit customers;
  - suppliers should monitor prepayment meters to check if they are being used initially and on an ongoing basis to ensure they are set at the correct level, are affordable and to avoid self-disconnection.

Non-adherence by suppliers to the key principles may suggest non-compliance with SLC 27.

Energy UK's Vulnerability Commitment

Energy UK is the trade association for the gas and electricity sector. Its members include the main energy suppliers in Great Britain.

Under Energy UK's Vulnerability Commitment, no vulnerable customer should be disconnected at any time of the year. You are considered to be vulnerable if you are unable to safeguard your welfare or the welfare of other members of your household because of 'age, health, disability or severe financial insecurity'.[19]

The Commitment complements and supports the regulations contained within suppliers' licences. Although not legally binding, the committment could be used as a negotiating tool to avoid disconnection if you believe that you should be treated as vulnerable or be given appropriate support to meet their needs.

Examples of what counts as 'vulnerable' include:[20]

- you care for an elderly person in your household;
- you have a disability or a chronic health condition;
- the household includes young children, aged six or under (or under the age of 16 during the winter moratorium);
- you have a mental health or a developmental condition;
- you cannot safeguard your welfare or the personal welfare of other members of the household.

Supplier signatories resolve to adopt a collaborative, proactive and transparent approach when dealing with vulnerable customers.[21]

It complements and supports existing licence requirements for the protection of vulnerable households, demonstrating a quality benchmark and best practice for compliance. Although not legally binding, the policy could be used as a negotiating tool to encourage signatory suppliers to provide additional support needs if you are vulnerable. The support includes:

- alerting you to risks of standing charge build-ups on prepayment meters during the summer (to avoid self-disconnection);
- ensuring uninterrupted supply from a prepayment meter once installed or smart meter recalibrated;
- providing alternative means of contacting suppliers in addition to telephone contact;
- providing paper billing communication where appropriate;
- never knowingly disconnecting a vulnerable customer at any time of year;
- providing a package of support (including energy efficiency and tariff advice and information) for customers using a prepayment meter;
- actively promoting digital inclusion for vulnerable customers;
- only using High Court enforcement officers to recover debts where appropriate for a vulnerable customer;
- signposting or assisting customers to maximise their income;
- working with all credible debt or consumer body organisations, to consider all the information available when setting up payment plans for customers;
- increasing customer awareness of support available to vulnerable households.

See p139 for more information about protections for people in vulnerable situations.

Breathing space debt respite scheme

Standard breathing space moratorium

In England and Wales, a standard breathing space is a moratorium that provides you with legal protection from supplier action for up to 60 days.[22] An application is submitted via an online portal, effective the day after initial registration.

The protections and prohibitions include a pause on most enforcement action, including:

- collecting or recovering arrears;
- commencing any legal action;
- obtaining a warrant;
- disconnecting fuel supply (unless on grounds of theft or illegality);
- taking steps to switch you to a prepayment meter to take payments;
- taking steps to collect payments through other means (such as deductions from a social security benefit);

- using a prepayment meter already installed to take payments, save for if you had agreed for the meter to be installed before the breathing space commenced.
- recovery action through a debt collection agency.

Generally, neither a creditor nor their agent may contact you about enforcement of a moratorium on debt during a breathing space period, including demanding payment, but they may contact you:

- for reasons not related to the moratorium fuel arrears – eg, ongoing liabilities or consumption;
- to respond to a query or complaint;
- about any action or legal proceedings a court has allowed to continue during the moratorium.

You are obliged to continue meeting your ongoing fuel consumption charges and engage in debt advice for the moratorium period. You can enter into one every 12 months.

A debt respite moratorium is a useful short-term mechanism to suspend recovery or enforcement action when in fuel arrears and unable to pay. It is designed to afford you time to obtain advice on the debt solutions available to you and/or put an appropriate debt solution in place. You can only apply through approved debt advisers who have authority to complete the online application. To find your nearest debt adviser, contact your local free advice agency.

The breathing space scheme also covers non-fuel debts and certain debts are excluded from the scheme altogether. See CPAG's *Debt Advice Handbook* for further details and CPAG's *Debt Advice Handbook Scotland* for debt solutions in Scotland – both are availabe free at cpag.org.uk/handbooks.

Mental health crisis breathing space moratorium

A mental health breathing space is a moratorium that provides you with legal protection from supplier action for the duration of time that you are receiving mental health crisis treatment, plus 30 days.[23] The protections and prohibitions available mirror those provided in a standard breathing space. To be eligible for a mental health breathing space, evidence of mental health crisis treatment must be provided by an approved mental health professional. There is no limit to the number of times you can enter a mental health crisis breathing space.

A mental health debt respite moratorium is a useful mechanism to suspend recovery or enforcement action when in fuel arrears and unable to pay for vulnerable customers during a mental health crisis.

---

3. **Arrears in another person's name**

You may not be liable for an electricity or gas bill which is in another person's name – eg, if your partner was previously responsible for the bill and has left home, if you are a joint tenant or sharer, or if the person responsible for the bill has died. In most cases, it is possible to reach a settlement by way of a new contract between the supplier and the person taking over responsibility for supply.

You cannot be held liable for the bill while there is a genuine dispute about liability – eg, where you have been charged for supply incurred by the previous occupier of your premises.[24] See Chapter 5 for who is liable for a bill. Under rules on joint and several liability, the supplier can try to reclaim the whole amount from one or all parties to an agreement. Any discount is at the supplier's discretion.

4. **Arrears as a result of estimated bills**

Estimated bills are a common way to accrue arrears. The former Energywatch indicated that where gas arrears built up over an extended period because of a succession of estimated bills, repayment of the arrears could be made over an equivalent, extended period if you would otherwise be caused hardship. This remains a sound principle.

Since 1 May 2018, suppliers have been prohibited from sending you a retrospective bill (back-bill), or otherwise recover, beyond 12 months.[25] These back-bills result from a supplier's failure to undertake an actual meter reading or problems with a supplier's billing system and only sending you a bill once an accurate meter reading is taken. This is subject to certain exceptions and does not apply if you have been obstructive or unreasonable, such as preventing a supplier from taking or receiving accurate meter readings, including obstructing access to the meter or tampering with the meter.[26] You are not at fault for failing to provide a supplier with an accurate meter reading.

If you cannot afford the rate of repayment of arrears because you have received a large back-bill, you should be allowed to repay the arrears at a rate you can genuinely afford (see p108). Your supplier may request that a prepayment meter be fitted as a way to manage arrears, particularly if you are only able to offer very low repayments. However, they are prohibited from an involuntary installation of prepayment meters or remote recalibration of smart meters into prepayment mode for the most vulnerable households (see p115).[27] Suppliers can apply for involuntary deductions to be made from benefits to recover arrears,[28] but since 1 April 2023, are prohibited for ongoing consumption.[29] If you are experiencing genuine financial hardship and would prefer not to have a prepayment meter, it is not safe or reasonably practicable or you have a vulnerability (eg, a mental impairment), your supplier should also offer you a range of other options for repayment. If it does not, contact Citizens Advice consumer service or Advice Direct Scotland for further advice. Also check your supplier's codes of practice on the payment of bills and prepayment meters. Involuntary installation of a prepayment meter, as with disconnections, should be a last resort for customers in payment difficulty.

If you disagree with a bill, you should pay a reasonable estimate of your usage. Once an accurate bill is produced by the supplier, you should seek a refund for overpaid sums or ask that overpaid sums be credited for future usage.

Where arrears have accrued because of estimated billing, ensure that your supplier has adhered to the minimum standards for meter reading (see p90). Standard Licence Condition 21B may also be useful. This sets out the minimum standards suppliers must follow and their responsibilities to ensure accurate and clear bills. It includes commitments to obtain and record the most up-to-date and accurate meter readings and that any payments are set at the right level. It is advisable to take your own readings regularly – at least once every three months – to ensure that a supplier's estimate of your consumption is correct. Suppliers usually amend estimated bills if you give them your own reading.

The roll-out of smart meters should, in theory, see the end of estimated billing as the meter sends information to your supplier remotely about how much energy you have used and allows accurate bills to be produced regularly. Where smart meters are already installed, suppliers must offer to provide or make available accurate monthly billing information based on consumption and billing information, if requested.[30]

Previous periods of consumption

If arrears have arisen because of a supplier's failure to read your meter accurately, you may wish to dispute your liability for the full amount of the arrears. See Chapter 6 for information on high bills.

If you need information on an earlier period of consumption concerning an estimated bill, ask your energy supplier for information on previous readings and the amount of energy used. Your supplier is required to comply with your request as soon as reasonably practicable.[31]

---

5. **Paying your arrears**

As the supply of energy is governed by contracts, it is open to you and your supplier to negotiate and find a solution to your arrears. However, because of the large number of customers of each supplier, energy companies may find it difficult to reach individual solutions. In legal theory – and in practice – it is possible for suppliers to clear arrears by an individual payment scheme, settlement payment agreement or even by the supplier writing them off, wholly or in part. This is even more likely in cases where suppliers have been at fault.

Unfortunately, it may be difficult to get a supplier to exercise any such option at first approach, since customer service staff may not be fully aware of the range of options legally available. Persistence may be necessary and unique proposals may need to be put into writing.

Before negotiating with your supplier, consider which way of repaying your arrears best suits your needs. Also consider the supplier's internal codes of practice, policy and procedures currently in place to recover arrears. Consider the practicalities of using a particular avenue and how convenient it is for you to make your payments – it is important to make an arrangement or settlement which you can keep. Chapter 4 looks at the advantages and disadvantages of the various methods of payment.

Generally, you will need to discharge arrears:

● through a short-term arrangement; *or*
● in instalments through a longer-term payment plan; *or*
● through a prepayment meter; *or*
● through the Fuel Direct scheme.

The ways these various options work are discussed below. The payment method available may also depend on your payment arrangements in the past. Your supplier is less likely to agree to your choice of method if you have a succession of broken arrangements. The supplier may take the view that a prepayment meter or benefit deductions (the Fuel Direct scheme – see p118) offers the best chance of secure and regular payment without increasing arrears.

Energy companies usually expect you to reach arrangements by telephone. It is advisable to back up any conversations in writing by email and enter into correspondence wherever possible, keeping copies. Keep a record of any failure to respond to raise in your defence at a later date should the matter result in court action.

Wherever possible, deal with the supplier's complaints or customer service department, as call centre advisers often know little about the relevant law or about ways a dispute may be lawfully settled. Some suppliers have appropriate extra care or support teams who may be able to get involved with a view to resolving problems if you have a need or vulnerability. Provide as much information about your financial situation as you can so that the staff can establish the most suitable method of payment for you.[32] Be prepared to provide information about your income and expenditure and, if you can, provide a detailed financial statement listing all your liabilities (see p109). Inform the supplier if anyone in your home is elderly, disabled, chronically sick, under five years old, has a mental health condition, if you claim a means-tested benefit, or if there are any other factors which cause you financial hardship, such as multiple debts, redundancy or a sudden change in circumstances.

If you are not satisfied with the options made available to you, consider using your supplier's complaints procedure. Citizens Advice consumer service can provide advice where there is a dispute about the choice of a meter or method of payment or if a deadlock situation is reached. If you are in a vulnerable situation the Extra Help Unit may help (see p206). The Energy Ombudsman may be able to intervene where the complaints system has been exhausted (see Chapter 14).

Consider applying for charitable assistance to repay or reduce arrears if you are experiencing serious hardship (see p126).

Short-term arrangements

Where problems with hardship are likely to be temporary, suppliers are often willing to come to a short-term arrangement to enable you to pay your bill in instalments, based on your ability to pay, as long as the outstanding balance is paid before your next bill arrives. If you ask for this arrangement regularly, a payment plan or a prepayment meter may be a better option.

Payment plans

Suppliers calculate an amount which you are required to pay on a weekly, fortnightly or monthly basis. This figure includes an estimated amount for current consumption and an amount for arrears.

Many suppliers add your arrears to your estimated annual consumption and then divide by 12 for a monthly figure or by 52 for a weekly figure. You may be told that this is the figure the computer says you have to repay in order to ensure that you will repay the arrears within a year. This is an arbitrary figure chosen by the supplier and has no legal basis. Often, the use of this formula means that you may be required to repay the arrears at a faster rate than you can afford. The overriding principle is that the method and rate of repayment should take account of your ability to pay.[33] If, for example, you can only afford to repay £3 a week, the supplier should simply add this figure to your estimated weekly consumption.

It is also important to ensure that the amount estimated for current consumption accurately reflects your use of fuel and that the supplier does not attempt to recover the arrears more quickly than you can afford by overestimating your consumption.[34] Ensure that you read your meter each quarter so that you can accurately track your consumption and, if necessary, ask for a review of the rate of your payments.

If you have not previously had any difficulty with your bill or you have previously been able to manage a payment plan, you should not be refused this as your preferred option. If paying regularly via PayPoint is convenient for you, say so.

Before contacting the supplier to implement a payment plan it is useful to complete a full financial statement outlining your income and expenditure (see p109). This shows you exactly how much disposable income you have. Use this information to work out how much you can afford to use to repay your energy debt. Once you have this figure, do not agree to a payment plan for more than this. This is for two reasons: firstly, you may try to meet these unrealistic and unequitable payments to the detriment of feeding, heating or clothing you or your family. Secondly, if you fail to meet the payments it may make your debt situation more complex, and could prejudice any future negotiations with your supplier. Therefore, resist any attempts, however persuasive, by your supplier to agree to a payment plan that is for more than you can realistically afford.

If you do not keep to the first payment agreement made, your supplier is likely to insist you have a prepayment meter rather than renegotiate a further arrangement. However, if there are legitimate reasons why an arrangement has been broken, such as a change of circumstances, this should not disqualify you, particularly if it is the only or most suitable method for you.

Some suppliers may allow you to have a payment plan in conjunction with a prepayment meter set to pay for current consumption only.

Preparing a financial statement

Stage 1: Work out your income and essential expenditure

Firstly, add up all the money you have coming in from your household income streams: wages, benefits, maintenance and any other income every week or month, depending on how you are paid. Check that you are receiving all the benefits to which you are entitled, available discounts and exemptions are afforded to you and that you are not paying too much tax. A free local advice agency, such as a law centre, Citizens Advice or welfare rights service, can help you with an income maximisation and benefit calculation. You can also get this assistance on the telephone from National Debtline free of charge. This is important because it could give you access to additional support, such as a Warm Home Discount.

Secondly, work out what you spend each month on essentials. Ignore any payments for arrears at this stage. Include your normal payments for the following items:

– rent or mortgage and any other loans secured on your home;
– gas (your average weekly or monthly bill over the last year);
– electricity (your average weekly or monthly bill over the last year);
– council tax;
– water charges;
– childcare;
– transport to work;
– food;
– clothing;
– other regular household expenses – eg, telephone, internet, insurance etc.

Be realistic, and remember that payments for housing arrears are a priority – eg, rent or mortgage. Work out what you need to live on over a long period and not over a week. Do not include current payments on loans, credit agreements or catalogues.

When you have done this, deduct the total of your expenses from your total income. The difference is what you have available to deal with your debts. If this is nothing, or your expenses are more than your income, seek advice.

Stage 2: Work out your debts

Make a list of everything you owe to everyone. Include:

- arrears of rent/mortgage;
- arrears of gas/electricity/water/telephone bills;
- the total amount owing (not just the arrears) on loans, credit cards, catalogues, credit agreements, etc.

Some debts must take priority because there are serious consequences if you cannot pay them. For most people these are:

- rent, mortgage or secured loans;
- council tax;
- magistrates' court fines;
- arrears of child maintenance.

If you are in arrears with any of these, contact the people and/or organisations you owe and try to arrange affordable repayments. If you explain your position fully, including any vulnerabilities you may have, they usually allow you a period to pay off your arrears. This may be a long period of time – particularly if you are in receipt of a means-tested benefit (see Chapter 11) or you have a low income. You may be able to reach an agreement to pay off mortgage arrears over the remaining term of the mortgage.[35] If you cannot reach an agreement, or if you think you have agreed to something you cannot afford, seek advice (see p126).

Deduct the total of what you have to pay on these priority debts from the amount you had available to pay all the debts. If there is nothing left, seek advice.

Now divide what is left fairly between all the other people you owe money to.

Stage 3: Work out how much to pay your creditors

To work out how to share this money between your creditors, there is a basic pro-rata rule: the more money you owe to one creditor, the bigger share that creditor gets.

Add up all your debts (except the priority ones you dealt with at Stage 2).

Next, work out what percentage of your total debt is made up by each individual debt. For example, if your total debt is £2,400 and you owe British Gas £120, the percentage of the total debt owed to British Gas is:

$$\frac{£120}{£2,400} \times 100 = 5\%$$

Take that percentage of the weekly or monthly amount you have available to pay your debts.

In the example above, if you have £15 a month available for debts, you should pay British Gas 5 per cent of that: £15 x 5% = £0.75 a month.

Once you have worked out all these details, contact all of your creditors. They all need to see your financial statement to understand why you will only be making a small payment to each of them. Fuel suppliers ought to accept whatever you can afford to pay using this calculation. They may try to argue that they should be priority creditors, but they must accept what you can reasonably afford to pay. Your electricity supplier may have adopted a policy of accepting low rates of repayment on a pro-rata basis with other creditors when revising its code of practice. Check your supplier's code of practice.

Prepayment meters

Prepayment meters can be calibrated to pay for gas or electricity before consumption. They can also be calibrated to pay for arrears over a period of time. For many prepayment meters (or remote-recalibrated smart meters), this means adjusting the meter to reclaim a fixed amount of arrears each week, irrespective of the amount of fuel used. A timing device in the meter registers the amount due towards the arrears each week. This amount is then deducted from the value of fuel paid for by top-ups, either when the meter is topped-up or over the week.

If you do not add credit to the meter every week, a build-up of these charges may result. Your supply is effectively disconnected until you can afford to pay these charges through your meter. This is known as '**self-disconnection**'. Self-disconnection can occur on a credit-calibrated mode prepayment meter if all credit is exhausted, including a fixed emergency credit. Signatories to Energy UK's Vulnerability Commitment (see p102) have agreed to alert prepayment customers of standing charge build-up during the summer, and encourage them to keep their meters topped-up during this time and avoid self-disconnection.[36] See p51 for help if you have self-disconnected.

If you deliberately limit or control your energy use to lengthen your available credit or prudently save money for other goods or services, this is called '**self-rationing**'.

Suppliers must actively manage consumer usage and self-disconnection for prepayment meter customers. Standard Licence Condition (SLC) 27A requires that suppliers provide appropriate emergency credit support (usually about £5) in situations of self-disconnection or self-rationing to ensure continuity of supply. They must also offer 'friendly hours' top-up points and 'additional support credit' if you are in a vulnerable situation. See p50 for more information.

Where an involuntary prepayment meter is installed (see p115), suppliers must automatically add a repayable £30 credit so you have a supply at the point of installation.[37] Suppliers must actively monitor prepayment meter ongoing usage to identify trends, including to consider if you are self-disconnecting and offer you support, as appropriate.[38]

On a smart meter, the emergency credit support can be accessed via the in-home display (IHD).

The emergency credit support provided needs to be repaid when you next top-up or agree an instalment plan, taking into account your ability to pay.[39]

The gas Quantum meter and similar 'smart card' electricity prepayment meters are more sophisticated in the way they are able to recover arrears. They recover an agreed fixed sum once each week and leave you with a certain minimum percentage of your credit – typically 30 per cent – for your current fuel supply. This means you always get some fuel for each credit you make.

The British Gas prepayment meter is set so that, where there is a build-up of weekly fixed charges, you are guaranteed the use of only 10 per cent of any credit you make for your ongoing supply. The remaining 90 per cent is used towards this part of your debt.[40] If your supplier offers this or a similar meter, you can find out the level of this setting from the meter itself. The information booklet supplied with the meter should give details of how to obtain information from the meter. These settings can be changed by the supplier. It may be worth pressing for a change in the settings or tariff if you are facing hardship as a result of the amount you are paying back, particularly given that such repayment arrangements must be calculated with your ability to pay.

Smart meters can be programmed remotely to operate in both credit and prepayment mode. You can agree with your supplier to pay in the way that best suits you. They facilitate greater payment flexibility and choice – eg, you can top-up credit instantly online, via text message or through your telephone, reducing the risk of 'self-disconnection'. You can also manage your budget better because the IHD shows your consumption, debt balance, emergency credit balance and provides low credit alerts.

A prepayment meter can sometimes be a good option if you have energy debts. Some rented properties already have prepayment meters to avoid fuel debts being left by previous tenants. The advantage is that you pay-as-you-go and cannot therefore run into more debt. It also means that once the debt is paid off the situation cannot resurface in the future. However, the disadvantages of a prepayment meter include the risk that if you are in serious financial difficulty or have a physical or mental impairment, the lights may literally go out. It is therefore important that you notify your supplier of particular vulnerabilities you have to mitigate the risk of self-disconnection. Ofgem's Consumer Survey 2020 found that of the four million households using prepayment meters, 21 per cent had self-disconnected their supply in the previous 12 months.[41]

It is rare for a voluntary request for a prepayment meter to be refused. If it is, contact Citizens Advice consumer service or Advice Direct Scotland. If you cannot have a prepayment meter for safety reasons or because you are particularly vulnerable, request a payment plan or request Fuel Direct if you receive a qualifying benefit. Suppliers cannot involuntarily install a prepayment meter without meeting a number of conditions detailed in SLC 28. If breached, it can result in enforcement action and substantial fines.

For repayment arrangements set up on a prepayment meter, suppliers must actively monitor its initial usage to identify trends, including considering if a different repayment plan or repayment method would be more suitable.[42]

If you have previously not been able to manage a payment plan, you may be offered a prepayment meter as your only option. If this is not convenient for you, try to renegotiate another payment plan – SLC 27 sets out alternatives including Fuel Direct.

You are not normally charged the cost of repositioning a meter to enable a prepayment meter to be fitted in these circumstances or for a smart meter set in prepayment mode.

Resisting a prepayment meter

Suppliers sometimes attempt to impose a prepayment meter– eg, if a payment plan breaks down or if you are unwilling or unable to pay a security deposit.

– In individual cases, Ofgem has a duty to make decisions about the reasonableness of the request for security, including the request for a cash security deposit or the imposition of a prepayment meter as an alternative.[43]

– Check the supplier's code of practice and point out its obligations, including licence obligations towards those in a vulnerable situation.[44] Try to negotiate an affordable payment plan in the first instance. Ensuring that a payment plan is affordable reduces the chance of it failing and avoids more difficult negotiations to reinstate a revised payment plan.[45]

– Check whether the supplier is a signatory to Energy UK's 'Vulnerability Committment'[46] which provides better safeguards and protections if you are in financial difficulties.[47]

– Where a supplier asks for a security deposit, you may need to show that you can manage a payment plan, perhaps by referring to other bills you have successfully managed to pay in instalments – eg, catalogue debts or consumer purchases. If negotiations fail, contact Citizens Advice consumer service.

– If it is not 'safe and reasonably practicable'[48] (see p114) for you to operate a prepayment meter, the supplier is in breach of its duty to supply and should offer you alternative means to pay charges or other arrangements to make it 'safe and reasonably practicable'.[49] Contact Citizens Advice consumer service.

– If you have entered into a breathing space scheme (see p103), fresh action to install a prepayment meter must not be taken (existing warrant proceedings may however continue, save execution of the warrant).[50]

– If you have entered into a breathing space scheme, a supplier must not use a prepayment meter already installed to take payments, except if you had agreed to the meter before the breathing space commenced.[51]

Prohibitions on installing a prepayment meter

Suppliers are prohibited or restricted from force-fitting prepayment meters under a warrant or recalibrating smart meters to prepayment mode in certain circumstances. A warrant should not be exercised and a prepayment meter installed or smart meter recalibrated where:

- it will be severely traumatic to you due to an existing vulnerability which relates to your mental capacity and/or psychological state, and it will be made significantly worse by the experience;[52]
- you are in financial difficulty and the supplier has not offered or discussed with you a range of debt repayment options first;[53]

- it is not safe and reasonably practicable in all circumstances for you to use a prepayment meter;[54]
- you are in the 'high risk' category (see p115);[55]
- you are in the 'medium risk' category (considered on a case-by-case basis – see p115);
- it is not a 'proportionate' measure in the debt recovery process. Suppliers must ensure that all debt recovery actions and costs and charges levied up to and including applying for a warrant are proportionate to the amount that is owed;[56]
- there are unpaid charges which are genuinely in dispute;[57]
- you have entered into a breathing space scheme (see p103).[58]

Prohibitions on warrant-related charges

Suppliers are prohibited from levying charges or costs associated with a warrant (including applying for and executing) where:

- you have a vulnerability which significantly impairs your ability to engage with the supplier;[59] *or*
- you have a severe financial vulnerability which will be exacerbated by warrant-associated charges or costs;[60] *or*
- you have entered into a breathing space scheme (see p103).[61]

In all other cases, warrant-related charges and costs are capped at £150.[62]

Is it safe and reasonably practicable for you to have a prepayment meter?
When a supplier becomes aware that it is not safe and reasonably practicable in all circumstances for you to use a prepayment meter, it should make alternative payment arrangements, move your meter, adapt your meter or replace it completely.[63]
What determines 'safe and reasonably practicable' is open to interpretation and has 'high risk' and 'medium risk' categories. These apply where you request or a supplier offers a prepayment meter, or it is considering installing (or installs) an involuntary prepayment meter. Relevant factors can include:
– a physical or mental disability, or other limitation, which prevents you from operating or understanding a prepayment meter or prevents you from travelling to local top-up outlets or operating top-up devices;
– you require an uninterrupted or regular fuel supply due to a relevant health condition – eg, an electric ventilator;
– local top-up outlets are located an impracticable distance for you to travel;
– the prepayment meter is located in an inaccessible location – eg, a locked room to which you do not have regular access, high on a wall or outside.
Where it becomes apparent that your household will, frequently or for prolonged periods, self-disconnect and risk causing you significant harm, it will not be considered safe or reasonably practicable for you to have a prepayment meter, either voluntarily or involuntarily. In these circumstances, the supplier must also conduct an affordability

assessment, provide meter care and aftercare support. If appropriate, raise a formal complaint with your supplier. Consideration should be given to guidance published by Ofgem.[64] You can also contact Citizens Advice consumer service or Advice Direct Scotland.

Involuntary prepayment meters

A supplier can seek to install a prepayment meter or recalibrate a smart meter to prepayment mode without your written or verbal consent.

In all cases, suppliers should individually assess the suitability of each household for involuntary prepayment meter, including considering if it is 'safe and reasonably practicable' (see p114). An involuntary prepayment meter *cannot* be installed for those highest at risk. They fall under the 'do not install' category.[65] A second group, those at medium risk, require further investigation by suppliers before proceeding with an involuntary prepayment meter or smart meter recalibration.[66]

'High risk' – involuntary prepayment meter cannot be installed

When a supplier considers that it is 'safe and reasonably practicable' for you to use a prepayment meter, and seeks to proceed with a prepayment meter, it must refrain from all involuntary installations for the highest-risk customers. These include households:

– where all occupants are aged 75 years and over (if there is no other support in the home);

– with children aged under two;

– which require a continuous supply for health reasons, including dependence on powered medical equipment – eg, heart/lung ventilators, dialysis equipment, stair lift, hoist, carelines, health alarms or refrigerated medication;

– which include someone with chronic, severe or terminal health conditions or those with a medical dependency on a warm home – eg, cancer, organ failure and cardiovascular/ respiratory disease (such as emphysema and chronic bronchitis);

– where no one can access, operate and/or top up the meter due to physical or mental incapacity or for technical reasons.

If you fall into this 'do not install' category, raise a formal complaint with your supplier. Consideration should be given to guidance published by Ofgem.[67]

'Medium risk' – further assessment required before involuntary installing a prepayment meter

Before a supplier can proceed with an involuntary prepayment meter, it must refrain from all involuntary installations for medium-risk customers. These fall into the 'further assessment needed' category. In making its assessment of 'safe and reasonably practicable', the supplier must consider a number of characteristics/circumstances/conditions, alongside the assumption that this group is in financial difficulty and likely to self-disconnect. It should be noted that the personal circumstances and characteristics are not absolute nor exhaustive. They include households:

- with children aged under five years;
- where someone has a serious medical or health condition such as a neurological disease (eg, Parkinson's, Huntingdon's or cerebral palsy), respiratory condition, nutritional issue (eg, malnutrition) and mobility limiting condition (eg, osteoporosis, muscular dystrophy or multiple sclerosis);
- where someone has a serious mental or developmental health condition (eg, clinical depression, Alzheimer's, dementia, Schizophrenia or learning disabilities and difficulties);
- temporary situations – eg, pregnancy or bereavement.[68]

In these circumstances, suppliers must conduct an 'ability to pay' assessment and provide meter care and aftercare support. If you fall into this 'further assessment needed' category, raise a formal complaint with your supplier. Consideration should be given to guidance published by Ofgem.[69]

Before an involuntary prepayment meter can be installed

Suppliers must follow certain processes before proceeding with an involuntary installation of a prepayment meter. The outstanding charges per fuel must be £200 or more (called the 'debt trigger') and be outstanding for three months or more after the date the bill was issued.[70] Three months preceding any execution of an involuntary prepayment meter, suppliers must also:[71]

- make at least 10 attempts to contact you through various communication channels, at various times of day;
- conduct a site welfare visit at least once, with audio or body cameras;
- make translation services and accessible formats – eg, braille;
- retain any assessment documentation and audio or body camera recordings;
- consider the cheapest payment option when calculating your ability to pay and offer you an affordable, sustainable repayment plan;[72]
- provide clear information relating to prepayment meter operation, including process and methods to pay and procedures in the event of disconnection;[73]
- provide you with easy access to a Supplier Priority Services team.[74]

Suppliers must accept information from you (or your representative) about your circumstances and your ability to pay,[75] including the conditions detailed in SLC 27.

If all engagement attempts have been exhausted, including during site welfare visits, suppliers can exercise their discretion to obtain a warrant for a prepayment meter to be installed or for a smart meter to be recalibrated to prepayment mode. In doing so, suppliers must also use their internal 'welfare officers'. Welfare officers are responsible for overseeing the safeguarding of consumer protection, particularly if they have not been able to establish with certainty your risk level and that it is 'safe and reasonably practicable' for a prepayment meter to be installed.[76]

At the point of warrant installation/recalibration, suppliers must place a repayable £30 credit per meter (or equivalent non-disconnection period) as a short-term credit/measure to remove the risk of you disconnecting.[77]

If it is subsequently determined that the involuntary prepayment meter is unsuitable, the prepayment installation/recalibration should be reversed to non-prepayment mode. If suppliers have been found to breach licence conditions and guidance, they must offer compensation reflective of any detriment suffered.[78]

Assessment of 'ability to pay' for involuntary prepayment meter

As with customers who are in payment difficulty under SLC 27, suppliers must also take into account your 'ability to pay' before proceeding to an involuntary prepayment meter. Suppliers must:[79]

- not threaten you with involuntary prepayment meter to try to secure a higher payment than is affordable;
- consider the cheapest payment option when calculating your ability to pay and offer you an affordable, sustainable repayment plan;
- consider alternative approaches to recovering the debt such as delaying repayment starting if the affordability assessment establishes that you can only currently afford to pay towards your ongoing energy usage.

Collecting arrears from a previous property on a prepayment meter

The Electricity (Prepayment Meter) Regulations 2006[80] and the Gas (Prepayment Meter) Regulations 2006[81] allow a prepayment meter to be used to recover a sum owed to a supplier for the supply of gas or electricity, including the provision of the gas and electricity meter, 'at any premises previously owned or occupied by the customer'.[82] Note that a supplier cannot recover sums unless it had previously entered into an agreement with you, which states in writing:[83]

- your name; *and*
- the charges you are required to pay in addition to those recovered from a previous property; *and*
- a guarantee that the supplier has verbally provided you with details of other payment options available to you; *and*
- the operation of the prepayment meter as regards recovery of debt and charging for ongoing consumption; *and*
- the implications of failing to make payments.

You can cancel the agreement by giving verbal or written notice to the supplier within seven working days of receiving the written terms of the agreement. Either party can terminate the agreement on provision of 30 days' verbal or written notice.

Vulnerable customers facing disconnection should refer to Energy UK's Vulnerability Commitment (see p102) and SLC 28.

Fuel Direct

The Fuel Direct scheme is a means to clear fuel arrears. It is also known as the DWP's 'third party deduction scheme'. It allows an amount to be deducted from your benefit at source by the DWP and paid directly to your energy supplier until the debt is cleared.

To be placed on the Fuel Direct scheme you must have a fuel debt and be in receipt of:

- universal credit (UC). Five per cent of your UC is deducted to put towards your outstanding fuel debt (see p191 for the amounts);[84] *or*
- pension credit, income support, income-based jobseeker's allowance (JSA) or income-related employment and support allowance (ESA). In some situations, deductions can be made from contribution-based JSA or contributory ESA. A fixed amount of £4.55 a week (during 2024/25) is deducted to address your arrears.

An additional amount can also be deducted to cover ongoing consumption, based on your previous annual bill, except where you are using a prepayment meter. This is to avoid future debt accruing and assist with budgeting in the future. See p190 for how the scheme works.

Fuel Direct should be used as an option, 'where available', when arrears have been incurred by vulnerable people.[85] A supplier may be at fault if it overlooks this option, as many people who fall within a vulnerable category are likely to be on a qualifying benefit. You must be contacted by the DWP to establish your wishes or have an opportunity to make representations before being placed on the scheme.[86]

If you are eligible for Fuel Direct and are willing to have arrears deducted from your benefit, request that your supplier and Jobcentre Plus implement this.[87] Be prepared to raise a formal complaint if the supplier will not implement Fuel Direct or if you face procedural obstacles or delays (see Chapter 14).

Fuel Direct deductions usually involve suppliers applying to the DWP for deductions for both ongoing consumption and arrears. However, since 1 April 2023, new deduction applications for ongoing fuel consumption, or a change in existing deductions, can only be made if a supplier obtains your consent first or you apply for it yourself.[88]

6. **Rate of repayment**

Fuel suppliers are required to make arrangements for the recovery of debts which take into account your ability to pay.[89] This applies whether you are offered a payment plan or a prepayment meter.

The rate of Fuel Direct deductions (see p191) is often used as a yardstick to determine the period over which a debt should be repaid within a payment plan or through a prepayment meter.

If you get universal credit, pension credit, income support, income-based jobseeker's allowance or income-related employment and support allowance, you may wish to consider the Fuel Direct scheme, but note that this would result in deductions for your arrears over a long period. This may not be appropriate if your arrears should be recovered at a lower rate and the deduction rate set is causing you financial hardship, particularly if you have existing deductions. Research has led to one charity recommending a lower minimum deduction rate of £1.[90]

Repayments below Fuel Direct rates

If your income is low, or roughly equivalent to means-tested benefit levels (eg, you get housing benefit or council tax reduction), argue that you should not repay your debt at a higher rate than the Fuel Direct rates.

There are many situations where a supplier should accept less than this level of repayment, particularly if your income is very low – eg, you may not be entitled to benefits because you work, but you have to pay childcare or mortgage expenses which are not taken into consideration; or your benefit is sanctioned; or you have multiple other priority debts.

Suppliers are primarily concerned with ensuring that you pay for your current consumption, and should accept payments of arrears over extended periods at rates which you can afford to sustain and are in line with your ability to pay,[91] even if this is very low. If you have multiple debts, your suppliers should be persuaded to treat fuel debts in the same way as other priority debts. If you cannot afford the rate of repayment sought, ask to pay at a lower rate. Provide your supplier with information about your income, necessary outgoings and other debts by sending a detailed financial statement (see p109). Under the Vulnerability Commitment (see p102), suppliers have committed to consider affordable payment offers, budget sheets and prepared Standard Financial Statements.[92] Ultimately, you could challenge the deductions from being made if they exceed the maximum sum permitted, even for a limited period, on the grounds that they are not in your 'best interests'.[93]

If the DWP makes a refusal decision, it is subject to legal challenge, including by judicial review. If the supplier refuses to accept lower payments, contact Citizens Advice consumer service or Advice Direct Scotland for advice.

If a supplier formally refuses a particular repayment rate but then subsequently accepts regular repayments from you at that rate, it is arguable that an agreement has been reached and agreed by virtue of the conduct of both parties. Similarly, if a supplier has promised not to take enforcement action or pursue a certain sum and you then act in reliance on that promise, it is arguable that the supplier cannot then renege on the promise. For example, if a supplier tells you that it is prepared to reduce part of a debt and you then repay the remainder, it should not be open to the supplier to take action regarding the unpaid balance at a later date. The rule on estoppel applies (see p122).

Arrears more than six years old

In England and Wales, where arrears for fuel accrued more than six years ago, recovery is statute-barred under the Limitation Act 1980, which imposes a six-year time limit on the recovery of contractual debts in law. The six years run from the date that the bill first fell due. Suppliers cannot issue legal proceedings after this date and it is a complete defence if they do. But this does not stop them from serving a demand for a bill or undertaking recovery action which is more than six years old. However, you are not under a legal obligation to pay if faced with a demand which relates to a debt more than six years old. If six years have passed, you should not admit or acknowledge the arrears or debt to the supplier. You should not make any payment towards the sum. Where legal action has been commenced within the six-year period (eg, the supplier has taken court action against you and obtained a judgment), then it can enforce the judgment even after six years but will need to seek the permission of the court to do so, and the court would take into account any failure on its part to act promptly. Enforcement action is not subject to the limitations under the Limitation Act 1980. Also remember that since 1 May 2018, suppliers are prohibited from sending you a retrospective bill (back-bill), or otherwise recovering, beyond 12 months.[94] You can therefore formally challenge any back-bill issued by a supplier with an ultimate redress leading to an investigation by Ofgem for a supplier's failure to adhere to its supplier licence conditions. This protection may not apply if you have behaved obstructively or unreasonably, preventing the supplier from accurately billing you. Complaint mechanisms are also available, such as complaining to the Energy Ombudsman. Get legal advice if the debt accrued under back-billing rules (see p83).

For fuel arrears in Scotland, statute-barred debts cease to exist after a period of five years, unless a decree has been issued by the court before the five-year limitation period. As with the Limitation Act 1980, creditors cannot issue legal action against you. See CPAG's *Debt Advice Handbook Scotland* for more information.

Paying for your current consumption

Whatever your debt repayment rate, you must also pay for your estimated current consumption over the year. It is important that this estimate is as accurate as possible, otherwise you may end up paying more than you can afford.

You can check the estimate provided by the supplier, either by using your own bills or by asking for details of the actual readings of your meter over a past period. Suppliers often have records for up to eight quarters. Try to make sure that the readings cover at least a year so that you make allowances for seasonal variations and any changes in your lifestyle or appliance usage. Calculate the number of units of fuel you have used over the period covered by meter readings, and then divide this figure by the number of weeks in that period to work out the number of units you use on average each week. Multiply that figure by the cost of the units of fuel. Then add on the amount of the standing charge for each week.

If you have not been in your property for long, the supplier's energy efficiency advisers should be able to advise you on the likely size of your bills if you provide them with details of the size of your home, family and the appliances you use.

Where you have a payment plan, ensure that your meter is read every quarter, either by you or the supplier, so that you can check the accuracy of your estimated current consumption and ensure that the amount you are paying is neither too low nor too high.

Lump-sum repayments

You should not be asked to pay lump sums of money as part-payment towards arrears conditional on you being allowed a prepayment meter; nor should you be asked to pay lump sums before being allowed to pay arrears in instalments if you are unable to pay your bill because of hardship. The supplier's licence specifically provides that it must allow you to pay your arrears in instalments, taking into account your ability to pay.[95]

However, a supplier might demand a part payment towards a debt before agreeing to a prepayment meter. This is contrary to the licence provisions, specifically Standard Licence Condition (SLC) 27. Refer a dispute arising from such a request to Citizens Advice consumer service or Advice Direct Scotland.

Breakdown of repayment arrangement

If a change of circumstances has occurred which has affected your ability to pay, ask the supplier to consider a revised payment arrangement. Suppliers are obliged to consider this under the licence conditions.[96] Your supplier may include a statement about changes of circumstances, payment difficulties or vulnerabilities in its code of practice. Note that the provisions within SLC can be enforced by Ofgem in individual cases, in contrast to the provisions within the code of practice, which are voluntary. Any special circumstances ought to be brought to the attention of the supplier.

If your circumstances have not changed, it may have been that the level of repayment was too high in the first place and the supplier had not acted in the spirit of the licence conditions, taking into account affordability, nor adhered to Ofgem's 'ability to pay' principles.[97] If this is so, ask for a revised payment arrangement based on a more detailed picture of your financial circumstances. For example, if you have obtained debt advice for the first time and your adviser has helped you to prepare a financial statement. Otherwise, you may be obliged to accept a prepayment meter or the Fuel Direct Scheme.

If you cannot manage the payment level you have agreed, always try to pay something, however small, and on your usual payment date, even if you are in the process of negotiating a new payment arrangement. Doing so demonstrates 'good faith'; you want to address your debt, but cannot afford to do so at the previously agreed level.

In the event of a dispute and a threat of disconnection, contact Citizens Advice consumer service or Advice Direct Scotland for advice.

7. **Waiver, full and final settlement of arrears and estoppel**

As the supply of gas and electricity is covered by contracts, general principles of the law of contract may be applied to assist you. The legal principles are complex, but there is no reason why they should not be applied to arrears. Simply giving you time to pay off arrears does not deprive the supplier of the right to take recovery action for the debt, but other principles of contract law protecting you may apply.

In some cases, an energy company may be prepared to waive its rights to recover arrears, or remit a debt, either wholly or in part. A number of doctrines of contract law, including waiver, full and final settlement and estoppel may be help a consumer with arrears in seeking a solution. These principles have yet to be tested in relation to fuel supply contracts, but for information on the general principles see textbooks on the law of contract.

Get legal advice before seeking a part payment or full and final settlement based on common law principles of contract; the law relates here to England and Wales and separate advice should be sought if considering settlement in Scotland.

In many cases, a supplier may prefer to reach a final settlement on arrears on commercial and economic grounds, rather than face the cost of recovery action through the courts for a debt. Under the small claims procedure of the county court, a supplier will not be able to recover legal costs if the sum claimed is under £10,000. This often makes taking action through the county court an uneconomic recovery option. The general attitude of suppliers is that they will issue court proceedings (including the magistrates' court – see Chapter 9) to install a prepayment meter.

Some suppliers may be prepared to accept a one-off lump sum payment of arrears as settlement to a dispute. In contract law, parties may seek to be discharged of their obligations under an agreement by varying the terms and one party accepting a lesser payment. Many civil disputes are settled privately between parties without recourse to court action by agreeing to conclude matters in a full and final settlement, rather than continue to court. The rules of court encourage parties to try to reach amicable settlements to legal claims, rather than using the court to settle disputes. There is no reason why reaching an agreement to pay a lesser sum as a full and final settlement to an energy debt should not be more widely used, as it is a common practice in other areas of commercial life.

Settlement by paying a lesser sum may be an option where you are in a position to switch supplier (although the successor company may be entitled to recover certain arrears if the debt is assigned, if a full and final settlement is not reached).

However, the legal rules can be complicated. Simply sending a small amount to an energy supplier is not sufficient to discharge arrears or a sum owed in interest.[98] The supplier is still lawfully entitled to recover the money, unless some benefit is derived from the terms you may offer to the energy supplier, along with the part-payment.

For part-payment to represent a settlement, the supplier must formally agree to waive its right to recover any sums in return for accepting a lump sum or by agreeing to relinquish some obligation upon itself, such as the requirement to read a meter or investigate a complaint. Alternatively, you might agree to a prepayment meter, varying the terms of an existing contract, in return for the supplier accepting a lesser sum in full and final settlement of the existing arrears. Where a supplier threatens legal action, it may be possible to reach a settlement whereby you make part-payment of the money owed in return for the supplier waiving its right to take legal action (thus saving itself the resources, time and expenses of litigation). You must make a clear offer to the supplier that you are willing to pay a smaller sum immediately towards clearing arrears and it is necessary for the supplier to agree and to waive the right of court action. Alternatively, the energy company may agree to waive its right to recover a sum in arrears if you have switched supplier. In some cases, you might agree to waive the right to issue a claim against the supplier, or withdraw any existing claim issued against the supplier or to Ofgem for a breach of the licence conditions. In such a case, the supplier will have derived a benefit (ie, not being subject to a complaint or legal claim) and may agree to accept a lesser sum. The conferring of benefits on both you and the company establishes a settlement to the debt.

Put forward your offer in open correspondence, in writing and clearly refer to acceptance being a full and final settlement of the sum and a waiver of further recovery action in future.

Any communications should be marked 'full and final settlement', including endorsing this on any final payment cheque and not be marked 'without prejudice' to ensure that it is binding upon both parties.

Example

Jean is a widowed pensioner who had been a customer of one supplier for many years. Before her husband died, he switched to a new supplier. The new company failed to read the meter and sent an estimated bill of over £1,000, which was carried over each quarter. Efforts to negotiate proved fruitless, and letters went ignored. Jean contacted her previous supplier who had kept records of her good payment history. Jean paid sums she could afford and repeatedly wrote to her new supplier offering to pay by instalments. No written response was forthcoming. The new supplier then threatened legal action to recover the arrears. On taking advice, she was recommended to pay 10 per cent of the bill in full and final settlement. She sent a cheque for 10 per cent of the outstanding amount and the letter was clearly marked 'cash this cheque only if you accept this sum in full and final settlement of the dispute'. She also endorsed the cheque 'full and final settlement cheque'. The new supplier cashed the cheque after Jean switched supplier, returning to her old energy company with whom she had a good payment record.

Four months after she returned to her old supplier, the new energy company presented her with a fresh demand. The letter in full and final settlement was cited in negotiations. It was argued that by cashing the cheque in response to the settlement letter the supplier had accepted the offer of settlement by Jean. Eventually, the supplier agreed to waive recovery and wrote off the arrears when it emerged that it had not read Jean's meter for over a year.

Disputes over whether a supplier has agreed to a full and final settlement may come down to a dispute of fact where the energy company has accepted payment. Legal advice should be taken in such cases.

Frontline staff may not be familiar with these principles, so you should seek to speak to the complaints handling team or a senior manager.

In some cases, a supplier may agree to forego the right to recover arrears for a period and not enforce a debt in return for a lesser sum in payment. During that period, the supplier cannot go back on the agreement and take action. What is known as the doctrine of '**estoppel**' operates. This provides that where a person acts in reliance on a promise made by another, that other person cannot then break the promise and take enforcement action. For example, where a supplier agrees to grant a three-month suspension on paying arrears and you act accordingly, the supplier cannot demand the money in the three months. The supplier is said to be 'estopped' from taking action in the period.[99]

8. **Switching supplier when you have arrears**

Where there is an unpaid bill, a supplier may block a transfer to another energy provider. This is also known as a 'debt objection' or 'debt blocking'.[100] This applies to debts owed for 28 days or more.

However, if you have a prepayment meter and have outstanding fuel debts of between £10 and £500, these can be assigned to a new supplier. The new supplier must consent to taking you as a customer and the assignment. The debt is then carried over to the new supplier and you pay it instead. Within this boundary, your existing supplier cannot block a transfer. This should encourage greater flexibility, energy efficiency, competitive tariffs, assist you in discharging your arrears and switching suppliers more easily, even when in debt. This process is known as the '**debt assignment protocol**' and is implemented in the Standard Licence Conditions.[101] The protocol is the mechanism used by suppliers to facilitate a transfer of supply to another supplier when an indebted prepayment meter customer requests a switch. Similarly, if you have a disputed debt of £500 or less transferred on to a prepayment meter, the supplier cannot block a transfer where charges are disputed in their entirety or there is supplier error.[102] The precise scope of this condition has yet to be tested by the courts or by the regulators.

One such situation may be where you have offered and paid a lesser sum in full and final settlement for an existing debt and accepted the imposition of a prepayment meter.

Suppliers are required to keep evidence of that request and of the reasons for it for at least 12 months after the request is made.[103] If a supplier objects to a transfer, it is required to give you formal notice as soon as reasonably practicable:[104]

- that an objection has been raised and the grounds of the objection; *and*
- how you may dispute or resolve such grounds; *and*
- that you have 30 working days to pay outstanding charges.

Suppliers must also offer you advice or information on:

- energy efficiency; *and*
- debt management; *and*
- alternative contracts that may be available to you.

Normally, within 90 days of taking over a supply, the new supplier is given a notice by the previous supplier to assign the charges. The new supplier must then pay the outstanding charges to your previous supplier. Your new supplier can then seek to recover the money from you. If the old supplier fails to act within prescribed time limits, the right of assignment may be lost.

In such cases, you should not be regarded as having failed to pay any charges for the supply of fuel:[105]

- if the supply is genuinely in dispute; *or*
- where charges are in relation to the provision of a gas meter.

Contact Citizens Advice consumer service or Advice Direct Scotland for advice on the position with charges and difficulties with a supplier; it may also be worth involving the Energy Ombudsman (see Chapter 14).

Ultimately, it is the county court in England and Wales and the sheriff court in Scotland which could be called upon to determine the matter (see Chapter 14). A debt which has been assigned is not enforceable if there is a dispute which you are prepared to raise as a defence. Only when the dispute has been resolved against you and a judgment given will any debt be legally enforceable. Alternatively, your new supplier also has discretion to waive charges or collect a lesser sum.

9. **Multiple debts**

For many people, fuel arrears are just part of a bigger problem of unpaid bills. It is beyond the scope of this book to give detailed advice about debts other than those for fuel. See CPAG's *Debt Advice Handbook* or *Debt Advice Handbook Scotland* – both are available free at cpag.org.uk/handbooks.

If you are seeking advice about your fuel debts, tell the adviser about all your other debts as well, so they can give you accurate and relevant advice.

Getting advice

Your local Citizens Advice can tell you what is available locally and can advise on multiple debts. There is also a national telephone helpline, National Debtline (tel: 0808 808 4000; webchat available at nationaldebtline.org). The Money Advice Trust produces a comprehensive self-help guide for dealing with multiple debts. The guide includes a very useful sheet to help you work out your own financial statement. Copies of this pack can be obtained from your local free advice agency and is also available from moneyadvicetrust.org.

You can also consult solicitors, law centres or advice agencies which provide debt advice. Certain charities also operate assistance schemes. Make sure that any advice you get is free and genuinely independent of your creditors.

Charitable assistance

Many of the fuel companies offer charitable assistance in the form of energy trusts to customers experiencing financial difficulty. Check whether your fuel supplier runs such a scheme.

You can only ask for help to clear arrears – you are usually expected to set up a regular payment arrangement to manage your future supply and prevent arrears accruing on your account again.

The qualifying criteria for these trusts are relatively broad. Some trusts accept applications from you, even if you are not their customer. You must be able to show that you are experiencing financial hardship, and that a payment from the trust will assist you to pay your future fuel bills. Make sure that you give as much information as possible about your circumstances including why you have had difficulty paying your energy bills. You are also required to complete a detailed financial statement listing your other commitments and any other debts you may have and provide evidence of your hardship, including wage slips, benefit entitlement letters and evidence of debts and ill health.

Before applying for assistance, you are recommended to meet with an adviser for support on addressing your debts, particularly as funds are limited.

Not all applications are successful and it can take a number of weeks for the trustees to decide about your case. The decision made by the trust is final and there is no right of appeal.

Some trusts offer further help in the form of 'further assistance payments' to meet the cost of boilers, white goods, energy-efficient appliances, funeral expenses and applying for bankruptcy. These can be useful if you have multiple debts and want to pursue any of these options but cannot meet the cost of doing so yourself. Check whether your supplier offers this type of help.

Administration orders

If you have multiple debts, you can apply to a county court in England and Wales for an administration order as a means of getting the county court to take over the administration of your debts.[106] This is a little used but extremely useful, provision whereby the court will decide how much you can afford to pay to each of your creditors. You make one monthly payment to the court, which then pays your creditors on your behalf.

To be able to obtain an administration order:

• you must have a county court or High Court judgment against you; *and*
• the total of your debts must be less than £5,000; *and*
• you must have at least two debts.

Administration orders are not available in Scotland.

Importantly, the court can reduce the amount of overall debt paid by order so that only a percentage of the total debts are to be paid – eg, ordering that the debtor pays into the administration order 25p for each £1 owed. So, a person with total debts of £4,000 would only be required to ultimately pay back £1,000 under the administration order.

In terms of fuel debt, the making of an administration order by a court must be the definitive statement of your ability to pay. Suppliers who seek to recover arrears outside the terms of the administration order could find themselves in contempt of court.

Suppliers, however, are not used to people putting their debts into administration orders. Always contact your supplier in advance to explain your proposed course of action. You also need to make arrangements to pay for your current supply. The supplier will almost certainly insist that you pay using a method which offers the supplier greater security, such as a prepayment meter, Fuel Direct or a payment plan using direct debit. The supplier is not permitted to recover arrears through any of these methods of payment without the leave of the court, since the court will take over the payment of arrears.

Apply for an administration order on Form N92 available from your local county court or gov.uk. There is no upfront fee to apply.

The court contacts your creditors and either makes the order by agreement or arranges a private hearing with a district judge to consider your application. In practice, few creditors bother to attend a hearing for an administration order, and in many cases, they may write off the debt completely at this stage.

The court has powers to cancel or vary the administration order once it is granted, if you fail to pay. However, if you do encounter payment problems, contact the court immediately to seek a variation of the order.

Advantages of an administration order

- The order usually runs for three years, although this is not automatic (check with the court). Provided you have paid your monthly payments, the rest of the debt is written off at the end of this period.
- Interest is frozen on accounts.
- Your creditors cannot chase you or take other court action against you while the order runs.
- You have to make only one payment each month.
- The court can reduce the amount of each debt owed by requiring only a percentage of the debt to be paid.
- It is possible for a charity or a third party to pay off the amount owing under the administration order in a lump sum.

Disadvantages of an administration order

- Your name appears on a register of court orders and you may find it hard to get credit.
- There is a court fee each time you make a payment. This cannot be more than 10 per cent of your debt – eg, if you owe £4,000, the total fee must be a maximum of £400.

Debt relief orders

In England and Wales, if you cannot pay your debts and you meet the eligibility conditions, you can apply for a debt relief order (DRO).

To qualify, you must satisfy the following.[107]

- You must be unable to pay your debts.
- Your total debts must be no more than £50,000.[108]
- Your total assets must not be more than £2,000, although you are also permitted to additionally own a vehicle worth up to £4,000[109] (or more if it has been adapted because you have a disability).
- Your disposable income after deducting allowable expenses must not be more than £75 a month.
- You do not own your home.
- You have lived, worked or had a property in England or Wales at any time during the last three years.
- You must not have been subject to a DRO within the last six years.
- You must not be involved in any other formal insolvency procedure at the time of application for a DRO.

Under a DRO, recovery action by creditors to obtain money from you is stopped and at the end of a set period (usually a year) the debts are cleared. So, for example, a supplier cannot take any further action against you such as disconnection in respect of fuel arrears included in a DRO.

Certain debts are excluded from a DRO and it will negatively affect your credit. See CPAG's *Debt Advice Handbook* for further details. Although you can include fuel arrears in the order, you are expected to meet the costs of future fuel consumption and should include these in your expenditure figures.

There is no upfront fee to apply for a DRO.[110]

DROs are administered by the Official Receiver through the Insolvency Service. You can only apply through an approved third party or intermediary. These are usually debt advisers who have authority to complete the online application. To find your nearest approved intermediary, contact your local free advice agency.[111]

Enforcement agents

In England and Wales, if you have fuel debts, enforcement agents – formerly bailiffs – (in Scotland, sheriff officers) may come to your home to take away your possessions. Enforcement agents cannot force entry to private dwellings in England and Wales for most types of debt, and in Scotland, forced entry is only possible as a last resort. If a company or its enforcement agents threaten to force entry, make a formal complaint to the supplier. In England and Wales, enforcement agents must give you seven days' notice that they will be calling at your property.[112]

Forced entry to your home in connection with an unpaid energy bill can only be by warrant of control (see Chapter 10). Even if enforcement agents gain entry and seize goods, the sums of money raised at auction rarely cover the enforcement agent and auctioneer fees and the debt remains.

Enforcement agents have a duty to notify the creditor and report the circumstances when there is evidence of vulnerability. The Ministry of Justice has produced standards as to what constitutes 'vulnerable situations' (see Appendix 3).[113]

In Scotland, sheriff officers cannot demand entry to your home unless a court order known as an 'exceptional attachment order' has been obtained. Forced entry cannot take place unless there is a person present who is at least 16, and is not, because of their age, knowledge of English, mental illness, mental or physical disability or otherwise, unable to understand the consequences of the procedure being carried out.[114]

Energy suppliers do not have powers to force entry simply to recover money – any power of entry can only be exercised under a warrant through a magistrates' court to disconnect a supply, not to seize possessions (see Chapter 10).

Notes

1. What are arrears
1 Sch 6 paras 1 and 2 EA 1989; Sch 4 UA 2000
2 Sch 2B para 7(1)(b) and (3) GA 1986

2. Protection when you are in arrears
3 Condition 26.4 SLC
4 Condition 26.5 SLC
5 Condition 26.1 SLC
6 Condition 26.1(a) SLC
7 Ofgem, *Consumer Vulnerability Strategy 2025*, October 2019
8 Condition 29 (gas) SLC
9 Condition 26.1(b) and (c) SLC
10 Enforceable principles placed on suppliers by Ofgem to treat consumers fairly, professionally, honestly and transparently in the way they behave, provide information and deliver customer service, see ofgem.gov.uk/publications/licence-guide-standards-conduct
11 Conditions 0 and 0A SLC (Standards of Conduct)
12 Energy UK, *The Vulnerability Commitment*, 2024, at energy-uk.org.uk/our-work/vulnerability-commitment
13 Condition 27.5 SLC
14 See the latest prices at gov.uk/government/collections/quarterly-energy-prices
15 Condition 27.6 SLC
16 Suppliers are accountable for the action of any third parties they work with, Conditions 13 SLC and 0.2 SLC
17 Condition 27.8 SLC
18 Ofgem, *Review of Suppliers' Approaches to Debt Management and Prevention*, June 2010
19 Energy UK, *The Vulnerability Commitment*, 2024
20 Energy UK, *The Vulnerability Commitment*, 2024
21 At the time of writing, the signatories are British Gas, EDF Energy, E.ON Next, Scottish Power, Octopus Energy, Utility Warehouse, OVO Energy, Ecotricity, So Energy, Outfox the Market, Utilita, Good Energy and E Energy

22 DRS Regs
23 DRS Regs

3. Arrears in another person's name
24 Sch 6 para 2 EA 1989

4. Arrears as a result of estimated bills
25 Condition 21BA.1 SLC
26 Condition 21BA.2 SLC
27 Condition 28 SLC
28 Sch 6 paras 8(4), 9(6) and 9(7) UC,PIP,JSA&ESA(C&P) Regs
29 Regs 2 and 3 The Social Security Benefits (Claims and Payments) (Amendment) Regulations 2023 No.232
30 Condition 21B.5A SLC
31 Condition 21B.9 SLC

5. Paying your arrears
32 Condition 27 SLC
33 Condition 27.8 SLC and codes of practice from suppliers
34 Condition 27.15 SLC
35 *Cheltenham and Gloucester Building Society v Norgan* [1996] 1 All ER 449
36 Energy UK, *The Vulnerability Commitment*, 2024
37 Condition 27A.7A SLC; Ofgem, *Involuntary PPM Code of Practice*, 18 April 2023, at ofgem.gov.uk/publications/involuntary-prepayment-meter-energy-supplier-code-practice
38 Condition 27A.1 SLC
39 Condition 27A.6 SLC
40 britishgas.co.uk/help-and-support/struggling-to-pay/paying-us-back-through-your-pay-as-you-go-meter
41 ofgem.gov.uk/sites/default/files/docs/2021/04/consumer_survey_2020_update_on_engagement.pdf
42 Condition 27.8A(g) SLC
43 Condition 27.3 and 27.4 SLC
44 Condition 0.1 and 0.3 SLC
45 Condition 27.8 SLC
46 Current signatories are British Gas, EDF Energy, E.ON Next, Scottish Power, Octopus Energy, Utility Warehouse, OVO Energy, Ecotricity, So Energy, Outfox the Market, Utilita, Good Energy and E Energy

47 Energy UK, *Vulnerability Commitment,* 2024
48 Condition 27.6(a)(iii) SLC; Ofgem, *Guidance: PPM (safe and reasonably practicable),* 13 September 2023, at ofgem.gov.uk/sites/default/files/2023-09/PPM%20Guidance_Safe%20and%20Reasonably%20Practicable.pdf
49 Condition 28.2 SLC
50 DRS Regs
51 DRS Regs
52 Condition 28.10 SLC
53 Condition 27.5 and 27.6 SLC
54 Condition 27.6(a)(iii) SLC; Ofgem, *Guidance: PPM (safe and reasonably practicable),* 13 September 2023
55 Ofgem, *Guidance: PPM (safe and reasonably practicable),* 13 September 2023, para 3.7
56 Condition 28.14 and 28.15 SLC
57 Sch 6 para 2 EA 1989; Sch 2B para 7 GA 1986
58 DRS Regs
59 Condition 28.11 SLC
60 Condition 28.11 SLC
61 DRS Regs
62 Condition 28.12 and 28.22 SLC
63 Condition 27.6(a)(iii) SLC; Ofgem, *Guidance: PPM (safe and reasonably practicable),* 13 September 2023
64 Ofgem, *Guidance: PPM (safe and reasonably practicable),* 13 September 2023; Ofgem, *Guidance on the interpretation of Safe and Reasonably Practicable for the purposes of Standard Licence Condition 28 of the Gas Supply Licence and the Electricity Supply Licence,* 31 March 2016
65 Ofgem, *Guidance: PPM (safe and reasonably practicable),* 13 September 2023, para 3.7
66 Ofgem, *Guidance: PPM (safe and reasonably practicable),* 13 September 2023, para 3.8
67 Ofgem, *Guidance: PPM (safe and reasonably practicable),* 13 September 2023, para 3.8
68 Ofgem, *Guidance: PPM (safe and reasonably practicable),* 13 September 2023, para 3.7
69 Condition 28.7 SLC; Ofgem, *Guidance: PPM (safe and reasonably practicable),* 13 September 2023, para 5
70 Condition 28.4, 28.22 SLC; Ofgem, *Guidance: PPM (safe and reasonably practicable),* 13 September 2023, para 5.2

71 Condition 28.7 SLC; Ofgem, *Guidance: PPM (safe and reasonably practicable),* 13 September 2023, paras 5.3 and 5.7
72 Condition 28.9(b) SLC; Ofgem, *Guidance: PPM (safe and reasonably practicable),* 13 September 2023, para 5.6
73 Ofgem, *Guidance: PPM (safe and reasonably practicable),* 13 September 2023, para 8.1
74 Ofgem, *Guidance: PPM (safe and reasonably practicable),* 13 September 2023, para 8.1
75 Condition 27.8 SLC; Ofgem, *Guidance: PPM (safe and reasonably practicable),* 13 September 2023, para 6.1
76 Ofgem, *Guidance: PPM (safe and reasonably practicable),* 13 September 2023, paras para 5.8 and 5.16
77 Ofgem, *Guidance: PPM (safe and reasonably practicable),* 13 September 2023, para 10.1
78 Ofgem, *Guidance: PPM (safe and reasonably practicable),* 13 September 2023, para 10.4
79 Condition 27.8 SLC; Ofgem, *Guidance: PPM (safe and reasonably practicable),* 13 September 2023, para 6
80 SI 2006 No.2010
81 SI 2006 No.2011
82 Reg 3(1)(a) E(PM) Regs; reg 3(1)(a) G(PM) Regs
83 Reg 4 E(PM) Regs; reg 4 G(PM) Regs
84 Sch 9 paras 6 and 8 SS(C&P) Regs
85 Condition 27.6 SLC (gas)
86 *Timson, Rex (On the Application Of) v SSWP* [2022] EWHC 2392 (Admin)
87 DWP, *A guide for energy suppliers ('Fuel Direct'),* 12 September 2024, at gov.uk/government/publications/how-to-request-deductions-from-benefit-a-guide-for-creditors/third-party-deductions-from-benefits-a-guide-for-fuel-suppliers
88 Social Security Benefits (Claims and Payments) (Amendment) Regulations 2023

6. **Rate of repayment**
89 Condition 27.8 SLC
90 StepChange, *The Problems of Third Party Deductions,* 14 September 2017
91 Condition 27.8 SLC
92 Energy UK, *Vulnerability Commitment,* 2024
93 Sch 6 para 4(4) UC,PIP,JSA&ESA(C&P) Regs
94 Condition 21BA.1 SLC

95 Condition 27.8 SLC
96 Conditions 27.5 to 27.8 SLC
97 Ofgem, *Key principles for ability to pay,* 3
     June 2010; conditions 27.5 to 27.8 SLC

7. **Waiver, full and final settlement of
   arrears and estoppel**
98 *Foakes v Beer* [1881-85] All ER 106;
     Pinnel's Case (1602) 5 Co Rep 117
99 *Central London Property Trust v High
     Trees House Ltd* [1947] 1 KB 1307

8. **Switching supplier when you have
   arrears**
100 Condition 14.4 SLC
101 Condition 14.6 SLC; Ofgem debt
     assignment protocol for prepayment
     meter customers, letter 12 May 2015
102 Condition 14.7 SLC
103 Condition 14.10 SLC
104 Condition 14.9 SLC
105 Sch 6 para 1(9) EA 1989; Sch 2B para 2B
     GA 1986

9. **Multiple debts**
106 s112 County Courts Act 1984; CCR 39
107 Sch 4ZA Insolvency Act 1986
108 The Insolvency Proceedings (Monetary
     Limits) (Amendment) Order 2024
     No.626
109 Insolvency (England and Wales)
     (Amendment) Rules 2024 No.622
110 gov.uk/government/publications/
     spring-budget-2024
111 See advicelocal.uk
112 Reg 6 Taking Control of Goods
     Regulations 2013
113 Ministry of Justice, *Taking Control of
     Goods: National Standards,* 6 April 2014
114 s18 Debtors (Scotland) Act 1987; s49
     Debt Arrangement and Attachment Act
     (Scotland) 2002

Chapter 8

· ·

Disconnection for arrears

This chapter covers:

1. When you can be disconnected for arrears

The most important power which suppliers have for non-payment of energy bills is to cut off your supply. The power to disconnect is considered more effective than the right to recover money through the court system.

Unfortunately, suppliers sometimes find it difficult to distinguish between deliberate non-payment and those who would pay but are suffering financial hardship or other problems. However, disconnection should only be a last resort in extreme circumstances, when all other methods of recovery have failed. It should not be used as a standard method of debt enforcement.

In practice, very few customers are now disconnected as a result of a failure to pay and it is increasingly becoming an outmoded and disused tool. However, debt and arrears have increased significantly. According to Ofgem,[1] between April and June 2024, there was an estimated £3.696 billion worth of gas and electricity debt and arrears, an increase of 43 per cent from the previous 12 months. For those with a gas repayment plan in place, average debts were £581, and for those with no repayment plan in place, average arrears were £1,329. For those with an electricity repayment plan in place, average debts were £687, and for those with no repayment plan in place, average arrears were £1,546. The proportion of customers repaying gas and electricity through a prepayment meter have increased to 55 per cent for electricity and 52 per cent for gas.

· · · ·

Ofgem has amended its domestic standards of conduct, imposing greater obligations on suppliers to ensure that disconnection is the last resort and vulnerable situations and circumstances are better identified.

The declining number of disconnections

In 2003, there were 15,973 disconnections of gas and 1,361 for electricity.[2]

As a result of the increased consumer protection, in 2022 there were 13 electricity disconnections and six gas disconnections in the UK.[3] This is an increase from 2021, where there were no disconnections for either electricity and gas. However, it represents a very small percentage of the number of customers in fuel debt during the same period and an even smaller percentage of all customers nationally.

It is important as a preliminary step to discover the cause of your arrears and identify whether you fall into a vulnerable group (see p139). If you or someone in your household is vulnerable, inform your supplier as soon as possible, preferably before arrears arise.

When the supplier can disconnect – electricity

Contract suppliers can only disconnect for arrears if the contract says so. If you are threatened with disconnection, check your contract carefully.

With any remaining tariff customers, a tariff supplier may disconnect your supply if you have not paid all charges due in respect of your electricity supply[4] within 28 working days after the date of the bill or other written request to pay.[5]

You must be given at least seven working days' written notice of the intention to disconnect[6] and cannot be disconnected for any amount which is 'genuinely in dispute'.[7] '**Charges due**' include any amounts for the electricity supply to any premises, including standing charges, meter provision, the provision of an electrical line or plant, or sums due under a green deal plan.[8] They do not include other charges such as those for credit sale agreements or for repositioning/ adapting a meter for a disabled person.[9]

Your supplier might attempt to wrongly include charges for periods when supply was disrupted and was not reconnected in a reasonable time. Check carefully that you are only being asked for the arrears for which you are liable.

Charges due can only be properly established on the basis of a meter reading. Estimates cannot be used, and you should not be disconnected based on an estimated bill. However, you must ensure you pay the amount you agree you do owe; otherwise there is an increased risk of disconnection. The supply can be cut off at the premises to which the bill relates.[10]

Failure to give the required notice of disconnection is an enforcement matter. Contact Citizens Advice consumer service or Advice Direct Scotland for advice urgently if you think your supplier intends to disconnect your supply.

When the supplier can disconnect – gas

Gas suppliers supplying under the terms of contracts and deemed contracts may disconnect your supply if you have not paid any charges due for gas within the 28 days following the date of the bill.[11] **'Charges due'** are any charges in respect of the supply of gas.[12] You are entitled to seven days' notice in writing of the intention to disconnect.[13] This is usually given in the final demand, which may arrive earlier than the 28 days above. A gas supplier is not entitled to disconnect your supply for any amount 'genuinely in dispute'.[14]

It is important to pay any undisputed part of the bill, as well as to maintain or establish a payment arrangement for ongoing fuel costs while resolving the dispute.

Note that public gas transporters may also disconnect your supply in certain circumstances (see p36).

Disconnection for assigned arrears

If you have switched supplier and you owe money to your previous supplier, the previous supplier can assign some of its debt to your new supplier in certain circumstances (see p124). The new supplier may cut off your supply as though it were the previous supplier if you fail to pay. You are entitled to a minimum of seven days' notice of the new supplier's intention to disconnect.[15] There is no right to disconnect when the entire bill is genuinely in dispute.[16] When there is a genuine dispute about the sum due and a real risk of disconnection, you should immediately formally register your dispute with the supplier in writing and request that it ceases disconnection action. You may also be protected from disconnection by conditions contained in your supplier's licence if you fall into one of the protected categories – ie, vulnerable persons or circumstances (see p139).

Disconnection when you pay in instalments

If you have an arrangement to pay in instalments, either for your current supply only or for your current supply plus an amount for arrears, the supplier is not entitled to disconnect for arrears while you keep to the terms of your agreement, since you are paying the amounts requested in writing.[17]

If you miss a payment, the supplier is entitled to disconnect for arrears from 28 working days after the date of your missed payment, but only if there are still charges due (see above), and providing you have been given seven working days' notice of the intention to disconnect. If your account is in credit, based on a reading of your meter and allowing for any standing and other charges, the supplier is not entitled to disconnect your supply.

In practice, rather than actually disconnect, suppliers are more likely to try to impose a prepayment meter. The supplier has to inform you of its intention to disconnect, subject to the notice period above, before being entitled to install a prepayment meter no less than 28 days from the date of your missed payment. A prepayment meter may be installed with your agreement at any time. This may also carry additional costs. If you have a smart meter, it can be recalibrated remotely from credit to prepayment mode. However, suppliers are not permitted to install a prepayment meter or recalibrate a smart meter to prepayment mode for certain groups of vulnerable people (see p113).

See p113 for how to resist a prepayment meter.

Alternatively, your supplier may decide that a security deposit is required just in case you do not keep to your agreement to pay by instalments.[18] The supplier must write to you to inform you of this. The supplier must give you notice that it intends to disconnect if you do not pay a security deposit. You can ask for a prepayment meter if you do not wish to pay a security deposit, unless a prepayment meter is not 'safe and practicable in all the circumstances' or it is 'unreasonable' to expect you to pay one.[19] See p37 for more about security deposits.

If the breakdown of your instalment arrangement has occurred because you cannot afford to pay, you may be able to arrange an alternative, more suitable, payment plan or payment method.[20] Remember, under their supply licence conditions, suppliers are required to make instalment arrangements based on what you are able to pay.[21] You can write to your supplier with a completed budget sheet and letter explaining what you can afford to pay (see p109).

In any event, the supplier must offer you a prepayment meter as an alternative to disconnection and as a payment option,[22] providing you do not fall into the high or medium risk group (see p115),[23] it is 'safe and practicable in all the circumstances' (see p114 – ie, not just at the point of installation but for the entire time it is used) and is 'calculated in accordance with' what you are able to pay.[24]

Payment arrangements fail for a variety of reasons. It might have been the wrong arrangement from the outset: the commencement date may not coincide with the receipt of income; the frequency of payments may not coincide with the receipt of income; or the amount for consumption or arrears may be set too high (or too low) and be unaffordable. There may have been a change in the household, lifestyle or appliance use. You may have been ill or in hospital. Failing to keep to an agreement should not automatically preclude the possibility of another one being arranged – it is essential to establish why a previous arrangement failed.

Under their supply licence conditions, suppliers are required to make instalment arrangements based on what you are able to pay.[25] A supplier found to be contravening the relevant licence conditions can be faced with regulatory action and enforcement by Ofgem. You should be prepared to raise a formal complaint if you feel that a supplier is failing to meet its licence conditions.

Fuel Direct (see p190) should also be considered as a payment option. Suppliers are expected to use '*where available*, a means by which payments may be deducted at source from a social security benefit received by that customer'.[26] The use of the words 'where available' suggests that a supplier may be at fault if it overlooks or ignores this option.[27] Fuel Direct deductions usually involve suppliers applying to the DWP for deductions for both ongoing consumption and arrears. However, since 1 April 2023, new deduction applications for ongoing fuel consumption, or a change in existing deductions can only be made if a supplier obtains your consent first or you apply for it yourself.[28]

2. Protection from disconnection

The following provisions may prevent disconnection in certain circumstances:
- condition 27 of the Standard Licence Conditions (SLCs – see below);
- the supplier's code of practice and internal policies may offer some protection (see p245);
- the Priority Services Register (see p142);
- Energy UK's Vulnerability Commitment (see p142);
- a breathing space scheme (see p143);
- if you claim certain means-tested benefits, Fuel Direct may be an option (see p190);
- if you are a tenant, your local authority may be able to help (see p204);
- help from social services (see p205).

Protection if you cannot pay your bill

Condition 27 of the Standard Licence Conditions

If you are threatened with disconnection because you cannot pay your bill, SLC 27 gives you the following rights.
- You are entitled to a payment arrangement to repay your arrears at a rate you can afford.[29]
- You can use, where available, a means by which payments may be deducted at source from a social security benefit such as Fuel Direct (see p190).[30]
- You may pay by regular instalments and through a means other than a prepayment meter.[31]
- If you have been unable to manage a payment arrangement, you must be offered a prepayment meter (if safe and reasonably practicable) as an alternative to disconnection. The meter must be set to recover arrears at a realistic rate which you can afford.[32]
- If you are a pensioner[33] or have children under 18, you should receive protection from disconnection in winter (see p138). If the supplier knows or has reason to believe you are such a customer, it *must not* disconnect you if you live alone or live with another pensioner or children under 18.[34] This provision applies even where there is suspicion of theft of electricity.[35]

- If you are below pension age and your household includes people who are of pensionable age, disabled or chronically sick, the supplier must take 'all reasonable steps' to avoid disconnecting your supply in winter.[36]
- You should be offered information about how you can reduce your charges by using fuel more efficiently.[37]

Winter

'Winter' is defined as the months of October, November, December, January, February and March.[38]

Suppliers are obliged to develop methods for dealing with customers in arrears under the terms of this condition. These set out the procedures which should be followed by each supplier and provide the practical mechanism for protecting your rights. Any departure from the methods may constitute a breach of your rights and could be referred to Ofgem for investigation.

Calculation of an instalment rate

Under SLC 27 a supplier must not disconnect you unless it has first taken all reasonable steps to arrange the repayment of outstanding charges. This means that your supplier must:

- 'take all reasonable steps' to discover your ability to pay and must take this into account when calculating instalments;[39] *and*
- provide you with energy efficiency advice;[40] *and*
- allow the following repayment methods:[41]
  - payment plan; *or*
  - Fuel Direct scheme; *or*
  - through a prepayment meter.

The supplier must also consider:

- relevant information provided by third parties, such as a social worker, carer, physician or health visitor, where it is available;[42] *and*
- where instalments will be paid using a prepayment meter, the value of all of the charges that are to be recovered through that meter.[43]

Suppliers should ensure that they properly and proactively take into account your ability to pay. This includes that your supplier:[44]

- has suitable credit management policies and guidelines;
- ensures that it actively communicates with you and establishes early intervention;
- understands your ability to pay;
- sets repayment arrangements relative to your ability to pay and personal observed circumstances;

- ensures all available information is obtained and taken into account when setting repayment rates;
- only sets default amounts when information about ability to pay is unavailable;
- sets default amounts subject to change once information about ability to pay is made available;
- sets reasonable default repayment rates;
- sets appropriate channels for you to quickly and easily raise concerns;
- proactively explores payment amounts and payment methods which are appropriate to your circumstances;
- makes you aware of debt advice services when in payment difficulty;
- pauses scheduled repayments for an appropriate period as part of your repayment plan and reviewing your repayment plan in accordance with your ability to pay at regular intervals before reinstating scheduled repayments;
- ensures that you understand any new arrangement made, including the rate of payment, method of payment, length of plan or recovery period and action to take if you experience difficulties;
- monitors any arrangement made, including for credit payment arrangements, to check for the occurrence of failure and, for prepayment meter arrangements, to check whether the meter is being used initially and on an ongoing basis;
- monitors any arrangement made, including review of a failed payment arrangement, discussing alternative and suitable payment arrangements or methods of payment.

You should provide your supplier with a detailed financial statement (see p109).

Protection if you are vulnerable or in a vulnerable situation

Vulnerability is complex, can be transient and is caused by a combination of factors. It can be temporary or permanent. Vulnerable customers are at particular risk of being treated unfairly, exploited or financially abused. Individual circumstances can vary, and people may move in and out of vulnerable categories, or be vulnerable under more than one heading.

In recent years, regulators have increased their focus on principles-based regulation, ensuring that suppliers pay attention to the needs of vulnerable consumers. In doing so, greater obligations under licencing conditions have been introduced that offer vulnerable people further protections, and these should be raised with suppliers.

Defining vulnerability

Ofgem defines vulnerability as when your personal circumstances and characteristics combine with aspects of the energy market to create situations where you are:[45]

– significantly less able than a typical consumer to protect or represent your own interests;
and/or

– significantly more likely to experience detriment, or for that detriment to be more substantial.

Ofgem also has an overarching vulnerability principle that you should be treated fairly if you are vulnerable or are in a vulnerable situation.[46]

Ofgem further takes into account the needs of people of pensionable age, those with a disability or chronic sickness, on low incomes and those living in rural areas.[47]

Statute also expects suppliers to consider the specific needs of other groups of consumers.[48]

Energy UK defines a customer as vulnerable if, for reason of age, health, disability or severe financial insecurity, they cannot safeguard their personal welfare or the personal welfare of the household.[49]

Potentially, vulnerable categories also include those listed in paragraph 77 of *Taking Control of Goods: National Standards* (see Appendix 3) as well as those included under SLCs 27 and 28B. Suppliers may also have their own definitions and codes of practice which you should consider before contacting them.

Under the Consumers, Estate Agents and Redress Act 2007, a vulnerable customer is defined as one whom a consumer advocacy body to which a complaint is referred is satisfied that it is not reasonable to expect to be able to pursue the complaint on their own behalf (see Chapter 14).[50]

The National Audit Office defines vulnerable people as those with characteristics or circumstances which can impair their ability to engage with or benefit from different services.[51]

Ofgem further recognises that vulnerability is transient and a number of characteristics and situations can exacerbate vulnerability and risk detriment, including:[52]

- physical or mental health conditions;
- cognitive impairment;
- digital exclusion;
- literacy or numeracy difficulties;
- English as a second language;
- speech impairment;
- being on a low income or unemployed;
- being a lone parent;
- being a full-time carer;
- living alone;
- relationship breakdown;
- bereavement;
- household changes;
- living in private rented accommodation;
- having a certain meter type – eg, prepayment or dynamic tele-switching meter;
- living off the gas grid;
- living in an energy-inefficient home.

Ofgem also recognises that how suppliers behave (action and inaction) can create or worsen a vulnerable situation, such as:

- failing to send regular or accurate bills;
- failing to regularly read meters;
- aggressive debt recovery or enforcement action;
- not receiving clear, accessible and timely information on bills and support available;
- failing to account for your needs or providing services to support your needs;
- lack of appropriate guidance and training for staff to understand your needs and your ability to pay;
- complex information on products or services;
- premium rate telephone numbers for customer services;
- lack of specially trained front-line staff to identify vulnerable situations;
- not monitoring self-disconnection from prepayment meter accounts;
- installing prepayment meters even when you do not pass the 'safe and reasonably practical' test;
- failing to take into account any vulnerable situation;
- not being a signatory or meeting the requirements of Energy UK's Vulnerability Commitment (see p142).

Supplier good practice and further system improvement opportunities are identified in Energy UK's *Vulnerability Commitment: good practice guide* to drive continuous improvement in offering and providing appropriate support.[53]

You are likely to get one of the following benefits if you fit within the definitions of a vulnerable consumer:

- universal credit (or one of the benefits it is replacing – see p180);
- pension credit;
- attendance allowance (or, in Scotland, pension age disability payment);
- disability living allowance;
- personal independence payment (or, in Scotland, adult disability payment);
- employment and support allowance;
- retirement state pension.

If you are entitled to such benefits but there has been a problem with your claim or your benefit has been sanctioned or suspended, quote these provisions in initial correspondence with a supplier.

Are you in a vulnerable circumstance?

Typical examples of you being in a vulnerable circumstance include the following.

– You are a carer for a sick, disabled or elderly person.
– You are dependent on medical equipment or machinery that is operated or maintained by electricity – eg, dialysis machine, feeding pump, stair lift, electric ventilators, oxygen concentrator or refrigerated medicine.

- You have a mental health or a developmental condition.
- You have no recourse to public funds and have inadequate means and capital.
- You are unable to communicate in English.
- You have recently faced life-changing events, such as a redundancy, bereavement or relationship breakdown.
- A support worker, care co-ordinator, social worker, health visitor or physician has indicated that a member of the household may be vulnerable.

If the supplier does not respond properly to the information about vulnerability, ignores information it holds, or if there is delay, you should consider raising a formal complaint, particularly as there is a potential breach of licence conditions. Also inform Citizens Advice consumer service or Advice Direct Scotland, which may refer you to the Extra Help Unit (see p206).

Condition 27 of the Standard Licence Conditions

Suppliers must conform to SLC 27 with regard to vulnerable customers who fall into arrears (see p137). This condition covers payments, security deposits, disconnections and final bills. They must also identify circumstances, needs and characteristics of vulnerable customers and satisfy themselves that their actions are resulting in vulnerable customers being treated fairly.[54]

Priority Services Register

Suppliers are prohibited from disconnecting a premises occupied by a customer eligible for the Priority Services Register (see p98) during the winter months (1 October to 31 March). You are eligible for the Priority Services Register if you are in a vulnerable situation.[55] The definition of a 'vulnerable situation' is wide-ranging (see p139–40).

Your supplier is required, at least once a year, to take 'all reasonable steps' to inform all customers about the Priority Services Register and how you can be listed on it if you are over pension age, disabled, have a hearing or visual impairment or long term health condition.[56] If you have different suppliers for gas and electricity, you need to register separately with both.

Vulnerability Commitment for vulnerable customers

Energy UK is the trade association for the gas and electricity sector. Its members include over 95 per cent of the energy suppliers in Great Britain, including British Gas, EDF Energy, E.ON Next, OVO Energy and Scottish Power.

Energy UK members have signed up to the **'Vulnerability Commitment'**. This means they resolve to never knowingly disconnect a vulnerable customer at any time of year where the household has children under the age of six (or under the age of 16 during the winter months (1 October to 31 March)) or where for reasons of age, health, disability or severe financial insecurity, you are unable to safeguard your welfare or that of other members of your household.[57] See p102 for more information.

If you can benefit from this policy, you should inform your supplier that you (or members of your household) are vulnerable and should therefore not be disconnected.

Protection under the breathing space debt respite scheme

If you have entered into a breathing space standard debt respite scheme (valid for up to 60 days) or a mental health debt respite scheme (valid for the duration of the mental health crisis treatment and another 30 days after that), suppliers must cease any recovery or enforcement action for the breathing space debts. In essence, this means that suppliers cannot:[58]

- take steps to disconnect your gas or electricity supply (unless on grounds of theft or illegality);
- get or execute a warrant;
- start any action or legal proceedings;
- contact you about enforcement or recovery;
- begin or continue existing recovery action through a debt collection agency;
- take steps to switch you to a prepayment meter to take payments;
- take steps to collect payments through other means (such as deductions from a social security benefit);
- use a prepayment meter already installed to take payments, save for if you had agreed for the meter to be installed before the breathing space commenced.

A breathing space starts the day after it is registered online. It therefore can be readily applied for to circumvent any attempts by suppliers to disconnect supply. During the intervening debt respite scheme moratorium period, efforts should be made to negotiate a settlement of the arrears. This is because, at the end of the moratorium, suppliers can resume or commence legal proceedings against you for the arrears, including disconnection. If not strategically handled, it will serve only to delay disconnection and not avoid it. You can only apply for a standard breathing space every 12 months and therefore any application must be made to ensure you get maximum protection and benefit from your supplier.

Other situations where disconnection should not occur
Examples of when supply will not be disconnected include:
– if you agree and keep to a payment plan;
– if the debt is in the name of a past customer, such as an ex-partner or previous occupier, and you have made arrangements to take over the supply;
– if the debt relates to arrears from a previous property;
– If the debt is for something other than fuel consumption;
– if the supplier has not discussed and assessed with you other means by which you may pay off the arrears first – such as a payment plan or prepayment meter;[59]

– if you have a genuine query or dispute about your bill and you have paid the part of it which you agree you owe;

– if the debt is due to a different supplier;

– if you have agreed to have a prepayment meter;

– if you have been adjudged bankrupt or a debt relief order has been approved and the debt relates to a period before the insolvency (but a supplier could insist on a prepayment meter or a security deposit paid as a condition of future supply);

– if you have entered into a standard or mental health debt respite scheme (including all enforcement and recovery related to the fuel arrears for the duration of the moratorium);

– you request to be placed on the Fuel Direct scheme;

– you have contacted social services for help (see p205) – you must tell the supplier that you are doing this.

It may be useful to suggest these alternatives to disconnection as the basis for negotiation with suppliers.

3. **Preventing disconnection**

There are reasons why you should always try to prevent disconnection.

- You cannot solve a debt problem by being disconnected. Even after you have been disconnected, the supplier still requires you to pay the money you owe and can take court action to recover the debt from you. You will also be charged a fee for the expenses of disconnecting the supply.

- If you later want your supply reconnected, you will have to pay any arrears still owing, plus the costs of disconnection and reconnection.

- If the supplier has had to obtain a warrant to disconnect your supply, you also have to pay the costs of obtaining the warrant (although an application may be made to the court to use its discretionary power to refuse the claimed costs). If you have produced a financial statement (see p108), this should be submitted to the court.

You may have to pay a security deposit as a condition of being supplied in the future following disconnection, or have a prepayment meter. If you are finding it difficult to meet your fuel costs, seek advice and let your supplier know about the difficulties you are experiencing as soon as you can. You are more likely to be able to obtain a solution which genuinely meets your needs if you have time to think about your proposals to the supplier, or what the supplier is prepared to offer you.

You should be able to prevent disconnection if you contact the supplier and:

- you arrange to pay your arrears at a rate you can afford; *or*

- you request to be put on the Fuel Direct scheme (see p118). A request may also be made by the supplier (except for ongoing fuel consumption); *or*

- you agree to accept a prepayment meter set to collect the arrears at a rate you can afford.

Disconnection most often occurs where there has been no contact between the customer and the supplier. Once you engage with the supplier, it must consider your situation and work with you to identify a suitable way for your supply to continue and for you to repay your arrears at a rate you can afford (see p118).

The codes of practice may make some provision for disconnection to be delayed, typically for 14 or 21 days, if you tell the supplier that you are going to ask social services (social work in Scotland) for help with the bill.

Usually, suppliers prefer you to contact them by telephone. It is safer in terms of establishing an agreement and ensuring that the correct information is received, to confirm everything in writing. If possible, send an email to your supplier to confirm what you have agreed to pay so that you have a record for future reference, and request that the supplier confirms the terms of the agreement in writing with you.

If all else fails you can still make representations at the warrant stage if the matter goes to the magistrates' (or sheriff) court (see Chapter 10). It is often possible to negotiate a settlement even at this point. You should always attend court, taking an adviser, representative or friend with you, if possible.

The availability of entering into a debt respite scheme should be explored (see p143). This can only be applied for every 12 months and is limited to 60 days (unless it is a mental health debt respite scheme, which is for the duration of mental health crisis treatment, plus 30 days).

4. At the point of disconnection

The supplier's right to enter your premises

The supplier may, with your consent, enter your premises to disconnect your supply, providing it has served you with a correct notice of disconnection and has published details of Standard Licence Condition (SLC) 27 on its website (see p137 and Chapter 10).[60] If you do not consent, the supplier must obtain a warrant from the magistrates' court (or sheriff court in Scotland). The costs of the warrant are added to your bill – these are generally around £75–£110 and the supplier may also charge for expenses legitimately incurred,[61] such as pre-warrant attendance charges and disconnection attendance. There is a large variation in the charges levied by suppliers. There is no standardised or agreed set of warrant costs across the energy industry and therefore the costs and charges levied by each supplier will differ. However, warrant-related charges and costs are capped at £150.[62]

Your home must be left no less secure than it was before entry. Suppliers sometimes change locks and leave a note telling you where to pick up a key. Any damage caused by legally gaining entry must be made good or monetary compensation paid. If the supplier fails to secure your premises and your possessions are stolen as a result, you can claim damages from the supplier, including for distress and discomfort as well as for expenses and loss of specific items. All losses arising out of the specific breach of contract or duty of care must be clearly pleaded and appropriate legal advice must be taken if such a claim is sought from the supplier.

Disconnecting external meters

In some cases, the supplier will disconnect your supply from the mains outside your property – which makes reconnection extremely expensive. It has yet to be tested in law to what extent, if any, a realistic offer to clear arrears may be grounds for a magistrates' court to refuse to issue a warrant of entry to disconnect, but magistrates would be expected to act reasonably and consider all the relevant circumstances.[63]

A warrant is not required for the disconnection of an external meter. Disconnection is lawful, providing the correct notices have been given (see p134). Despite this, most suppliers will still obtain a warrant.

Disconnecting smart meters

Smart meter technology means that suppliers can disconnect your supply remotely without visiting your home. Ofgem has addressed this by modifying and strengthening the existing protection contained in SLC 27 for all vulnerable customers.[64] Suppliers must be able to show that they have:

- taken proactive steps and a risk assessment to establish whether anyone in the household is vulnerable and has additional needs;
- made sure that written contact with you is in plain English and that it includes details of sources of help, such as Citizens Advice consumer service;
- made a number of attempts to contact you using different methods such as telephone and email and at different times of the day;
- visited the property and looked for any visual signs indicating vulnerability;
- checked whether the property is unoccupied, either on a temporary or permanent basis;
- considered whether the occupancy of the property has changed.

Last-minute negotiations

If the supplier agrees not to disconnect at the last minute, but an official turns up to carry out the disconnection, the disconnection should not be agreed to, and the official should be asked to contact the supplier's office. Many suppliers accept payment on the doorstep, but some make an extra charge to cover their expenses. Always get a receipt to establish payment.

Some electricity suppliers' disconnection officials routinely carry prepayment meters with them and will offer you one as an alternative, even at this late stage. If you accept the meter, check that it has been set to collect arrears at a rate you can afford. If it has not, ask the supplier to change the setting. Do not be put off by such statements as 'it cannot be changed' or 'it is set at the factory'. This is not the case. It is unlikely that a gas supplier would try to fit a prepayment meter straight away – the system has to be purged and re-lit first.

If you refuse to allow entry, the supplier has to obtain a warrant in the magistrates' court or may disconnect from the road. This costs more, unless you are able to negotiate keeping your supply and paying off the arrears at a rate you can afford in the meantime (see Chapter 7).

5. Getting your supply reconnected

The supplier must reconnect the supply within 24 hours if:[65]
- you pay your outstanding bill, together with the expenses of disconnection and reconnection and any security deposit; *or*
- you reach an agreement with the supplier to pay off the arrears in instalments as a condition of being reconnected.

Where you pay or reach an agreement outside working hours, the 24 hours begins at the start of the next working day.[66] If the supplier does not reconnect you within the 24 hours, you are entitled to a £30 compensation payment within 10 working days, unless there is an exception (see p91).[67] If the supplier does not pay on time, it has to pay you an extra £30 for the delay. Payment is typically made as a credit to your energy account. You can alternatively request it to pay you by cheque or bank transfer.

If you are registered on the supplier's Priority Services Register, you should be given priority reconnection if supply is interrupted.

In practice, if you agree to accept a prepayment meter set to collect the arrears, the supplier will reconnect your supply. You may have to pay the expenses of disconnection and reconnection separately, but usually they are added to your arrears and collected in instalments through the meter.

If you do not want your supply reconnected

The supplier continues to submit bills regardless of whether or not you want your supply reconnected. You may also incur standing charges. If you do not pay, it may seek recovery of the debt through the small claims court or sell on or assign the debt to a third party (such as a debt collecting agency). In practice, few suppliers or debt collectors try to recover through the county court, preferring to send letters in the hope of payment. The reason is that in a small claims court action legal costs cannot normally be recovered. As a result, it would cost more to take a case to court than would be recovered, particularly if you have no disposable income, assets, savings or valuable property.

Assuming you agree you are liable for the bill, try to negotiate payment in instalments before any legal action. Otherwise, if the supplier has issued a claim in the county court, you may respond by completing Form N9A[68] and asking to pay in affordable instalments. In these circumstances, a county court order is usually granted, with payment in instalments. As long as you honour the terms of the order, further enforcement action should not be taken against you. If the court has already made a court order for payment of the whole debt at once ('forthwith'), you could apply to have the order varied to payment by instalments. This is undertaken by making an application on Form N245 to suspend a warrant or vary payments made by a court order. Note that this procedure does not apply to warrants granted by magistrates' courts (see Chapter 10).

There is a fee of £14 for this application, unless you are exempt on grounds of low income, for which you have to complete an application for fee exemption on Form EX160. The court should not order you to pay an amount you cannot afford – even if this means you can only afford £1 or £2 a month. However, the courts have established that where a judgment debtor applies to pay a judgment debt by instalments, they must put forward a realistic payment schedule for the outstanding debt and a reasonable time frame. If this test is not met, a court should refuse the judgment debtor's application.[69]

You are not liable for the supplier's legal costs if you lose in the small claims court, which is why suppliers seldom commence recovery proceedings for sums under £10,000 (see Chapter 14). The supplier is only able to claim for its fee in starting proceedings. The fees for issuing a money claim online are cheaper than the fees for a paper claim.

Court fees (paper form) [70]

Sums up to £300	£35
Sums from £300.01–500	£50
Sums from £500.01–1,000	£70
Sums from £1,000.01–1,500	£80
Sums from £1,500.01–3,000	£115
Sums from £3,000.01–5,000	£205
Sums from £5,000.01–10,000	£455

In Scotland, you can apply for a time to pay direction before a decree (court order). If you break this arrangement by allowing three instalments to pass unpaid, you lose the right to pay by instalments. If you allow a decree to pass without defending or seeking time to pay, you have to wait until the supplier seeks to enforce the decree before you can ask for a time to pay order. You may be liable for the supplier's costs if you lose your case, but only if the debt is over £200. If the value is between £200 and £1,500, the maximum amount awarded to the successful party is £150. If the value is between £1,500 and £3,000 the amount awarded is 10 per cent of the value of the claim. See CPAG's *Debt Advice Handbook Scotland* for more information.

The costs of disconnection and reconnection

Charges for disconnection and reconnection must be 'reasonable' and must reflect the actual costs involved.[71] Charges vary between suppliers. You will need to contact your supplier to find out how much it charges for disconnection and reconnection.

Ultimately, the question of what is a reasonable cost may be determined by a court. Citizens Advice consumer service or Ofgem may also be able to examine charges. Operators may waive costs at their discretion, particularly in light of financial vulnerability, and in some cases (eg, where costs appear to be excessive) it may be argued that a supplier is under a duty to mitigate its loss. Legal advice should be sought.

6. Disputes: unlawful disconnection

If you dispute that the supplier is entitled to disconnect, you can ask Citizens Advice consumer service or Advice Direct Scotland to intervene. They can order the supplier to reconnect or continue your supply pending a decision on your dispute.

Unlawful disconnection is an enforcement matter. Suppliers can be forced to comply with the law by Ofgem. If the supplier ignores the order, you can apply for a court order to enforce it, including by applying for an injunction.

If disconnection was unlawful, you do not have to pay the costs of disconnection or reconnection. You may also have a claim for compensation, for any costs you have incurred as a result of the unlawful disconnection along with any other damages (including to reputation, loss of supply, expenses, inconvenience and distress) that may arise from how a supplier acted when disconnecting your supply and legislative breaches. These claims may be pursued through the civil courts (see Chapter 14).

For example, a supplier may wrongly disconnect a supply, arising from a mistake by a contractor who visits a household. This can be a problem in multi-occupation buildings or where a contractor suspects the occupants are squatters. In such a case, immediately contact the supplier and be prepared to back up a demand for reconnection with an action through the courts (see Chapter 14). An emergency injunction may be sought to order reconnection and a claim for damages included as a result of nuisance and losses caused by being without a supply. In an emergency case, an injunction can be sought outside normal court hours.

Prepayment meters and arrears

In theory, it should not be possible to get into arrears by using a prepayment meter. However, in practice, arrears may be transferred from a previous supplier when you switch supplier or they may be set on a prepayment meter if you accept a prepayment meter as an alternative to disconnection and you pass the 'safe and reasonably practical' test (see p114).

A problem associated with prepayment meters is that households may self-disconnect simply by not topping up the meter due to lack of money or if standing charges build up over the summer months. If you think this may happen to you, consider using one of the other methods of making payments such as Fuel Direct or ensure the debt deduction rate agreed is affordable to you. Standard Licence Condition 27A requires that suppliers provide appropriate emergency credit support in situations of self-disconnection or self-rationing of prepayment meters to ensure continuity of supply (see p50). Suppliers have committed also to alert you of the risk of standing charge build-up on prepayment meters during the summer. Ensure that you provide your supplier with as much information as you can about your circumstances. If you feel that a prepayment meter is being imposed upon you, contact Citizens Advice consumer service or Advice Direct Scotland.

If you have arrears from a previous supply, you may be faced with bills from both your current supplier and your previous supplier. In such a situation, you should pay for your current energy consumption first before paying any arrears to your former supplier, to avoid building up arrears on your ongoing account. Treat the arrears on your old account as a non-priority debt (see Chapter 7). If you have any disposable income after addressing your priority expenditure, such as rent, council tax and current fuel supply, negotiate an affordable repayment plan with your former supplier just as you would with any other unsecured creditor.

7. Complaints about disconnection

To complain about disconnection by an energy supplier, first contact the company concerned. Energy suppliers are subject to regulations setting out how to respond to a complaint (see Chapter 14). They are required to have a complaints procedure in place and must comply with it in relation to each complaint they receive.[72] If raising a complaint, you should request a copy of the supplier's complaints policy as well as codes of practice or policy documents on:

- payment of bills and arrears;
- disconnection;

- prepayment meters;
- services for vulnerable people.

Both Ofgem and the Energy Ombudsman can refuse to investigate a complaint until you have given the supplier a reasonable opportunity to deal with the problems raised and remedy them. If you need help to make your complaint, get advice from Citizens Advice consumer service or Advice Direct Scotland. If your complaint has not been resolved to your satisfaction within eight weeks you can ask Ofgem or the Ombudsman to investigate your complaint.

Ofgem investigates potential breaches of the Standard Licence Conditions. Where companies fail, Ofgem uses its enforcement powers to ensure compliance. It can also impose financial penalties on suppliers and order consumer redress, including compensation.

Provided you have exhausted the supplier's internal complaints procedure, Ofgem can investigate your complaint about disconnection against:

- a gas transporter for:
  - disconnection of, or a threat to disconnect, your gas;
  - refusal to reconnect your supply following disconnection;
- a gas supplier for:
  - cutting off, or a threat to cut off, your gas;
  - refusal to reconnect your supply following disconnection;
  - the failure of a prepayment system;
- an electricity supplier, distributor or licence holder for:
  - disconnection of, or a threat to disconnect, your electricity;
  - refusal to reconnect your supply following disconnection;
  - the failure of a prepayment system.

For more information on complaints, see Chapter 14.

Notes

1. **When you can be disconnected for arrears**
   1 Ofgem, *Debt and Arrears Indicators*, Q2 2024 at ofgem.gov.uk/publications/debt-and-arrears indicators
   2 Department of Trade and Industry Fifth Report, House of Commons, 1 February 2005

3 Ofgem, *Customer Service Data*, Q1 2022 – Q4 2022; ofgem.gov.uk/energy-data-and-research/data-portal
4 Sch 6 paras 1 and 2 EA 1989; Sch 4 UA 2000
5 Sch 6 paras 2(3) EA 1989; Sch 4 UA 2000

6 Sch 6 paras 2(2)(b) EA 1989; Sch 4 UA 2000
7 Sch 6 paras 2(2)(a) EA 1989; Sch 4 UA 2000
8 Sch 6 paras 2 EA 1989; Sch 4 UA 2000
9 Sch 6 para 27 EA 1989; Sch 4 UA 2000
10 Sch 6 para 1(6)(a) EA 1989
11 Sch 2B para 7(1)(b) and (3) GA 1986
12 Sch 2B para 7(1) and (3) GA 1986
13 Sch 2B para 7(1) and (3)(b) GA 1986
14 Sch 2B para 7(5) GA 1986
15 Sch 2B para 7(4) GA 1986
16 Sch 2B para 7(3) GA 1986
17 Sch 2B para 7(5) GA 1986
18 s20(1)(a)(b) EA 1989; s11 GA 1986 (as amended); Condition 27 SLC
19 Condition 27.3 SLC
20 Conditions 20.1, 27.5 and 27.6 SLC
21 Condition 27.8 SLC
22 Condition 27.9 SLC
23 Ofgem, *Guidance: PPM (safe and reasonably practicable)*, 13 September 2023, para 3.7
24 Condition 27.6(a)(iii), 27.8, 27.8A and 27.9 SLC
25 Condition 27.8 SLC
26 Condition 27.6(a)(i) SLC
27 See Condition 27.5 and 27.6 SLC
28 DWP, *Guidance: guide for energy suppliers ('Fuel Direct')*, 12 September 2024, at gov.uk/government/publications/how-to-request-deductions-from-benefit-a-guide-for-creditors/third-party-deductions-from-benefits-a-guide-for-fuel-suppliers; Social Security Benefits (Claims and Payments) (Amendment) Regulations 2023

2. Protection from disconnection
29 Condition 27.6(a)(iii) and 27.8 SLC
30 Condition 27.6(a)(i) SLC
31 Condition 27.6(a)(ii) SLC
32 Condition 27.6(a)(iii) and 27.8 SLC
33 As defined in s48(2B) GA 1986, Sch 4 para 1 Pensions Act 1995 and Condition 1.3 SLC
34 Condition 27.10 SLC
35 Condition 12A 11(d) SLC
36 Condition 27.11 SLC
37 Condition 27.6(b). Also see Condition 31.2(a) and (b) SLC
38 Condition 1 SLC
39 Condition 27.8 SLC
40 Condition 27.6(b) SLC
41 Condition 27.5 and 27.6 SLC
42 Condition 27.8(a) SLC
43 Condition 27.8(b) SLC

44 Condition 27.8A SLC
45 Ofgem, *Consumer Vulnerability Strategy 2025*, October 2019; Ofgem, *Consumer Vulnerability Strategy*, 4 July 2013
46 Condition 0.1 and 0.9 SLC
47 Ofgem, *Consumer Vulnerability Strategy 2025*, October 2019
48 s3A(3) EA 1989; s4AA(3) GA 1986
49 Energy UK, *The Vulnerability Commitment*, 2024, at energy-uk.org.uk/our-work/vulnerability-commitment
50 s12(2) CEARA 2007
51 National Audit Office, *Vulnerable Customers in Regulated Industries*, 31 March 2017
52 Ofgem, *Consumer Vulnerability Strategy 2025*, October 2019
53 Energy UK, *Vulnerability Commitment: good practice guide*, 1 October 2024, at energy-uk.org.uk/publications/2024-vulnerability-commitment-good-practice-report
54 Condition 0.1 and 0.3(d) SLC
55 Condition 26 SLC
56 Condition 26 SLC
57 Energy UK, *The Vulnerability Commitment*, 2024
58 DRS Regs
59 Condition 27.9 SLC

4. At the point of disconnection
60 Condition 27.12 SLC
61 Sch 6 para 2(1)(b) EA 1989; Sch 2B para 73(b) GA 1986
62 Condition 28.12 and 28.22 SLC
63 *Associated Provincial Picture Houses v Wednesbury Corporation* [1948] 1 KB 223, per Lord Greene
64 Condition 27 SLC

5. Getting your supply reconnected
65 Reg 6 EG(SP)S Regs
66 Reg 6(4) EG(SP)S Regs
67 Reg 8 EG(SP)S Regs
68 Available from gov.uk/government/publications/form-n9a-form-of-admission-specified-amount
69 *Diana Loson v (1) Brett Stack (2) Newlyn PLC* [2018] EWCA Civ 803
70 Court Form EX150A; gov.uk/make-court-claim-for-money/court-fees
71 Reg 6(1)(a) EG(SP)S Regs

7. Complaints about disconnection
72 Reg 3(1) GE(CCHS) Regs

Chapter 9

Theft and tampering

This chapter covers:
1. Introduction (below)
2. Tampering with a meter (p154)
3. Theft of fuel (p158)
4. Disconnection of the supply (p162)
5. Theft from meters (p166)
6. Removal of meters (p167)

1. Introduction

Unlike most other goods, gas and electricity are delivered to you without the supplier being present. Suppliers cannot see what you are doing with their meter or the fuel they have supplied. This makes suppliers vulnerable to theft. This can occur from bypassing a meter completely or fixing it to run slower, interfering with wires, connecting to the network directly or using a supply without informing the supplier so that actual usage rates cannot be measured or recorded. Perhaps because of this vulnerability, suppliers sometimes make allegations of theft on flimsy evidence. The consequences of such allegations against you can be severe, as a supplier has the power to disconnect your supply without having to go to court to prove the allegations first.

Theft from, or tampering with, a meter are criminal offences and can result in both criminal prosecution and civil proceedings to recover the alleged debt. However, it is important to realise that not in every case of alleged tampering will you necessarily have to pay for damage or alleged stolen fuel.

A full discussion of criminal law and practice is outside the scope of this book. If you might be liable for prosecution, seek specialist legal advice on your position and how to respond.

If you are legally liable to pay for any loss caused by theft or tampering, a supplier or transporter may be entitled to disconnect the supply, although this right does not follow automatically from liability (see p162).

There are regulatory arrangements in place which require suppliers to detect, investigate and prevent theft of electricity and gas.[1] While doing so, suppliers must still ensure that they treat customers fairly and take into account vulnerability. By **'vulnerability'**, the regulations mean customers who are of pensionable age, disabled or chronically sick or if the customers will have difficulty in paying all or part of the charges resulting from any theft of fuel.[2] Both gas and electricity suppliers have implemented a centralised theft risk assessment service to tackle this issue.[3] ElectraLink is the dual-fuel energy theft risk assessment service provider. The theft risk assessment service aims to provide a data analytics service. This will help assist suppliers' efforts to detect theft by using data to profile the risk of gas or electricity theft at premises. When taking any steps, suppliers and any representatives are required to treat you 'in a manner which is fair, transparent, not misleading, appropriate and professional'.[4]

Meter ownership

The theft of gas or electricity or interference with a meter often causes damage to the meter itself. The supplier of the gas or electricity and the owner of the meter may not be the same company. Nearly all gas meters are owned by National Grid in its role as the main public gas transporter and electricity meters are owned by the privatised electricity suppliers in their role as distributors of electricity. If you are disconnected for theft or tampering, it will normally be one of these companies that actually carries out the disconnection even if you have a contract with a different supplier for the actual supply of gas or electricity.

---

2. Tampering with a meter

Evidence of tampering

As a supply of gas or electricity is charged for based on metered consumption, the most obvious unlawful method of reducing a potential fuel bill is to interfere with a meter to prevent it from registering or to reduce the amount it has registered.

It is a criminal offence to interfere with an electricity meter, punishable with a fine of up to £1,000.[5] An offence is committed where you alter the register of a meter or prevent the meter from duly registering the quantity of electricity supplied. It is a criminal offence to damage any electricity line, plant or meter, punishable with a fine of up to £1,000.[6]

It is a criminal offence to interfere with gas fittings, service pipes and meter equipment, punishable with a fine of up to £1,000.[7] An offence is committed where you alter the index of a meter or prevent the meter from duly registering the quantity of gas supplied.

The offence of abstracting electricity is committed where you dishonestly use electricity without due authority or dishonestly cause electricity to be wasted or diverted.[8] The test to be applied is that you were being dishonest by the standards of ordinary people.[9] The offence may be tried in the magistrates' court or the

Crown Court. On conviction in the magistrates' court, you can be fined or imprisoned for up to six months (for offences committed before 2 May 2022) or 12 months (for offences committed on or after 2 May 2022);[10] while on conviction in the Crown Court, the maximum penalty is five years' imprisonment. This penalty would be reserved for the most serious cases.[11]

There are sometimes tell-tale signs on a meter that has been tampered with – eg, the seals are cut or missing, meter dials are not moving, the meter dial is not visible, the meter casing is damaged, cracked or badly scratched or a small hole has been drilled in the side, odd wires or pipes out of place by meters or a prepayment meter is still working without credit. These descriptions are included not as a guide to people who might want to attempt tampering, but for advisers who may have no knowledge of what tampering involves and may need to identify and establish if meter interference has taken place commensurate with theft.

Never assume that an allegation of tampering is correct, whatever technical evidence is quoted by the supplier. The evidence is not always clear-cut and the supplier's experts do not always get it right. You can get your own expert (look for an 'electrical engineer', 'gas engineer' or 'gas installer') to examine the meter for an objective assessment.

Meter tampering is not always seen when the meter is read in the usual way. All meter technicians or readers should be trained in detection, but they are only there for a short time. Holes or cracks may be on the far side of the meter in a dark cupboard and therefore difficult to spot. In some cases, the dividing up of properties into separate self-contained dwellings and the resultant variations as to the addresses of occupiers can give rise to problems.

Theft due to tampering can be detected by unusual consumption patterns – eg, if the bills suddenly decrease or show a reduced consumption or if they increase or show heightened consumption after the installation of a new meter. A meter examiner will then come to look at the meter, normally accompanied by a colleague (see Chapter 10) and sometimes by the police. If signs of tampering are detected consistent with theft, the meter will be removed and the supply disconnected. If no evidence is detected there and then showing illegal abstraction, the meter may be taken away for further examination, but a replacement should be left so that the supply is not disconnected straight away. Some electricity suppliers are prepared to install another meter immediately, usually a prepayment meter. However, when a gas supply is disconnected, the system must be purged and relit before the gas supply can be restarted. The technicians who carry out the disconnection are unlikely to have both the expertise and the authority to do this.

With smart meters, the scope for unlawful tampering is reduced as the meter can be controlled remotely and the level of consumption can be regulated without the supplier having to physically remove the meter. If a smart meter is hacked to under-report energy usage, the offences described in this chapter apply.

Examining the evidence and the law

If a supplier alleges that a meter has been tampered with, there are three key areas to consider.

- You must establish exactly what is alleged. On what basis has the supplier found that the meter has been tampered with? In some cases, it will be obvious that the only explanation for damage to a meter is tampering – eg, there is physical evidence of deliberate damage. In other cases, there may be alternative explanations – eg, if meter seals are missing, it may be that these are company seals which were never put on, or were removed by the supplier but not replaced, or have been removed by someone else. Any evidence the supplier has should be presented to you so that you can comment. However, take care in any comment you make, as it is unlikely that you will be cautioned about anything you say possibly being used against you in court.

- You should investigate whether the supplier has evidence that it was you, and not someone else – such as a landlord or neighbour – who tampered with the meter. Usually, the supplier will not know who undertook the tampering. This can make it more difficult for the supplier to take action against you than if it had clear evidence of your involvement. It will help if you can explain why it has been tampered with – eg, if you know that the meter was taken over from a previous occupier who had tampered with it or that it was damaged by builders. However, evidence that the meter was interfered with while in your custody can, depending on the circumstances, be sufficient to convict you of electricity theft,[12] although not an essential ingredient.[13] The evidence must identify the date or dates on which the alleged tampering occurred.

- Where a case is brought against more than one person in a household, or against a married couple, evidence is needed against all persons, not just one, to sustain a prosecution or conviction. It should be shown that:[14]
  - each person agreed to obtain electricity which would not be paid for; *and*
  - each of them knew the means to be adopted to achieve that end – namely tampering with the meter; *and*
  - one of them, to the knowledge of the other(s), who was ready to assist if needed, tampered with the meter so that electricity could be obtained without payment; *and*
  - each of them knew that electricity which had not been paid for, and which neither of them intended to pay for, was being used by them in their home.

If a supplier alleges you are liable for theft or tampering, find out which legal provision it relies on. Different considerations apply when dealing with different parts of the law. Usually, the supplier points to particular provisions in the Gas Act, Electricity Act or Utilities Act, as appropriate, but liability can also arise under general common law principles or under your contract with your supplier.

General common law principles

In England and Wales, when you receive or take on a meter, you become 'bailee' of it. A **'bailee'** is under a duty to take 'reasonable care' of bailed property (in this case, a meter).

In Scotland, 'bailment' does not apply, but the concept of **'restitution'** may be used – ie, if you are in possession of goods which do not belong to you, you are under an obligation to look after them until the owner returns for them.

If you intentionally damage a meter, you could be liable to pay compensation to the supplier. The supplier can issue a civil claim for damages and theft losses, or you may be prosecuted for criminal damage, which is an imprisonable offence. It is entirely a matter for the police and Crown Prosecution Service to decide whether a case is dealt with by caution or prosecuted in court. Only a small amount of damage may constitute an offence. On conviction, the court can order you to pay compensation to the supplier to remedy the cost of the damage. Questions of vulnerability are considered before any decision to impose liability for loss arises (see p153).[15]

Contractual liability for meter damage

If you are supplied under a contract, your contractual duty is no higher than your duty as a bailee (see above), but in the past, some suppliers have claimed that customers should pay for damage to a meter even though they had done nothing wrong or were not negligent. For example, if a burglar damaged your meter, you would not normally have to pay for the damage under your duty as a bailee unless your negligence allowed the burglar to enter your home. Read your contract carefully because the relevant terms contained there may go wider. However, if the term is so wide that it could be regarded as unfair under the Consumer Rights Act 2015, then it should not bind you, and you should refer it to the Financial Conduct Authority (see Chapter 14).

Responsibility for meters under the Gas and Electricity Acts

In nearly all cases the meter will have been provided by a gas supplier or transporter, or hired/loaned by an electricity supplier and, under these circumstances, the meter is its responsibility.[16]

If you hire the meter, you may have to enter into a hire agreement with the supplier. Suppliers have no powers to impose conditions about the care of the meter in such an agreement that go further than those allowed under the Acts or their licence conditions.

There are three specific meter offences under the Acts, each punishable by a fine of up to £1,000:[17]

- damaging or allowing damage to any meter, gas fitting or electrical plant or line;
- altering the meter index or register by which consumption is measured;
- preventing the meter from registering properly.

In each case, the offence can only have been committed if the act was done intentionally or a result of culpable negligence – ie, if it was your fault.[18]

If you are prosecuted for either of the latter two offences, possession of artificial means for altering the way the meter is registering will be taken as *prima facie* evidence that you caused the alteration.[19] If such artificial means are not found, a conviction would be difficult to obtain, especially if the case concerns a property in multiple occupation or where there has been a burglary.

3. **Theft of fuel**

Theft of gas and dishonest use or 'abstraction' of electricity are criminal offences.[20] Penalties include fines or imprisonment, offences being triable either in the magistrates' court or the Crown Court before a jury. You can be convicted of theft even if there is no damage or evidence of interference with a meter.[21] The offence of **'abstraction'** is committed where there is use of electricity without the authority of the electricity supplier by a person who has no intention of paying for it under section 13 of the Theft Act 1968.[22] The offence may be committed where electrical or electronic equipment is used in premises you do not have permission to enter, or where equipment is used for a purpose for which permission is not given.[23]

The key to an offence is the question of dishonesty. If you genuinely believed you were entitled to use the fuel or had paid or would be paying for the fuel concerned, then the elements of the offence cannot be proved. The issue of what is honest or dishonest use is the standard applied by a jury as being the standards of honest, ordinary people.[24] Dishonesty in the context of an offence of abstraction requires knowledge that electricity was being consumed, coupled with an assumption that it would not be paid for. A genuine belief and intention that you will pay for the electricity you have used – even in a case where a person reconnects a supply without the permission of the electricity company – will provide a defence.[25] It is an offence to dishonestly use electricity without due authority, so a defence may exist where a person honestly believed they had been authorised to use the electricity.[26] For example, if only one person in a multi-occupation household knows about the unlawful consumption but other occupants are ignorant of it, only the person with knowledge may be convicted of the offence. It is improper to infer guilt simply based on a close relationship between household members where an offence has occurred.[27]

Prosecutions may arise in connection with other offences which involve the improper use of electricity – eg, where electricity is stolen to facilitate the cultivation of drugs. Liability can also be imposed where third parties have been knowingly hired to carry out work such as altering the arrangements for electricity supplies to premises to commit criminal offences. Deliberate attempts, even if no electricity or gas is illegally abstracted or no loss is incurred by the supplier, will also be prosecuted.[28]

The supplier is entitled to recover the costs of any fuel which has been stolen from the person liable. However, as with tampering, suppliers are more likely to address the issue of the stolen fuel by other means – ie, by threatening disconnection. Where the company transporting gas to your home (normally National Grid) is different from the actual supplier, the transporter also has the right to recover the value of the stolen gas.[29]

Note: just because your name is on a gas or electricity bill, it does not establish you as living at a property. You are simply a consumer of fuel under contract at the address but this does not mean you are living in the property, either as a trespasser or otherwise.[30]

Use of gas or electricity by squatters

Squatting in residential premises is a criminal offence.[31] This does not change the legal position with the existing supply of gas or electricity provided to a person living as a squatter where, for example, a supply has already been arranged. Provided the squatter genuinely intends to pay for the fuel supplied, no offence of theft is committed.

It is important that the supplier is notified as to the use as soon as practicable and that an undertaking of willingness to pay is given. If a squatter moves into premises, uses electricity or gas and then moves out without the intention of paying for it, an offence is committed.

Sentencing for abstraction offences

Guidance on the sentencing for extracting electricity offences under section 13 of the Theft Act 1968 has been issued by the Sentencing Council.[32] A wide range of punishments may be imposed, from an absolute discharge to imprisonment. The maximum penalty in the magistrates' court is six months' imprisonment. The maximum penalty is five years' imprisonment in the Crown Court for the most serious offences, usually involving the commission of other crimes. Most offences are prosecuted through the magistrates' court and the most common sentence is a fine. The Crown Court may set an unlimited fine, but in both the Crown Court and the magistrates' court the level of any fine is linked to your ability to pay it.[33] Where a fine remains unpaid, it may be enforced as a civil debt recoverable through the court machinery, with imprisonment for default where a debtor can pay but fails to do so. The court may also make a compensation order.[34]

Many factors affect the level of punishment imposed by the court – eg, the motive and any underlying reasons which led to the offence. Aggravating factors which may lead to a higher penalty include stealing fuel over a lengthy period, electricity being extracted from the property of another, attempts to conceal or dispose of evidence, the impact on the community and your previous criminal record.[35] The court may also consider the risk to life or property accompanying any offence and any damage, for example, where a fire is caused.[36] Factors which may reduce the penalty may include personal vulnerability, previous good character, being a sole or primary carer for dependent relatives and taking steps to address offending behaviour. Credit will also be given for a plea of guilty.[37]

Poverty and necessity are not a defence to stealing fuel.[38]

Investigation of fuel theft

When detecting and investigating allegations of fuel theft or abstraction, suppliers must provide you with clear, timely and accurate information and advice, detailing in plain and intelligible language:[39]

- the grounds underpinning their allegations of theft; *and*
- the basis for the calculation of charges; *and*
- the steps you must take to dispute the allegations; *and*
- the steps you must take to reinstate supply if it is disconnected.

Accuracy of meters and estimates of stolen fuel

In cases of alleged tampering or theft of fuel, suppliers will try to recover the cost of fuel stolen by estimating the consumption during the period of tampering or theft. This often leads to a dispute about whether or not a meter has recorded consumption accurately. Either party can refer the matter for consideration to a meter examiner (see p91).

If the consumption has been under-recorded, whether because of tampering or otherwise, extra charges will be due. Suppliers will claim that, since the meter has been tampered with, consumption must be estimated. If you dispute an estimate and want to challenge it, ask the supplier what assumptions and calculations were used. Just because a meter has been tampered and interfered with, it does not necessarily mean that fuel was successfully stolen – the onus is upon the supplier to prove that it was. There are various ways suppliers estimate consumption. One measure is to compare your consumption during the period of tampering with your normal rate of consumption, either before the meter was interfered with or after its replacement. To produce an accurate figure, the comparison should be over at least a year, as consumption tends to increase in winter.

This method may not be appropriate in your case because, for example, your pattern of consumption has changed, or you have recently moved home, or because the supplier claims tampering began after the meter was last read or inspected. There is another method based on the number and type of appliances you use. Suppliers make assumptions about the running costs of appliances and how often you use them. Look at the findings critically to see if they bear any relationship to your actual usage. Suppliers sometimes assume the existence of appliances which you do not actually have, or that you use the appliances you do have for maximum periods and at maximum settings.[40]

Also note when the supplier is alleging that any tampering began. Evidence of tampering may be clear, but not the start date or the period during which it took place. For example, the more times the meter has been read, the less likely it is that tampering would not have been noticed by a meter reader, which shortens the period during which the tampering is likely to have started. Under condition 12 of the Standard Licence Conditions (SLCs), the supplier must take all reasonable steps to prevent and detect:[41]

- the theft or abstraction of electricity at premises supplied; *and*
- damage to any electrical plant, electric line or metering equipment through which such premises are supplied with electricity; *and*
- interference with any metering equipment through which such premises are supplied with electricity.

Under condition 12A SLC, suppliers must take all reasonable steps to detect, investigate and prevent theft or abstraction of gas or electricity. As a result, all electricity suppliers must inform the owner of a meter if they detect or suspect any signs of tampering.[42] Suppliers must also behave in a fair, transparent, appropriate, professional and truthful manner in executing these obligations and take into account if any occupants are of pensionable age, disabled or chronically sick and/or will have difficulty in paying all or part of the charges arising of theft.[43] Performance of these obligations is undertaken by suppliers' 'revenue protection units' – specialist departments designed to detect and handle cases of fuel theft and abstraction.

If a meter examiner has been called in, they will decide the amount of extra fuel you should be charged for. You can instruct your own electrical expert (look for an 'electrical engineer' or consult Ofgem for licensed meter companies) to undertake an independent examination and assessment for you. See Chapter 14 for other methods of solving disputes about charges.

Inspection of meters

There are two points to make about the inspection of meters which have been allegedly tampered with.

- A supplier is supposed to take all reasonable steps to read your meter at least once a year.[44] A supplier is also obliged to inspect your meter generally for the purposes of investigating, detecting and preventing potential theft or abstraction of supply as part of its requirements in condition 12A SLC.[45] If the supplier claims that the meter has been tampered with for more than one year (hence it can try to claim more than one year's worth of stolen fuel), you can point out that this suggests it has breached its obligations to read the meter or take all reasonable steps to investigate, detect and prevent theft or abstraction of supply. You cannot rely on the supplier's obligations against back-billing in avoiding payment for more than one year's worth of stolen gas or electricity.

In normal circumstances, this is where a supplier is limited to billing you for energy use consumed within the preceding 12 months. This is because fuel theft is deemed as you behaving obstructively or manifestly unreasonably, which is exempt from the back-billing rules.[46]

- In cases of alleged tampering or theft of fuel, suppliers often remove meters quickly. Electricity suppliers must keep meters they have removed because of tampering until Ofgem says otherwise.[47] Meter providers state in their relevant code of practice the minimum length of time they will keep a damaged meter. In the event of legal action, you will need to have your own expert inspect the meter, so check that the meter is being retained correctly and, if necessary, quote the code of practice.

4. **Disconnection of the supply**

If a supplier alleges theft or tampering, it may want to disconnect the supply until you arrange to pay for the loss. You should seek legal advice if the supplier intends to bring a civil claim against you based on theft, if you have not been charged or convicted of any offence in the criminal courts.

Disconnection powers arise under several different provisions and it is useful to find out which power the supplier is relying on. Each power has its own limitations and it is important to make sure they are not exceeded. In particular, the powers to disconnect for damage to, or tampering with, a meter are different from the power to disconnect for arrears. The supplier should clarify which power it is exercising when seeking to disconnect a supply. For instance, longer notice must be given before disconnection for arrears takes place, but in tampering cases, only 24 hours may be given for gas[48] and no notice at all for electricity, on the basis that the tamperer could be forewarned to get rid of the evidence. See Chapter 10 for the supplier's rights to enter your home to carry out the disconnection.

Injunctions

If suppliers exceed their powers (eg, by refusing to reconnect your supply unless you pay excessive charges), you may be able to obtain an interim court order or injunction (an 'interlocutory injunction') requiring them to reconnect the supply until the dispute is resolved and a final determination is made. An injunction can be an effective remedy against the irreparable harm caused by the infringing party supplier. Sometimes, the threat to seek an injunction may be sufficient to persuade a supplier to reconnect.[49] **Note:** applying for an injunction can be costly. You must pay a court fee of at least £365[50] and should also get advice from a solicitor before using this remedy. A court fee is payable unless you are exempt on grounds of low income, in which case you have to complete an application for a fee exemption on Form EX160. You must also satisfy the legal test to succeed in the injunction application. Legal Aid is not available for advice about this type of debt, so you would need to meet the cost of instructing a solicitor yourself. See Chapter 14 for more information.

Specific powers of disconnection

There are three specific meter offences under the Electricity and Gas Acts which are discussed on p907. If any of the offences are committed in respect of a gas meter or fitting, the supplier can only disconnect the supply of the person who has committed the offence. This is also the case with the offence of damaging an electricity meter or electrical line or plant.[51]

However, if anyone tampers with an electricity meter to commit one of the other two offences, the supplier can disconnect the supply from the premises regardless of whether the person who committed the offence is the actual customer, and whether or not other users of electricity live there.[52]

Suppliers' rights to enter your home to disconnect are dealt with in Chapter 10. However, it is worth pointing out that gas suppliers and transporters do not have the right to enter to disconnect for theft or tampering unless they have given 24 hours' notice[53] or have a warrant from a magistrate or, in Scotland, a sheriff or Justice of the Peace.

To get a criminal conviction, it must be proved beyond all reasonable doubt that an offence has been committed. The onus is on the supplier to prove you have committed an offence. However, to exercise its power to disconnect the supply, the supplier needs only to be able to prove it (with evidence) on the balance of probabilities – ie, it is more likely than not.[54] This test is easier to satisfy than that required to prove a criminal offence. It is important to note that there does not have to be an actual conviction before the power to disconnect can be used.

The supplier can disconnect the supply (and has no obligation to reconnect) until the matter has been remedied.[55] In the case of tampering with a meter, this includes paying for the cost of any damage to the meter and any stolen fuel, but the two should be treated separately. Tampering is normally carried out to reduce the fuel bill, which amounts to theft. However, if a meter has been damaged or tampered with, this does not necessarily mean any fuel has successfully been stolen and proof of damage or tampering is not proof that any money is owing in respect of fuel. (For example, tampering can inadvertently result in the meter actually registering a higher consumption.) Therefore, unless the supplier can show that, on the balance of probabilities, the damage in question caused financial loss other than the cost of replacing the meter, piping or equipment, the matter will be remedied once that cost has been met.

Challenges to disconnection of stolen fuel

Where theft of gas or electricity has been established and the amount is not 'genuinely in dispute',[56] no grounds exist to challenge the disconnection of fuel supply as a consequence of theft.

However, even when disconnecting fuel supply as a result of theft, the supplier must take into account whether any of the occupants of the premises are of pensionable age, disabled or chronically sick. If you fall into one of these categories, your supplier must use disconnection as a last resort for non-payment of charges arising from theft. A prepayment meter should be offered as a means of repayment and the supplier must not disconnect premises during the winter.[57]

Vulnerable customers facing disconnection should refer to Energy UK's Vulnerability Commitment (see p102), SLC 27 and SLC 28.

Save for an interlocutory injunction when a supplier behaves *ultra vires*, there is no further legal protection from disconnection, including entering into a breathing space scheme (see p103). This scheme usually provides legal protection from supplier enforcement and recovery action (including disconnection) for up to 60 days (or for the duration of time that you are receiving mental health crisis treatment, plus 30 days).[58] However, in cases of theft of fuel, the scheme provides no protection.

Charges for stolen fuel

Before demanding payment for stolen fuel, the supplier needs to have evidence on the balance of probabilities (ie, it is more likely than not) of fuel theft by an intentional act or by culpable negligence.[59]

Often the supplier assesses an amount of fuel it thinks has been stolen and demands payment before it reconnects. It can only do this if it can prove that there was a theft and that it was caused by the damage in question.[60]

If the supplier can prove that fuel has been stolen, and can justify its assessment of its value, then it can disconnect for non-payment. However, suppliers cannot use this power if the amount charged is 'genuinely in dispute'. [61]

Even when charging for gas lost as a result of theft, the supplier must take into account whether any of the occupants of the premises are of pensionable age, disabled or chronically sick when deciding how to recover any sum owed.[62] If you fall into one of these categories, your supplier must use disconnection as a last resort for non-payment of charges arising from theft. An instalment plan or a prepayment meter should be offered as a means of repayment and the supplier must not disconnect premises during the winter.[63] The supplier must also take into account your 'ability to pay' all or part of the charges for gas lost as a result of theft, including when calculating instalments.[64] This includes giving due consideration to information provided by third parties and the value of all of the charges that are to be paid via the prepayment meter. Before requiring payment of charges because of theft, the supplier must have evidence that the theft was an intentional act or as a result of your culpable negligence.[65] The supplier must also take all reasonable steps to identify whether you will have difficulty in paying all or part of the charges arising from theft.[66]

Also check carefully any charges for disconnection and reconnection. Gas suppliers are limited by the Gas Act to recovering their 'reasonable expenses'. Otherwise, there is nothing that says exactly what charges can be included, but they must be linked directly to the disconnection and the reasons for it. Typical charges include:

- meter replacement – it is possible for tampering to take place without the meter actually being damaged, so do not pay for a meter to be replaced that is capable of being re-used without repairs;
- gas fitting isolation, restoration and repair – check that gas fittings are not charged for in their entirety if they have not been tampered with;
- visits to your home – check that travel costs and the number of visits are reasonable;
- administration costs of investigation and calculating fuel used but not paid for – check that charges are reasonable;
- general administration – check that this is not wholly or partly double-counted within some other charge (such as debt recovery).

Disconnection for safety reasons

Gas transporters and electricity suppliers have powers to disconnect your supply for safety reasons. A tampered meter can be in an unsafe condition (although not always, as with a meter which is simply missing its seals).

Electricity suppliers can disconnect your supply if they are not satisfied that your meter and wiring are set up and used to prevent danger and not to interfere with the supplier's system or anybody else's electricity supply.

Gas transporters have similar powers for 'averting danger to life or property', including dealing with and preventing gas escaping.[67] The powers to disconnect are accompanied by rights to enter your property to inspect the relevant fittings and carry out such disconnections (see Chapter 10).[68]

Neither gas transporters nor electricity suppliers have to give notice for disconnection in emergencies. Electricity suppliers must send you a written notice as soon as they can, telling you the reason for the disconnection. If you wish to challenge the decision to disconnect your supply, contact Citizens Advice consumer service. It can refer the matter to Ofgem if a decision on the dispute needs to be enforced (see Chapter 14).

Gas transporters must send you a written notice within five days of the disconnection, telling you the nature of the defect, the danger involved and what action has been taken. If you want to object, you have 21 days to appeal to the Secretary of State for Environment, Food and Rural Affairs against the disconnection. The meter stays disconnected until the fault is remedied or the appeal is successful. Reconnection without the consent of the appropriate authorities (ie, the gas transporter or the Secretary of State) is a criminal offence.[69]

When the supply is disconnected for safety reasons, a supplier may provide alternative appliances (eg, electric heaters and cookers) although this is unlikely if tampering is thought to be involved.

Gas suppliers are obliged by their licence conditions to provide a free, annual gas safety check for installations and appliances if you are eligible for the Priority Services Register (see p98). The check includes a basic examination and minor work. If any additional work is necessary, there may be a charge. To qualify, you must request the free safety check yourself and you must own your home, receive an income-based benefit; *and*

- live alone; *or*
- live with other adults, all of whom are eligible (pensionable age, disabled or chronically sick); *or*
- live with others, at least one of whom is under five years old.[70]

In the case of tenants, this obligation is normally upon the landlord. Landlords are obliged to ensure that gas appliances, pipework, fittings and chimneys/flues provided for tenants are safe and annually checked for continued use. A gas safety check must be carried out within 12 months of the installation of a new appliance and annually after that by a Gas Safe Registered engineer.[71]

5. **Theft from meters**

Any form of interference with a meter, whether by electronic interference or some method specifically devised to obtain fuel belonging to another without payment, constitutes an offence under the Theft Act 1968.

Very few prepayment coin-operated meters remain. However, if your coin meter is broken into, you have two problems:

- convincing the supplier that you were not responsible for the theft; *and*
- the supplier may want you to pay not only for damage to the meter, but also for the stolen contents of the meter.

If you discover a coin meter theft:

- report it to the police as soon as practicable and obtain a crime reference number. This will help rebut allegations that you are responsible;
- ask to see your supplier's codes of practice and internal policies or staff guidelines. Some of these are not published, so that they cannot be taken advantage of dishonestly, but it is always worth checking as they may be more generous than the minimum provisions of the law;
- check your home insurance policy to ascertain if a claim can be made for theft from prepayment meters.

6. Removal of meters

When tampering is suspected, suppliers (and gas transporters and shippers) have powers to remove, inspect and reinstall meters.[72] Suppliers must install a replacement meter of the same type,[73] and leave the supply connected on the same terms as before, unless they are exercising powers to disconnect the supply itself. Replacement rather than repair will also occur whenever the internal parts of a meter come to the end of their working life.[74]

The supplier can disconnect the supply by whatever means it thinks fit if it is doing so because of non-payment, and recover any expenses incurred.[75] This includes removing the meter without replacing it. A gas supplier must give seven days' notice,[76] and two days' notice by an electricity supplier.[77] This notice is usually given in the final demand. **Note:** the meter cannot be removed if any amount is 'genuinely in dispute'.[78] To gain entry into the property, the supplier must get your contsent or a warrant. After the notice period expires, a supplier may break into the premises, if not given access, and remove the meter.

An electricity company can disconnect a supply and remove a meter even if legal proceedings under the Theft Act are not pursued. Several court decisions have held that disconnection could be justified where the supplier could produce, on the balance of probabilities, the civil standard of proof that unlawful abstraction had occurred, even though there may have been no criminal conviction.[79]

Notes

1. Introduction
1 Condition 12A SLC
2 Condition 12A.1(b)(ii) SLC
3 Condition 12A SLC
4 Condition 12A.1(b)(i) SLC

2. Tampering with a meter
5 Sch 4 para 11 EA 1989
6 Ch 27 Sch 7 para 6(1) UA 2000
7 Sch 2B para 10(1) GA 1986
8 s13 TA 1968
9 *R v McCreadie and Tume* [1992] 96 Cr App R 143; *Ivey v Genting Casinos* [2018] AC 391

10 s32 Magistrates' Courts Act 1980; The Criminal Justice Act 2003 (Commencement No.33) and Sentencing Act 2020 (Commencement No.2) Regulations 2022 No.500
11 Sentencing Council Guidelines, 1 February 2016, available at sentencingcouncil.org.uk/offences/magistrates-court/item/abstracting-electricity
12 *Semple v Hingston* [1992] Greens Weekly Reports 21:1201
13 *R v McCreadie and Tume,* [1992] 96 Cr App R 143, CA
14 *R v Hoar* [1982] Crim LR 606

15 Condition 12A SLC
16 Sch 7 para 10(2) EA 1989; Sch 2B para 3(3) GA 1986
17 Sch 7 para 11(1) EA 1989; Sch 2B para 10(1)(a) GA 1986
18 Sch 7 para 11(1) EA 1989; Sch 2B para 10(1)(a) GA 1986
19 Sch 7 para 11(2) EA 1989; Sch 2B para 10(3) GA 1986

3. Theft of fuel
20 s13 (electricity) and s1 (gas) TA 1968; in Scotland, the common law offence of theft
21 *R v McCreadie and Tume* [1992] 96 Cr App R 143, CA
22 *R v McCreadie and Tume* [1992] 96 Cr AppR 143, CA
23 See, for example, *R v Riley* [2011] EWCA Crim 3066
24 *Ghosh* (1982) 75 Cr AppR 154
25 *Collins and Fox v Chief Constable of Merseyside* [1988] Crim LR 247; *Boggeln v Williams* [1978] 1 WLR 873
26 s13 TA 1968
27 *Collins and Fox v Chief Constable of Merseyside* [1988] Crim LR 247
28 Criminal Attempts Act 1981
29 Sch 2B para 9 GA 1986
30 *Doncaster BC v Stark and Another* [1997] CO/2763/96, 5 November 1997, Potts, J; *Frost (Inspector of Taxes) v Feltham* [1981] 1 WLR 452
31 s144 Legal Aid, Sentencing and Punishment of Offenders Act 2012
32 Sentencing Council Guidelines, 1 February 2016
33 *Re Churchill (No.2)* (1967) 1 QB 190
34 Sentencing Council Guidelines, 1 February 2016
35 Sentencing Council Guidelines, 1 February 2016
36 *R v McKay (Grant) and Another* [2017] EWCA 2299 CA (Crim)
37 s144 Criminal Justice Act 2003
38 *Southwark LBC v Williams* [1971] 2 All ER 175
39 Condition 12A.12(g) (gas) SLC
40 Appliance running cost calculator: citizensadvice.org.uk/consumer/energy/energy-supply/save-energy-at-home/check-how-much-your-electrical-appliances-cost-to-use
41 Condition 12.1(a)-(c) (elec) SLC
42 Condition 12A SLC
43 Condition 12A.1(b) SLC
44 Condition 21B.4 SLC
45 Condition 12A.1(a) SLC

46 Condition 21BA.2(c) SLC
47 Condition 12A SLC

4. Disconnection of the supply
48 Sch 2B para 24(2) GA 1986
49 *Gwenter v Eastern Electricity plc* [1995] Legal Action, August 1995, p19
50 Form EX50, gov.uk/government/publications/fees-in-the-civil-and-family-courts-main-fees-ex50
51 Sch 2B para 10(2) GA 1986; Sch 6 para 4(3) EA 1986
52 Sch 6 para 6 EA 1986
53 Sch 2B para 24(2) GA 1986
54 Condition 12A.11(e) SLC
55 Sch 4(6)(5) UA 2000
56 Ch 24 Sch 4(2)(2) UA 2000
57 Condition 12A.11 SLC
58 DRS Regs
59 Condition 12A.11(g) SLC
60 *R v Director General of Gas Supply ex parte Smith* [1989] (unreported); *R v Minister of Energy ex parte Guildford* [1998] (unreported)
61 Sch 6 para 2 EA 1989; Sch 2B para 7 GA 1986
62 Condition 12A.11 SLC
63 Condition 12A.11 SLC
64 Condition 12A.11 SLC
65 Condition 12A.11(g) SLC
66 Condition 12A.11(b) SLC
67 Reg 4 GS(RE) Regs
68 Reg 5 GS(RE) Regs
69 ss17(2) and 29 EA 1989; s18(2) GA 1986; regs 4, 6, 7, 9 and 10 GS(RE) Regs; reg 29(4) The Electricity Supply Regulations 1988 No.1057
70 Condition 29.1 (gas) SLC
71 Reg 36A GS(IU) Regs as amended

6. Removal of meters
72 Ch 24 Sch 4 (7) UA 2000
73 Ch 24 Sch 4(7)(3) UA 2000
74 Ch 24 Sch 4(9) UA 2000
75 Ch 24 Sch 4(2) UA 2000
76 Sch 2B GA 1986
77 Ch 24 Sch 4 UA 2000; Sch 6 and 7 EA 1989
78 Ch 24 Sch 4(2)(2) UA 2000
79 *R v Director General of Gas Supply ex parte Smith* [1989] QB 31 July (unreported); *Director of Gas Supply ex parte Sherlock & Morris N Ireland* [1996] QB 29 November (unreported); *R v Seeboard PLC & Another ex parte Robert Guildford* [1998] 18 February 1998, per Ognall, J

Chapter 10

· ·

Rights of entry

This chapter covers:
1. Entering your home (below)
2. Right of entry with a warrant (p171)

1. Entering your home

The Gas Act 1986 and the Electricity Act 1989 give suppliers and gas transporters certain rights and powers to enter your home. Suppliers do not have any entry rights other than those under the Acts. These rights of entry can only be exercised if:

* you consent; *or*
* the supplier obtains a warrant from a magistrates' court (in Scotland the sheriff court, a Justice of the Peace or a magistrate); *or*
* there is an emergency and to avert danger.

Suppliers emphasise that they will only disconnect your supply as a last resort and where all other measures have failed. However, in practice, this is not always the case. Some suppliers may seek a warrant to disconnect ahead of adopting alternative ways of addressing the arrears – eg, by arranging Fuel Direct or affordable payment arrangements. Suppliers' licences also contain conditions requiring them to take all reasonable steps to recover unpaid charges through available means before disconnection.[1] Suppliers are required to train their representatives and to ensure that they behave appropriately when visiting your home and do not install a prepayment meter if you are psychologically vulnerable and that would be made significantly worse by the experience. Suppliers can only install prepayment meters without permission (called an 'involuntary prepayment meter') or remotely switch a smart meter to prepayment mode if they have taken every step to check the household's circumstances, including by undertaking a site welfare visit.[2] They are also required to identify the circumstances, needs and characteristics of vulnerable customers and satisfy themselves that their actions are resulting in vulnerable customers being treated fairly.[3] Suppliers and their agents should also be aware of paragraphs 70 to 78 of *Taking Control of Goods: National Standards* (see Appendix 3).[4]

These standards are intended for use by all enforcement agents, public and private, and the creditors (in this instance the fuel suppliers) that use their services. This national guidance does not replace local agreements or legislation, and you should check any codes of practice published by individual suppliers. The standards are not legally binding. They can, however, offer a useful benchmark to determine what you can reasonably expect if suppliers instruct agencies to collect debts on their behalf.

Legal powers

Electricity and gas suppliers and gas transporters have the right to enter your home to:[5]

- inspect fittings or read the meter – no advance notice has to be given;
- disconnect supply on non-payment of bills (this does not apply to gas transporters). Electricity suppliers must give one working day's notice, and gas suppliers 24 hours' notice (this may be waived on grounds of public safety or tampering);
- discontinue supply or remove a meter under their powers in connection with theft and tampering (see Chapter 9). Gas suppliers must give 24 hours' notice;
- discontinue supply or remove a meter where it is no longer wanted. Electricity suppliers must give two working days' notice and gas suppliers 24 hours' notice;
- replace, repair or alter pipes, lines or plant. Electricity suppliers must give five working days' notice (unless it is an emergency, in which case notice must be given as soon as possible afterwards), and gas suppliers seven days' notice.

Notice should be given in writing and can be served by post or by hand, or by attaching it to any obvious part of the premises. Once any required notice has been given, suppliers may use these rights at any reasonable time. 'Reasonable' is not defined but should be taken to mean at reasonable times of the day – ie, not late at night, on religious festivals and public holidays such as Christmas Day, or when the supplier knows that it would cause you difficulty.

If your supply is disconnected for any reason other than safety, gas suppliers and transporters also have the right to enter your home to check that the gas supply has not been reconnected without consent.

Electricity suppliers do not have the power to inspect or read the meter if you have written to them asking for the supply to be disconnected and this has not been done within a reasonable time.

A gas transporter also has the right to enter your home if it has reasonable cause to suspect that gas is, or might be, escaping, or that escaped gas has entered your premises, in order to do any necessary work to prevent the escape or to avert danger to life or property.

Officials representing the supplier or transporter must produce official identification when using the above powers.

If you intentionally obstruct an official exercising any of the above powers of entry, you can be fined up to £1,000. However, you cannot be punished if the official does not have a warrant.[6]

Suppliers must leave the premises no less secure than they found them and must pay compensation for any damage caused.

Always check that the correct person is named in the warrant application and that the fuel debt does not relate to another person – eg, a previous resident.

Licence conditions

Gas and electricity suppliers operate under licences issued by Ofgem (see Chapter 1), which has powers to force the suppliers to keep to the conditions in their licences (see Chapter 14). Licence conditions state that gas and electricity suppliers must send details of their policies on entering customers' homes to Ofgem for approval.

Suppliers' codes of practice require the following.[7]

- Suppliers' representatives visiting or entering your home must be fit and proper persons – eg, they must have no relevant criminal convictions.
- Each representative must be identifiable, including by driving marked vehicles, wearing appropriate clothing and carrying a suitable photocard.
- Each representative must be fully trained about the legal powers discussed above.
- Suppliers must operate password schemes for pensioners, disabled or chronically sick customers. If you want one, you can have a password known only to you and the supplier to identify genuine representatives.
- Representatives must be able to tell you where you can get further help or advice about the supply of gas or electricity.

Check your supplier's website for its code of practice or phone and ask for a copy.

---

2. Right of entry with a warrant

If you do not consent to the supplier entering your premises in accordance with any of the above rights, or there is no adult to give such consent, the supplier or transporter can get a magistrates' warrant (or the Scottish equivalent). In an emergency, a supplier does not need to get a warrant, but can obtain one nevertheless if entry is obstructed despite the emergency. The issue of a warrant is governed by the Rights of Entry (Gas and Electricity Boards) Act 1954.[8] Although the application is dealt with through the magistrates' court, the application is a civil matter, not a criminal matter.

To get the warrant, the supplier must apply to the magistrates' court or, in Scotland, to the sheriff court. The warrant is granted if the court is satisfied that:

- entry to the premises is reasonably required by the supplier; *and*
- the supplier has a right of entry, but that right is subject to getting consent to enter; *and*
- any conditions the supplier is supposed to meet in order to exercise the right of entry (eg, to give notice) have been met.

Also, the court must be satisfied that:
- if the right of entry does not itself require notice, 24 hours' notice has been given after which entry was refused; *or*
- there is an emergency and entry has been refused; *or*
- the purpose of entering would be defeated by asking for consent – eg, if tampering is suspected.

A warrant is only valid if it is signed by the Justice of the Peace (or the sheriff in Scotland).

In recent years, the practice has been to use the warrant system to fit prepayment meters (or remotely recalibrate smart meters from credit to prepayment mode) rather than actually disconnect a supply. In 2022, there were 19 disconnections for gas/electricity debt in the UK.[9] See p113 if you do not want a prepayment meter imposed.

A warrant of entry remains in force for 28 days. If entry is not sought within this period, the warrant lapses.[10]

A warrant for entry and disconnection may be quashed or set aside by the court where it has been obtained against the wrong person or premises. The supplier must act exactly by the terms of a warrant. If you are unhappy with an entry by warrant, check its wording precisely.

A warrant for entry and disconnection may not be executed if you have entered into a breathing space standard debt respite scheme or mental health debt respite scheme (see p103).[11]

Notice of application for a warrant

There is no general requirement under the 1954 Act for the supplier or court to inform you that an entry warrant is being applied for, or has been issued. You have no right to be notified or be present at the hearing. However, your supplier may state in its code of practice that it will inform you and it is a general principle in English law that you should not have your rights affected without notice of some kind being served upon you.[12] Under the Humans Rights Act 1998, it may be possible to argue that a person affected by the warrant should be notified of the hearing and allowed to make representations to the magistrates' court. This point has yet to be tested, but Article 6 of the European Convention on Human Rights ensures the right to a fair trial and representation in legal proceedings which affect the rights of a person, including civil obligations. The State is under a duty to ensure the effective protection of rights.[13]

Typically, a supplier serves a notice informing you that you may attend. Some letters may state that the police may be in attendance. This is wrong and misleading. The police should not be involved because the warrant is a civil matter, not a criminal one. The police have no power to enforce the warrant, as it is a private dispute between you and the supplier. Only if there is a threat of violence at the property (such as a breach of the peace) should there be any involvement by the police, and then only to restrain a breach of the peace such as a fight. A complaint should be made where a letter contains such a suggestion.

Contacting the supplier in advance

Wherever possible, you or your representative should contact the supplier in advance of the hearing as there is still the possibility of negotiation.

In some cases, the supplier may withdraw the application before the hearing, particularly if the application may be contested or if you are vulnerable. Reference should be made to *Taking Control of Goods: National Standards* (see Appendix 3) in a case of vulnerability. Consideration should also be given to Standard Licence Condition (SLC) 27, Ofgem's code of practice for involuntary installation of prepayment meters[14] and whether a supplier is a signatory to Energy UK's Vulnerability Commitment. If a supplier disregards the guidance, a complaint can be made, as well as the matter being brought to the attention of the magistrates' court.

Representations should be made in writing, and may be emailed or faxed direct to the customer relations or the complaints department. Your supplier should provide you with the contact details for the department which deals with complaints. An explanation of the vulnerability and an outline of the issues should be included.

If a defence can be shown, or there are factors the court should consider, mention these. You should be prepared to provide further details and attend the court hearing.

Prohibitions on exercising a warrant

Suppliers are prohibited from exercising a warrant and levying prepayment meter warrant charges for the most vulnerable customers. A warrant should not be exercised and a prepayment meter installed where it would be severely traumatic to a customer due to an existing vulnerability which relates to their mental capacity and/or psychological state and it would be made significantly worse by the experience.[15]

Suppliers must also apply the 'proportionality principle' when exercising a warrant. This is that the warrant action and costs are proportionate to the amount of the outstanding charges.[16] In addition to a general prohibition on exercising a warrant, suppliers are prohibited from charging you in respect of any costs associated with issuing a warrant where you have:

- a vulnerability which has significantly impaired your ability to engage with the supplier or an agent about the recovery of a debt;[17] *or*
- severe financial vulnerability which would be made worse by charging you any costs associated with a warrant.[18]

Historically, suppliers have charged warrant costs back to affected customers, which has placed customers in further debt. However, the total amount of charges that a supplier can recover for installing prepayment meters under warrant for customers in debt is now capped at £150.[19] It is likely that these changes will protect the most vulnerable from experiencing unnecessary and avoidable hardship and force suppliers to only use prepayment meters as a last resort.

If you have entered into a breathing space standard debt respite scheme (valid for up to 60 days) or a mental health debt respite scheme (valid for the duration of the mental health crisis treatment and another 30 days after that), suppliers are prohibited from exercising a warrant during the moratorium.[20]

Disconnection of smart meters without a warrant

Suppliers are bound by the same rules applicable to those on non-smart meters about disconnection of supply. However, as they have remote access to your meter, and do not have to gain physical access to your property to switch off the supply, they do not have to apply for an entry warrant.

Powers of entry simply in respect of the debt

A supplier (or an enforcement officer acting on its behalf) authorised to collect a fuel debt (alone or with any other civil debt) does not have the power to force entry to a domestic dwelling. The protection covers the outer door which serves as the private entrance of your home. The protection remains in force whether the debt is being enforced through either the county court or the High Court.[21]

Restrictions on disconnection

SLC 27 provides that a supplier should not disconnect in winter (see p137) and that disconnection should be a last resort. When contacting the supplier or its agent, mention these restrictions, and at court where appropriate.

The approach of the court

The court should not grant the warrant unless it is satisfied that the legal requirements have been met; but in practice, courts tend to rubber-stamp suppliers' applications for warrants in the absence of the customer. However, the Court of Appeal has emphasised the importance of carefully scrutinising warrant applications to gain entry to private homes.[22] The position of the courts has also in recent years been subject to investigation by the Business, Energy and Industrial Strategy and Justice Committees.[23] Magistrates have discretion under the 1954 Act and are expected to exercise that discretion reasonably in each case, considering all relevant factors, disregarding irrelevant ones and not acting perversely.[24] If you suspect that your supplier will be applying for a warrant, write to them. You should set out why a warrant should not be granted and send a copy to the court, asking that it be shown to the magistrate (or other Scottish court officer) who will deal with the application. Letters and representations should be addressed to the Justices' Chief Executive stating that you wish to attend the hearing and make representations at any application. Letters may be emailed or faxed to the court in urgent cases.

However, as a result of magistrates' court reorganisation and the recent closure of some courts, administration is not always efficient and it may be necessary to attend the court in advance to seek an adjournment, or alternatively on the day set for the hearing. If attending in advance, ask to speak to the duty legal adviser about the application.

Adjournments

If you cannot attend court for a good reason, you may seek an adjournment. The application should only be made if you genuinely intend to contest the warrant application at a later date. Write a letter to the court requesting an adjournment of the warrant application, to allow you to attend or be represented. In an emergency, if you cannot get to court, you may be able to obtain the adjournment by telephone. If you are in a vulnerable situation or circumstance, or if the disconnection is being investigated by an official body, these may be grounds for an adjournment. Reasonable consideration should be given to an application to adjourn.

It is important not to leave the matter to the last minute. Act promptly yourself and, in cases where the energy company has failed to respond to representations, this should be put forward as a reason for the delay.

The court may also be willing to adjourn the hearing where there is a contradiction between the information contained in the summons or notice of hearing for the warrant and the evidence produced in court on behalf of the supplier.[25]

On attending court it may be possible to negotiate with the agent representing the supplier and, in some cases, it may be possible to have the warrant application withdrawn on the day of the hearing. This is more common than for a contested warrant hearing to go ahead. In some cases, simply attending court and being prepared to contest the warrant leads the supplier to withdraw the application.

You may represent yourself in court, be represented by a lawyer, or may be assisted by a 'McKenzie friend' (see p262).

Proportionality and Human Rights Act principles

The court has discretion whether to grant a warrant and must act reasonably.[26] In considering whether to exercise its discretion to grant a warrant, the court should have regard to human rights principles under European law including the 'doctrine of proportionality' – ie, any legal measures applied against citizens of member states and affecting their rights must be proportional to the ends achieved.

The law has yet to be tested, but it is at least arguable that an application for a warrant to gain entry to disconnect electricity or gas may be a disproportionate measure in the case of a vulnerable household – eg, a lone parent receiving only benefit income. In a case of fine enforcement, the High Court held that enforcement activity may be disproportionate as a measure and contrary to Article 8 of the European Convention on Human Rights (protecting rights to the home and family life).[27]

Applying the principle of proportionality, it would appear open to a magistrates' court to decline to issue a warrant where a debt is relatively small and the hardship caused to a vulnerable household would be severe. A magistrates' court should consider the position of any children residing in the property and any disabled people who may be affected. It is therefore important that a financial statement (see p108) and details of all persons residing in the property are provided to the court at the hearing. If you are too ill to attend, send details to the court in writing in time for the hearing.

Similarly, it has not been determined whether it is correct for an energy company to pursue a warrant where another option may be available – eg, Fuel Direct or a payment plan. You should certainly raise any failure to do so at the hearing, as your supplier must consider these options under SLC 27.

It should be noted that under SLC 28.15, suppliers should not exercise a warrant where such action would be disproportionate in the context of the amount of the outstanding debt and charges.[28]

Defects in the 1954 legislation

From anecdotal evidence and experience, it appears that a number of major suppliers have doubts as to the applicability of the 1954 Act. The legislation dates from when energy companies were state owned and supplies were not provided on a modern contractual basis. The legislation as envisaged in 1954 was not designed to accomplish the instalment of prepayment meters, which amount to a change in the terms and conditions of supply. Therefore, there is an argument that the use of a warrant to fit a prepayment meter is not within the powers granted under the Act as envisaged in 1954 and that you can legitimately object to the change in the terms and conditions. Sometimes, energy companies are reluctant to tackle these arguments in court and may withdraw the warrant.

If a warrant application is challenged in court, questions should also be asked about the cost of the application. Some suppliers (or companies acting on their behalf) will add £300 or more for the cost of seeking an individual warrant against one person, even though they may be making 10 or more such applications at the same time. The court has discretion about costs. This means you can ask the magistrates' court to consider costs and whether they are reasonable. Ofgem has also capped the charges for the installation of prepayment meters to £150.[29] If suppliers seek to levy large charges and costs, they could be referred to Ofgem or Citizens Advice consumer service for examination as to fairness.

Liability for negligence and improperly obtained warrants

A gas or electricity operator is protected against liability in civil law for acts in accordance with executing the warrant. However, a gas or electricity operator who gains entry under a warrant remains liable for any wrongful acts or defaults committed during the course of executing the warrant against the premises or where a warrant has been obtained in bad faith or for an improper purpose.[30] Therefore, a fuel operator may be liable to action in negligence, trespass or nuisance where the warrant is executed against the wrong premises or where damage is caused in the process of disconnection. If a supplier knowingly tries to force entry without a warrant this is a criminal offence, such as criminal damage. Pecuniary losses which arise from wrongful disconnection may be recovered and can include claims for damage to reputation.[31] A householder who resists such entry is entitled to use reasonable force.[32] A warrant should not be granted for entry to premises where the debt relates to the unpaid bills of a previous occupier and a new occupier has moved in.[33]

Appeals from the magistrates' court

Rights of appeal from the magistrates' court on a point of law lie to the High Court under section 111 of the Magistrates' Courts Act 1980 (known as 'case stated' appeals) and also to the High Court by judicial review.[34] Seek legal advice before attempting such an appeal and, if you appeal, notify the supplier that you are doing so.

Any application by 'case stated' must be commenced within 21 days of the decision of the magistrates' court. In an appeal by judicial review, this must be commenced as soon as possible, and in all cases within three months of the decision. An application may be made to obtain a quashing order to cancel out the warrant where it should not have been made in law, where there was procedural unfairness or the decision to issue the warrant was unreasonable in law.

Judicial review is a two-stage process, first requiring an application for leave. An injunction may be sought at the leave stage to prevent the enforcement of the warrant or, if a warrant has been granted, it may be set aside by the High Court.[35] It is always best to seek legal advice before attempting such an appeal or application. However, there is no automatic right to apply to the court for injunctive relief, such as an adjournment or stay of a warrant once issued. See Chapter 14 for more information.

Notes

1. Entering your home
1 Condition 27.9 SLC
2 Condition 28.10 SLC
3 Condition 0.1 and 0.3(d) SLC
4 Ministry of Justice, *Taking Control of Goods: National Standards*, 6 April 2014
5 Sch 6 paras 6(1) and (2) and 7(1) and (2) EA 1989; Sch 2B paras 16, 17, 23(1), 24, 24(2), 26, 27 and 27(1) GA 1986
6 s1(3) RE(GEB)A 1954
7 Code of Practice on Procedures with Respect to Site Access (Electricity); Arrangements in Respect of Powers of Entry; Authorisation of Officers (Gas)

2. Right of entry with a warrant
8 s1(3) RE(GEB)A 1954; this applies to Scotland under s11(7)
9 Ofgem, *Customer Service Data*, Q1 2022-Q4 2022, available at ofgem.gov.uk/publications/ infographic-energy-company-performance
10 s101 EA 1989, amending s2 RE(GEB)A 1954
11 DRS Regs
12 *Craig v Kanssen* [1943] 1 KB 256
13 ECHR Article 6; *Rommelfanger v Germany* (1989) 62 DR 151 and *Diennert v France* (1996) 21 EHRR 554
14 Ofgem, *Involuntary Prepayment Meter Energy Supplier Code of Practice*, April 2023, available at ofgem.gov.uk/ publications/involuntary-prepayment-meter-energy-supplier-code-practice
15 Condition 28.10 SLC
16 Condition 28.15 SLC
17 Condition 28.11(1) SLC
18 Condition 28.11(2) SLC
19 Condition 28.12 SLC
20 DRS Regs
21 *Semayne's Case* (1603) 5 Co Litt 91a; Sch 12 Part 2 Tribunals, Courts and Enforcement Act 2007
22 *O'Keegan v Chief Constable of Merseyside* [2003] 1 WLR 2197
23 committees.parliament.uk/work/7360/ prepayment-meters-warrants-and-forced-installations

24 *Associated Provincial Picture Houses v Wednesbury Corporation* [1948] 1 KB 223
25 s123(2) Magistrates' Courts Act 1980
26 *Associated Provincial Picture Houses v Wednesbury Corporation* [1948] 1 KB 223
27 *R (on the application of Stokes) v Gwent Magistrates' Court* [2001] JPN 766; [2001] EWHC 569 (Admin)
28 Condition 28B(4) SLC
29 Condition 28B(3) SLC
30 *O'Keegan v Chief Constable of Merseyside* [2003] 1 WLR 2197
31 *Say (t/a Corby Café) v British Gas Trading Ltd* [2010] EWHC 3946 (QB)
32 Criminal Damage Act 1971; *Vaughan v McKenzie* [1969] 1 QB 557
33 See *R (on the application of MS Superstore Ltd) v Luton and South Bedfordshire Court* [2013] EWHC 551 (Admin), CO/1046/ 2011
34 CPR 54
35 See *R (on the application of MS Superstore Ltd) v Luton and South Bedfordshire Court* [2013] EWHC 551 (Admin), CO/1046/ 2011

Chapter 11

Fuel and benefits

This chapter covers:
1. Benefit entitlement checks (below)
2. Universal credit, pension credit and other means-tested benefits (p180)
3. Cold weather payments, winter fuel payments and Scottish heating payments (p181)
4. Help with fuel-related housing costs and service charges (p186)
5. Impact of charitable payments on benefits (p188)
6. Local welfare assistance schemes (p189)
7. Budgeting advances and budgeting loans (p189)
8. Fuel Direct (p190)

1. Benefit entitlement checks

If you cannot afford to pay for fuel or something related (eg, maintaining a boiler or replacing a heater), get specialist benefits advice to make sure that you are receiving all the financial help you are entitled to.

Do not assume that you are not entitled to any help or to more help than you are already getting. Whatever your circumstances, your local Citizens Advice, advice centre or welfare rights service should be able to provide you with a benefit check free of charge. You can use the advicelocal.uk website to find a free advice service.

In Wales and Scotland, you can get a free benefit check via the government-funded energy efficiency schemes:
- in Wales, Nest: freephone 0808 808 2244;
- in Scotland, Home Energy Scotland (through its *Find funding* service): freephone 0808 808 2282.

If you are refused a benefit and need to challenge the decision, consult CPAG's *Welfare Benefits and Tax Credits Handbook* and get advice. If you are not entitled to any benefits, see Chapter 12.

2. Universal credit, pension credit and other means-tested benefits

If you are struggling to afford fuel, check your eligibility for means-tested benefits. If you are working-age, check your eligibility for universal credit (UC). If you have reached state pension age, check your eligibility for pension credit (PC). Entitlement to these benefits is based on your income, savings and other capital. They are administered by the DWP.

You might already be receiving UC, PC, or one of the older means-tested benefits: income support (IS), income-based jobseeker's allowance (JSA) or income-related employment and support allowance (ESA).

All of these benefits can help with household expenses including energy costs. If you get one of these benefits, it may make you eligible for:
- cold weather payments and Scottish heating payments (see p181);
- a Warm Home Discount (see p47).

You may also be able to pay for your fuel and any arrears through direct deductions from your means-tested benefit. This is the Fuel Direct scheme (see p190) and can be particularly useful where you are at risk of disconnection.

Note:
- For more detailed information about these benefits, see CPAG's *Welfare Benefits and Tax Credits Handbook*.
- See p186 for information about housing benefit (HB), which is also means-tested.

Universal credit

Universal credit (UC) is the main means-tested benefit for working-age people. It is replacing the following benefits which are sometimes referred to as 'legacy benefits': IS, income-based JSA, income-related ESA, HB and tax credits.

You are usually eligible for UC if you are between 18 and pension age. However, some 16- and 17-year-olds can claim, as can some pension-age people including those who have younger partners. You can claim UC whether or not you are working. You must usually meet basic conditions about education status, residence and capital.

You must accept a 'claimant commitment' to qualify for UC. This is an agreement that you will meet certain work-related requirements, which might include attending work-focused interviews, work preparation, work search and work availability. You may have no or limited work-related requirements because of your personal circumstances (eg, because of your health or caring responsibilities).

UC includes amounts for adults and dependent children, and can also include amounts related to disability or ill health, caring responsibilities, childcare costs, rent, and some housing costs such as service charges and ground rent payable by home owners. See p186 for information on fuel-related housing costs and UC.

Pension credit

Pension credit (PC) is a benefit for people who have reached state pension age. Your state pension age depends on your date of birth. You can check the date you will qualify at gov.uk/state-pension-age.

PC has two different elements:

- **guarantee credit**, designed to bring your income up to a certain level; *and*
- **savings credit**, which is intended to 'reward' you for making provision for your retirement above the basic state retirement pension. The savings credit is being phased out, though some people can still qualify.

If you get PC, you qualify for a winter fuel payment (or pension-age winter heating payment in Scotland) and, if you get the guarantee credit, you may be in the 'core group' of people entitled to a Warm Home Discount (see p47).

---

3. Cold weather payments, winter fuel payments and Scottish heating payments

In England and Wales, cold weather payments and winter fuel payments provide extra financial help during periods of cold weather. They have different eligibility rules.

In Scotland, you may be able to get:

- winter fuel payments (these will be replaced by pension-age winter heating payments from winter 2024);
- winter heating payments, which have replaced cold weather payments for Scottish residents and have different eligibility rules;
- child winter heating assistance if your family includes a severely disabled child (see p185).

Payments in England, Wales and Scotland are tax-free and do not affect other benefits you get.

Cold weather payments

Cold weather payments are payments made to pension credit (PC) claimants and some universal credit (UC), income support (IS), income-based jobseeker's allowance (JSA) and income-related employment and support (ESA) claimants.

Cold weather payments are intended to assist with the extra costs of heating when the weather has been exceptionally cold for at least seven consecutive days.

A period of cold weather

This is a period of seven consecutive days during which the average of the mean daily temperature, as forecast or recorded for that period at your designated local weather station, is equal to or below zero degrees celsius.[1]

Who qualifies

You qualify for a cold weather payment if:

- a period of cold weather has been forecast or recorded for the area in which your normal home is situated;[2] *and*
- you have been awarded PC (guarantee or savings credit) for at least one day during the period of cold weather. You also qualify if you have been awarded UC, IS, income-based JSA or income-related ESA for at least one day during the period of cold weather *and*:[3]
  - your UC includes an increase for a disabled or severely disabled child; *or*
  - your UC includes the limited capability for work or limited capability for work-related activity element (or would except that you get the carer element instead) and you are not in employment or gainful self-employment during the period of cold weather or on the day it is forecast; *or*
  - your IS or income-based JSA includes a disability, severe disability, enhanced disability, disabled child or pensioner premium; *or*
  - your income-related ESA includes the pensioner premium, severe disability premium, enhanced disability premium or the work-related activity or support component; *or*
  - you are responsible for a child under five; *or*
  - you are getting child tax credit which includes a disability or severe disability element.

You might qualify even if you are not getting one of these benefits, but you are getting support for mortgage interest. The rules on this are complicated so get advice if you think this might apply to you.

You do not qualify for the cold weather payment if:

- you are living in a care home; *or*
- usually, if you are a 'person subject to immigration control'.

Amount of payment

£25 is paid for each week of cold weather.[4]

Claiming and getting paid

You do not need to make a claim for a cold weather payment. The DWP should automatically pay you if you qualify. A payment cannot be made more than 26 weeks after the last day of the winter period (1 November to 31 March) in which the cold weather period fell.[5]

If you are overpaid a cold weather payment, you might have to repay it and, in some circumstances, you may have to pay a penalty.

Challenging a decision

If you do not receive a cold weather payment to which you think you are entitled, submit a written claim and ask for a written decision. If you are refused, ask for a revision of the decision within one month of receiving the decision. If you are still unhappy with the outcome, you can appeal to the First-tier Tribunal.

Winter fuel payments

A winter fuel payment is a yearly tax-free payment to help people pay for their heating in the winter. Getting the winter fuel payment does not affect any other benefits you may get.

Note: the rules have changed for 2024. It is now required that you (or your partner if you are in a couple) are entitled to a means-tested benefit or tax credit. In Scotland, winter fuel payments are being replaced in winter 2024 by a new Scottish benefit, pension-age winter heating payment. The rules are the same as those described below for winter fuel payments.

Who qualifies

You qualify for a winter fuel payment if:[6]

- you have reached pension age by the end of the **'qualifying week'**. This is the week beginning on the third Monday in September; *and*
- on any day during the qualifying week, you (or your partner if you are in a couple) are entitled to UC, PC, IS, income-based JSA or income-related ESA, or child tax credit (CTC) or working tax credit of at least £26 for the tax year 2024/25;
- on any day during the qualifying week, you are ordinarily resident in England, Wales or Scotland. **Note:** you may also be entitled if you live in Switzerland or in a European Economic Area (EEA) country, excluding Cyprus, France, Gibraltar, Greece, Malta, Portugal and Spain; *and*
- you claim in time (if a claim is required – see below); *and*
- you are not excluded under the rules below.

Exclusions

You are excluded from entitlement if, during the qualifying week:[7]

- you are serving a custodial sentence (throughout the week); *or*

- you have been receiving free inpatient treatment for more than 52 weeks in a hospital or similar institution; *or*
- you are living in residential care and have been for at least 12 weeks; *or*
- you are a person subject to immigration control (although there are exceptions).

Amount of payment

The amount of a winter fuel payment is:
- £300, if you reached the age of 80 in or before the qualifying week (ie, you were born before 23 September 1944) or you are in a couple or a polygamous marriage and the other member of that couple or marriage has reached that age; *or*
- £200, in any other case.

Note that you will not get the extra pensioner cost of living payment given in 2022 and 2023. It stopped in winter 2023.

Claiming and getting paid

Most people get the winter fuel payment automatically. DWP records of your circumstances can be used to show that you are entitled without you having to claim.[8]

Otherwise, you must claim a winter fuel payment by 31 March following the qualifying week.[9] To try to ensure you receive your payment before Christmas, submit your claim *before* the qualifying week. Claim via the winter fuel payment helpline on 0800 731 0160 (Relay UK: dial 18001 then 0800 731 0160) or download a claim form from gov.uk/winter-fuel-payment/how-to-claim.

Payments are usually made between mid-November and Christmas.

Challenging a decision

Decisions can be challenged by a mandatory reconsideration request and appeal. To get a decision, you may have to submit a written claim and request a written decision.

Winter heating payments

Winter heating payments are paid annually by Social Security Scotland (SSS) to Scottish residents with a low income. They have replaced cold weather payments in Scotland. In winter 2024/25, the winter heating payment is £58.75.[10] You qualify if on at least one day during the 'qualifying week' (which starts on the first Monday in November) you get a qualifying means-tested benefit and you are resident in Scotland.[11]

The qualifying benefits are:[12]
- UC, but only if:
  - your award includes a disabled child addition; *or*

- you are responsible for a child under five *and* you are not in employment or gainful self-employment; *or*
- you have been assessed as having, or are treated as having, limited capability for work or work-related activity, *and* you are not in employment or gainful self-employment; *or*
- PC (guarantee or savings credit); *or*
- IS, income-based JSA, or income-related ESA, but only if:
  - you are responsible for a child under five; *or*
  - you are also getting CTC which includes a disabled child element; *or*
  - your applicable amount includes a disability, severe disability, enhanced disability, disabled child, pensioner or higher pensioner premium; *or*
  - you get income-related ESA and have been assessed as having, or are treated as having, limited capability for work or limited capability for work and work-related activity.

Payments are made in February or March, usually to the same account into which your qualifying benefit benefit is paid. Payment is not affected by any other income or savings you have. Normally, you do not have to apply: payment should be made automatically. If you think you are eligible but have not received a payment, contact SSS.

If you are not happy with a decision about winter heating payments, you can ask within 42 days for the decision to be looked at again. This is called a 'redetermination'. You can make the request later than this, if you have good reason. SSS should carry out a redetermination within 16 working days. Following redetermination, you have a right of appeal.

Child winter heating payment

Child winter heating payment is an annual payment from SSS to families in Scotland with a severely disabled child. In winter 2024/25, it is £251.50.[13] To qualify, your family must include a child aged under 19 who is entitled to an eligible disability benefit (the highest rate of the care component of disability living allowance/child disability payment or the enhanced rate of the daily living component of personal independence payment/adult disability payment) on at least one day in the 'qualifying week'.[14] This is the week beginning on the third Monday in September. If your child is awarded a disability benefit later than this date but their award is later backdated to cover it, child winter heating assistance is payable.[15]

Your child must usually live in Scotland, but may also be eligible if they live in Switzerland or certain EEA countries.[16]

Payments are made in November, usually to the same account into which the disability benefit is paid. Payment is not affected by any other income or savings the child or anyone else in the family has. You can get a payment for each severely disabled child in your family who meets the qualifying conditions. Usually, you do not have to apply: payment should be made automatically. If you think you are eligible but have not received a payment by mid-December, contact SSS.

If you are not happy with a decision about child winter heating payment, you can ask within 42 days for the decision to be looked at again. This is called a 'redetermination'. You can make the request later than this, if you have good reason. SSS should carry out a redetermination within 16 working days. Following redetermination, you have a right of appeal.

4. Help with fuel-related housing costs and service charges

Universal credit housing costs element and fuel costs

Universal credit (UC) can include a housing costs element. This generally means help with rent, but it can also cover certain service charges.[17]

If you live in the social-rented sector (eg, local authority or housing association) or you are an owner-occupier, your UC can include help with service charges if payment of the charge is a condition of your right to occupy your home, and the charge is for certain types of specified service. This includes fuel costs for communal areas, but not fuel costs relating to your own home.[18]

If you live in the private-rented sector, service charges for fuel costs can be included in your housing costs element, but the total help you can get towards your rent and service charges is restricted by the local housing allowance, based on the market rents in your area.[19]

Housing benefit and fuel costs

Housing benefit (HB) is a means-tested benefit to help low-income households with rent payments. You may be able to get HB whether you are in work or out of work. For most people, HB is being replaced by UC, but you can still make a new claim for HB when you live in certain kinds of housing – eg, supported accommodation.[20]

HB does not assist with most fuel costs that you pay with your rent. However, the following charges may be met by HB.
- Service charges for communal areas, as long as they are separately identified from any other charge for fuel used within your accommodation.[21] Communal areas include access areas – eg, halls, stairways and passageways.[22] In sheltered accommodation only, rooms in common use (eg, a TV room or dining room) can also be included.[23]
- Charges for the provision of a heating system (eg, for boiler maintenance), if they are separately identified from any other fuel charge.[24]

How fuel charges are calculated

With the exception of those charges listed above, HB does not cover fuel charges which are included in your rent – eg, heating, hot water, lighting and cooking. If you have this kind of fuel charge included in your rent and the amount of your fuel charge can be identified (eg, in your rent agreement, rent book or letter from your landlord), the amount specified is deducted from the total amount of your rent before your HB is calculated.[25] As a result, HB may not cover the full accommodation charges that you are contractually expected to meet. For example, if your rent is £70 a week and your rent agreement states that this includes £15 for heating, £55 would be counted as rent in assessing your entitlement to HB.

If the local authority considers that the amount you pay for fuel is unrealistically low compared with the cost of the fuel provided, or if this charge contains an unknown amount for communal areas, it may instead apply a flat-rate deduction (see below). This does not apply if you are a council tenant as the regulations assume that your fuel charges are as specified in your tenancy agreement.[26]

A flat-rate deduction is also made if the amount of fuel charges is not specifically identified as part of your rent.[27]

Flat-rate deductions from housing benefit

Fuel deductions – weekly deductions for ineligible fuel charges

If you and your family occupy more than one room:

	2024/25
Heating	£35.25
Hot water	£4.10
Lighting	£2.85
Cooking	£4.10
Total	**£46.30**

If you and your family occupy one room only:

Heating alone, or heating with either hot water or lighting or both	£21.10
Cooking	£4.10

If fuel is supplied for more than one purpose, the appropriate charges are added together. If you are a joint tenant, the deductions are shared between you, usually according to your share of the rent.[28]

The local authority must notify you if it has used flat-rate deductions in calculating your entitlement to benefit. It must also explain that these can be varied if you can produce evidence of the actual or approximate fuel charge.[29] The flat-rate deductions can be varied accordingly. The *Housing Benefit Guidance*

Manual used by local authorities says that the lower rate applies if you occupy one room, even if you share a kitchen or bathroom.[30] Argue for the lower rate deduction if you are forced to occupy one room due to disrepair, damp or mould growth in your home.

Discretionary housing payments

Your local authority can make a discretionary housing payment (DHP) if you are entitled to HB or the housing costs element of UC (for rent) and you require additional help to meet your housing costs. You must show why your benefit does not cover your full rent – eg, because you are affected by benefit cap or the bedroom tax. In Scotland, the Scottish government funds DHPs to fully mitigate the bedroom tax and benefit cap, so if you apply to your local authority for a DHP for a loss of benefit due to the bedroom tax or benefit cap, you should receive one.[31]

You must usually complete an application form. DHPs are discretionary, so there are no rules about whether or how much you will be paid. You cannot apply for a DHP specifically to cover charges which are excluded from HB or the housing costs element of UC – eg, most fuel charges.

There is no right of appeal against a DHP decision, but you can ask the local authority to review its decision. If a local authority acts unreasonably regarding making a decision, it can be subject to judicial review or you can make a complaint to the Local Government Ombudsman.

Support for mortgage interest loans

You can apply for a secured loan from the DWP to help you to pay your mortgage interest or the interest on a loan for certain repairs and home improvements. You usually need to be getting UC, pension credit, income support, income-based jobseeker's allowance or income-related employment and support allowance. You should get advice before accepting a loan.

---

5. Impact of charitable payments on benefits

Charities sometimes step in to help with fuel or reconnection costs, particularly when vulnerable people have been disconnected. Citizens Advice and other advice agencies can help with applications for charitable payments.

Most charitable or voluntary payments which are paid regularly are disregarded as income for means-tested benefits. A one-off or occasional payment may count as capital but is very unlikely to affect benefit entitlement unless it takes your capital above the limit for the benefit you are on.

For detailed information about the effect on benefits of regular and irregular payments for fuel, and the treatment of payments as income or capital, see CPAG's *Welfare Benefits and Tax Credits Handbook*.

6. Local welfare assistance schemes

Some local authorities in England and the devolved administrations in Scotland and Wales have local welfare assistance schemes. These schemes may be able to help you with fuel-related costs such as connection and installation charges, draught-proofing and heaters. To find out about the scheme where you live, contact your local authority or local advice agency.

7. Budgeting advances and budgeting loans

Universal credit budgeting advances

Budgeting advances of universal credit (UC) are extra amounts of UC to help you with certain expenses – eg, buying essential household items, or paying for necessary home maintenance. Budgeting advances must be repaid, usually by deductions from future UC payments. The minimum amount of advance is £100. The maximum is £348 if you are single and not responsible for a child, £464 if you are a couple and not responsible for a child or £812 if you are responsible for a child (whether you are single or in a couple).

You can ask for a budgeting advance for whatever you need, but if you are refused you cannot appeal. To qualify:[32]
- you must usually have been getting UC (or a 'legacy benefit' – see p180) for at least six months; *and*
- your earnings from work must be below a specified level (£2,600 in the previous six months if you are single, or £3,600 if you are in a couple); *and*
- your savings must be below a specified level (£1,000 plus the maximum amount of advance you are entitled to); *and*
- you must not have any outstanding budgeting advance still to repay; *and*
- the DWP must be satisfied that you can repay an advance.

Social fund budgeting loans

A budgeting loan is the equivalent of a budgeting advance for people who claim means-tested benefits other than UC. The loan is repayable, usually by deduction from ongoing benefit entitlement. The minimum amount of a loan is £100. The maximum is £348 if you are single, £464 if you are a couple and £812 if you or your partner claim child benefit. If you have other social fund debts, your total debt cannot exceed £1,500.

You may get a budgeting loan if:[33]
- you are getting pension credit, income support, income-based jobseeker's allowance or income-related employment and support allowance, and have been getting one of these benefits for the past 26 weeks (disregarding one or more breaks of 28 days or less);
- you are not involved in a trade dispute; *and*
- you do not have too much capital (the limit is £1,000, or £2,000 if you or your partner are aged 63 or over).

The budgeting loan must be for one or more of the following:
- furniture and household equipment;
- clothing and footwear;
- maternity expenses;
- funeral expenses;
- rent in advance and/or removal expenses;
- improvement, maintenance and security of the home;
- travelling expenses;
- expenses associated with seeking or re-entering work;
- hire purchase and other debts for any of the above items.

8. Fuel Direct

The Fuel Direct scheme allows an amount to be deducted from your benefit entitlement and paid directly to your energy supplier to cover your ongoing energy costs and/or your energy arrears. Fuel Direct is also known as part of the DWP 'third party deduction system'.

To be on the Fuel Direct scheme you must be in debt for mains gas or mains electricity and get universal credit (UC), pension credit (PC), income support (IS), income-based jobseeker's allowance (JSA) or income-related employment and support allowance (ESA). Deductions can be made from contribution-based JSA or contributory ESA if you have an 'underlying entitlement' to the means-tested version of the benefit – ie, where, if you were not receiving the contribution-based type of benefit, you would instead be getting the means-tested type at the same rate.[34]

Note: the DWP can only make Fuel Direct payments for ongoing energy costs when your energy supplier applies for them and you consent to the deductions being made.[35] However, it can make Fuel Direct payments for energy arrears with or without your consent.

Deductions

If you get universal credit

Deductions can be made from UC for an energy debt and (where appropriate) to pay for your ongoing consumption of mains gas and electricity.[36] Where you are working or self-employed, earning over a certain level and getting UC, you are not able to have a deduction for fuel debt made from UC.[37]

The monthly amount that can be deducted from UC for a fuel debt depends on your age and on whether you are single or a couple.

Monthly deductions for fuel debts

	2024/25
Single, under 25	£15.58
Single, 25 or over	£19.67
Couple, both aged under 25	£24.46
Couple, one or both aged 25 or over	£30.88

These amounts are based on 5 per cent of the standard allowance for your circumstances.

In addition, an amount can be deducted for ongoing energy costs, unless this is not required – eg, if you already have a prepayment meter. If a deduction is made for ongoing energy costs as well as fuel debt, the maximum amount that can be deducted for both the energy debt and ongoing consumption is 25 per cent of the total of your standard allowance and any child elements you receive, unless you give your consent to a higher deduction being made.[38]

Deductions from UC for ongoing energy costs cannot continue once the energy debt is cleared.[39]

Deductions can be made from UC for other debts, such as rent arrears, housing costs and water charges. A maximum of three deductions can be made at any time.[40]

If you get pension credit, income support, income-based jobseeker's allowance or income-related employment and support allowance

Deductions can be made from your benefit if:[41]

- your arrears for gas or electricity are greater than £90.50 (in 2024/25); *and*
- you continue to need a fuel supply; *and*
- it is in your best interests, or those of your family, for direct payments to be made.

Deductions are normally refused if:

- the above do not apply; *or*
- your supplier does not agree to you paying this way; *or*

- you have a prepayment meter which has been reset to collect arrears. (If your prepayment meter is for current consumption only, however, you could still have any arrears paid by Fuel Direct.)

Deductions can be made to cover arrears, or just to cover weekly costs after the debt has been cleared, or both.[42]

- **For arrears.**
  - The maximum statutory deduction that can be made for electricity or gas is £4.55 for each fuel debt in 2024/25.
  - There is a maximum combined deduction of £9.10 for gas and electricity arrears.[43]
- **For ongoing energy charges.**
  - Your supplier gives the DWP an estimate of your weekly consumption. This is usually calculated by looking at your consumption over the past year. If the amounts suggested seem high, ask for an explanation – errors are not uncommon. Check that your supplier is relying on real meter readings in reaching its estimates.
  - The final decision on the amounts deducted rests with the DWP decision maker, who is not bound to accept the supplier's estimates.[44]
  - The maximum deduction that can usually be made is 25 per cent of your PC 'minimum guarantee' or IS, JSA or ESA 'applicable amount'. If you get child tax credit (CTC), this calculation is 25 per cent of the total of your CTC, child benefit and PC minimum guarantee or IS/JSA/ESA applicable amount combined (before housing costs are included). This includes the combined amount of the deductions for arrears and current consumption.[45]

Other debts can also be paid by direct deductions from benefit, and payment of these may be in competition with payments for fuel. The number of deductions for arrears is limited to a maximum of three and a priority order applies. If you have both gas and electricity arrears, the DWP decides which debt takes priority.

How to arrange Fuel Direct

Contact the DWP and your supplier if you want to pay by Fuel Direct. The decision to include you in the Fuel Direct scheme is made by the DWP. The DWP then contacts your supplier to check that it agrees to your paying in this way and gets the figure to pay for your current consumption.

Before agreeing to deductions, check that you are the person liable for the bill (see Chapter 5).

If disconnection is being threatened, let your supplier know that you are arranging or want them to arrange Fuel Direct. Suppliers normally delay disconnection for a limited period if they know you are trying to do this.[46] Continue to stay in regular contact with your supplier, informing it about the progress of your application. Take the name and extension number of the person arranging Fuel Direct for you and always keep a note of when you called. It helps if you keep copies of letters/forms in the event of difficulties. If there are any delays, the supplier can be asked to delay disconnection for a longer period. Check with the DWP that your application has been received and is being dealt with. If disconnection is imminent, ask the DWP to phone the supplier to confirm that Fuel Direct is being arranged and that written confirmation will follow.

Deductions are made by the DWP before you receive your benefit. If you disagree with a decision about deductions, you may be able to appeal.

Challenging the deduction amount for ongoing energy use

If you disagree with the amounts proposed by the supplier, ask the DWP for a different deduction. You must provide information about the assumptions in your own calculation. You will need to conduct your negotiations with care to ensure that the DWP or the supplier does not assume that you are refusing to join the Fuel Direct scheme, as this could ultimately lead either to disconnection or to the imposition of a prepayment meter. If the DWP does not agree to accept your calculations, you could always accept the supplier's calculation to ensure entry to the scheme, and then challenge the decision.

Do you want to change the amount of the deduction?
The deduction for arrears is a fixed amount and cannot be varied. However, the figure for your current consumption is not fixed and is usually reviewed regularly. It is important to ensure that deductions are based on an actual reading of your meter. If the supplier bases its calculations on estimated readings, the amount of your deductions is likely to be wrong. Ask the DWP to review the amount of deduction if you think the amount is too much or not enough.[47] The DWP can ask the supplier to provide its calculation.

You may wish to request a review if you can provide evidence that your actual consumption is likely to be different. You may want to do this if:
– a meter reading shows that the supplier's calculation is based on wrong information;
– your consumption has increased or decreased because of a change in your circumstances (eg, the birth of a baby, a child leaving home, working from home), a change in a heating system, energy efficiency improvements (eg, insulation, double glazing, draught proofing), or changes to how you use fuel as a result of energy advice.

You can request a review at any time a relevant change occurs. It is sensible to get the supplier's agreement to this first.

Change of circumstances

You have a duty to advise the DWP of any changes in your circumstances. This is a normal requirement for benefit awards, but is particularly important with respect to changes in energy supplier in you have a Fuel Direct arrangement. If you switch your gas or electricity supplier, you must immediately notify the DWP.

Sanctions

Benefit sanctions may affect the operation of Fuel Direct, reducing the amount of money from which it is possible to make a deduction. Benefit sanctions can be appealed, so seek advice if you are sanctioned.

Notes

3. Cold weather payments, winter fuel payments and Scottish heating payments
1   Reg 1(2) SFCWP Regs
2   Reg 2(1) and (2) SFCWP Regs
3   Reg 1A(2) and (3) SFCWP Regs
4   Reg 3 SFCWP Regs
5   Reg 2(6) SFCWP Regs
6   Reg 2 SFWFP Regs
7   Regs 2 and 3 SFWFP Regs
8   Reg 5 SFWFP Regs
9   Reg 4(1)(c) SFWFP Regs
10 Reg 9(1) WHA(LI)(S) Regs
11 s30 and Sch 4 SS(S)A 2018; regs 2 and 4 WHA(LI)(S) Regs
12 Reg 4 WHA(LI)(S) Regs
13 Reg 10 WHACYP(S) Regs
14 Reg 4 WHACYP(S) Regs
15 Reg 8 WHACYP(S) Regs
16 Reg 4(1)(c) WHACYP(S) Regs

4. Help with fuel-related housing costs and service charges
17 Reg 25(2)(c) and Sch 1 para 7(1), (2) and (4) UC Regs
18 Sch 1 para 8 UC Regs
19 Sch 4 para 3(3) UC Regs
20 Reg 2(1) and 6A(2) UC(TP) Regs; Sch 1 paras 3A and 3B UC Regs
21 Sch 1 paras 5 and 6(1)(b) HB Regs; Sch 1 paras 5 and 6(1)(b) HB(SPC) Regs
22 Sch 1 para 8 HB Regs; Sch 1 para 8 HB(SPC) Regs
23 Sch 1 para 8 HB Regs; Sch 1 para 8 HB(SPC) Regs
24 Sch 1 para 8 HB Regs; Sch 1 para 8 HB(SPC) Regs
25 Sch 1 para 6(1) HB Regs; Sch 1 para 6(1) HB(SPC) Regs
26 Sch 1 para 6(1)(a) HB Regs; Sch 1 para 6(1)(a) HB(SPC) Regs
27 Sch 1 para 6(2) HB Regs; Sch 1 para 6(2) HB(SPC) Regs

28 Reg 12B(4) HB Regs; reg 12B(4) HB(SPC) Regs
29 Sch 1 para 6(4) HB Regs; Sch 1 para 6(4) HB(SPC) Regs
30 para A4 4.912-4 HBGM
31 Scottish Discretionary Housing Payment: Guidance Manual, paras 2.3, 5 and 6

7. Budgeting advances and budgeting loans
32 Regs 12-15 The Social Security (Payments on Account of Benefit) Regulations 2013 No.383
33 Social Fund Directive

8. Fuel Direct
34 Sch 9 para 1(2) and (3) SS(C&P) Regs
35 Sch 9 para 6(2)-(3A), SS(C&P) Regs; Sch 6 para 8(4)-(4A) UC,PIP,JSA&ESA(C&P) Regs; regs 2 and 3 The Social Security Benefits (Claims and Payments) (Amendment) Regulations 2023 No.232
36 Sch 6 para 8 UC,PIP,JSA&ESA(C&P) Regs
37 Sch 6 para 8(5) and (6) UC,PIP,JSA&ESA(C&P) Regs
38 Sch 6 para 3(3) UC,PIP,JSA&ESA(C&P) Regs
39 Sch 6 para 8(2) UC,PIP,JSA&ESA(C&P) Regs
40 Sch 6 para 3(1)(b) UC,PIP,JSA&ESA(C&P) Regs
41 Sch 9 para 6(1) SS(C&P) Regs
42 Sch 9 para 6(4) SS(C&P) Regs
43 Sch 9 paras 1(1) and 6(2) SS(C&P) Regs
44 Sch 9 para 6(4) SS(C&P) Regs
45 Sch 9 para 8 SS(C&P) Regs
46 See supplier's code of practice for customers who need help with paying their bills
47 Sch 9 para 6(4) SS(C&P) Regs

Chapter 12

. . . .

Energy efficiency and other sources of help

This chapter covers:

1. National energy efficiency schemes

Energy efficiency is part of the UK and devolved governments' national energy strategies, which have the shared goals of reducing harmful emissions into the environment and tackling fuel poverty. It is widely accepted that the main cause of fuel poverty in the UK is a combination of low household incomes, high fuel costs and poor energy efficiency. In Scotland, a fourth driver of fuel poverty is recognised: how energy is used in the home, where a lack of knowledge on reducing consumption safely contributes to people's fuel poverty.[1]

Often people cannot afford to adequately heat their homes because they are not sufficiently insulated or in a poor state of repair, or because expensive or inefficient appliances are being used. Substantial savings in fuel bills can be achieved by introducing energy efficiency measures and adopting more energy-efficient behaviours.

Successive governments have acknowledged that energy efficiency should play a central role in improving living conditions for the fuel poor in the UK. Fuel poverty is a devolved matter, with separate definitions, targets and strategies adopted by each nation.

An official overall UK figure for fuel poverty is no longer measured. However, fuel poverty charities estimate that fuel poverty currently affects over 6 million households.[2]

There are now several officially accepted ways to define and measure fuel poverty in the UK. According to the original definition, a household is fuel poor if over 10 per cent of its disposable income is spent on fuel. This definition has been retained in Wales and Northern Ireland. England uses the 'low income high costs' indicator to measure fuel poverty. This is a relative measure of fuel poverty, which also measures the 'fuel poverty gap' – the reduction in required spending for a household not to be considered fuel poor. In Scotland, a household is in fuel poverty if its fuel costs (necessary to meet the requisite temperature and number of hours as well as other reasonable fuel needs) are more than 10 per cent of the household's adjusted net income and, after deducting these fuel costs, benefits received for a care need or disability and childcare costs, the household's remaining income is not enough to maintain an acceptable standard of living.[3]

This chapter looks at what help and support is available, how to access it and who is eligible. See also Chapter 13 for information on how you can exercise your rights against low-standard properties.

Energy Company Obligation

The Energy Company Obligation (ECO) is a UK government energy efficiency scheme, overseen by Ofgem, designed to help reduce carbon emissions and tackle fuel poverty by placing legal obligations on larger energy suppliers to deliver energy efficiency measures to domestic premises. ECO is distributed via a grant and is paid for by a levy on all domestic electricity bills.

ECO4 commenced on 1 April 2022 and will run until 31 March 2026. Through targeted support, it aims to reduce the number of supported households by focusing on the lowest-income households in the worst-quality properties. ECO4 is being delivered consistently across Great Britain.

Home Heating Cost Reduction Obligation

This is the sole focus of ECO4 and is also known as the Affordable Warmth Obligation. It provides free heating and hot water saving measures (eg, electric storage heaters), insulation (eg, cavity wall insulation), glazing and some micro-generation technologies to low-income and vulnerable households. It delivers this support through a whole house approach to maximise the energy efficiency and clean heat improvements to a property.

If you live in **social housing**, you might be eligible for help with insulation or installing a heating system if your home has an energy efficiency rating of E, F or G. Contact your local council to find out if it is taking part in the scheme.

You are eligible if you are an **owner-occupier or live in a private rented property** (although you will need the landlord's permission) and a member of your household gets a qualifying benefit. At the time of writing, this included the following benefits (check gov.uk/energy-company-obligation for the latest information):[4]

- child benefit;
- universal credit;
- pension credit (guarantee credit or savings credit);
- income-related employment and support allowance;
- income-based jobseeker's allowance;
- income support;
- tax credits (child tax credit and working tax credit);
- housing benefit.

If you own your home, it must have an energy efficiency rating of D, E, F or G. If you rent from a private landlord, the property must have an energy efficiency rating of E, F or G.

LA Flex

LA Flex utilises local authorities' localised and communal knowledge to target residents who may benefit from ECO4, but are not captured within the scheme's standard eligibility criteria (see above).[5] LA Flex can help if you are a 'fuel poor' owner-occupier or private tenant, are not in receipt of eligible benefits and are vulnerable to the effects of living in a cold home.[6] In addition, some non-fuel-poor homes are eligible for solid wall insulation projects, as long as a proportion of the households in the project are in fuel poverty or living in the cold.

Local authorities set their own criteria to determine which households are supported. Funding is only available to owner-occupiers and private rented sector tenants. If a local authority decides to participate in the scheme, it must publish a statement of intent on its website.

Great British Insulation Scheme

The Great British Insulation Scheme is a UK government energy efficiency scheme (formerly referred to as ECO+). It is overseen by Ofgem and is designed to deliver improvements to the least energy-efficient homes in Great Britain to tackle fuel poverty and help reduce energy bills. Eligible activity commenced on 1 April 2023 and is intended to run until March 2026. The scheme obliges medium and large energy companies to deliver measures that result in reduced energy usage.

The scheme complements ECO4. Yet unlike ECO4's 'whole house' approach, this scheme mostly delivers single insulation measures.

As well as supporting low-income and vulnerable households, it is also available to those living in homes with an energy performance rating of D, E, F or G, and within council tax bands A–D in England and A–E in Scotland and Wales. Check your Energy Performance Certificate at gov.uk/find-energy-certificate.

Renewable Heat Incentive

The Renewable Heat Incentive (RHI) is a payment for people living in England, Wales or Scotland for generating heat from renewable sources. RHI payments are partly intended to offset the cost of installing and running a renewable system. Instalment payments are made quarterly for seven years. The scheme closed to new applicants on 31 March 2022.

Households are paid for every kilowatt hour (kWh) of energy produced. The level of payment varies depending on the technology and the system size.

The eligible technologies (only specific makes and models[7]) are:
- biomass (wood burning) boilers and biomass pellet stoves;
- air source heat pumps;
- ground source heat pumps;
- solar thermal panels.

Feed-in tariffs

Under this scheme, energy suppliers must make regular payments to householders and communities in Great Britain who generate their own electricity from renewable or low-carbon sources such as solar panels or wind turbines. The scheme closed to new applicants on 1 April 2019.[8]

The tariffs are paid for every kWh of electricity you generate using a renewable electricity system. They apply to households, landlords and businesses. Tariffs can change as often as every three months. Comprehensive tables showing rate changes are available from Ofgem.[9]

Feed-in tariffs (FITs) provide three benefits.
- You get a payment for electricity produced, even if you use it yourself. Tariffs are paid for up to 20 years and vary depending on the type and scale of the installation. FITs payments are exempt from income tax. The eligibility period starts on the eligibility date and lasts for:
  - solar photovoltaic (PV) – 20 years (25 years for those with an eligibility date before 1 August 2012);
  - wind – 20 years;
  - hydro – 20 years;
  - anaerobic digestion – 20 years;
  - micro-combined heat and power (micro-CHP) – 10 years.
- You get additional payments for electricity exported to the grid.
- Your electricity bills are reduced as you use energy produced by the renewable technology.

Where ownership of a property changes, ownership of the generating technology also changes, and the FITs payments transfer to the new occupier.

Smart Export Guarantee

On 1 April 2020, the government introduced a replacement for FITs. The Smart Export Guarantee (SEG) requires some electricity suppliers (SEG licensees) to pay small-scale generators (SEG generators) for low-carbon electricity which they export back to the national grid, providing certain criteria are met.

If you have one of the following measures, you could benefit from the SEG (provided you meet the rest of the eligibility criteria) up to a capacity of 5MW, or up to 50kW for micro-CHP:

- solar PV;
- wind;
- micro-CHP;
- hydro;
- anaerobic digestion.

The rate you are paid, the contract length and other terms are determined by the SEG licensee. If you are thinking of applying for a SEG tariff, you should shop around to see which tariff is best for your circumstances.

You are paid by your licensee for the electricity you export back to the national grid. SEG tariff rates must always be above zero. SEG payments are calculated by using export meter readings.

Help with gas connections

The government has set obligations on the eight gas distribution networks (GDNs) in Great Britain to deliver assistance to their consumers. The current obligation (known as RIIO-GD2) runs from 2021 to 2026 and is monitored by Ofgem.

As part of this obligation, the Fuel Poor Network Extension Scheme enables customers who are in fuel poverty to switch to natural gas by helping towards the cost of connection to the gas network.

Each GDN covers a separate geographical region. They are owned and managed by the following companies. Contact them to find out what support is offered in your area:

- Cadent Gas Ltd – West Midlands, the North West, East of England, South Yorkshire and North London;
- Northern Gas Networks Limited – the North East (including North, West and East Yorkshire and Northern Cumbria);
- Wales and West Utilities Limited – Wales and the South West;
- SGN – Scotland and Southern England (including South London).

Advice and assistance from suppliers

Providing guidance on energy efficiency for customers is a licence condition for gas and electricity suppliers.[10] Each supplier must produce a code of practice on using energy efficiently. It should be published on the supplier's website, or you can request a copy by telephone.

Suppliers have trained staff offering advice on ways to save energy and cut your energy bills. In some areas, they can also arrange for an adviser to visit your home and recommend ways of saving energy and money.

You may also be sent booklets on energy efficiency, including details of grants and the supplier's own schemes. Ofgem monitors the energy efficiency activities of the 'big six' energy companies.

Many suppliers also have funds, foundations and trusts that can provide a range of support and assistance, particularly to vulnerable customers (see p208).

2. Energy efficiency schemes in England

Home Upgrade Grant scheme

The Home Upgrade Grant scheme (HUG) aims to upgrade the energy efficiency of properties off the gas network in England. It intends to enable the installation of multiple measures in these homes to substantially improve performance. The policy intent is to improve off-gas grid homes up through the energy efficiency scale. As a minimum, energy performance ratings of F or G should be upgraded to D or above and band D or E homes to C or above.

To be eligible for HUG, you must own and live in the property, not use a gas boiler as your home's main heating system and have an energy performance rating of D, E, F or G. You usually must have a household income of £36,000 a year or less. You might still be eligible if you earn more than that in some postcode areas.

Your local authority will survey your home and suggest ways to make it more energy efficient. It will organise and pay for any improvement work it agrees with you.

Check if you are eligible and apply at gov.uk/apply-home-upgrade-grant.

3. Energy efficiency schemes in Wales

The Welsh government's Warm Homes scheme, which includes Nest and Arbed, provides funding for energy efficiency improvements to low-income households.

Nest

All households in Wales can access the Nest scheme for advice on fuel tariffs and saving energy and for a benefit entitlement check.

Those living in the hardest-to-heat private sector properties and who get a means-tested benefit can apply for free home improvements such as a new boiler, central heating system, hot water cylinder insulation or renewable energy technologies – eg, solar panels.

To qualify for Nest home improvements, the property must:
- be your own home, privately rented or shared-ownership – if you rent, you must have the landlord's permission (those who rent from a local authority or a housing association are not eligible);
- have an energy performance certificate (EPC) ratings of E, F or G.

You or someone who lives with you must get one of the following:[11]
- universal credit;
- pension credit;
- housing benefit;
- council tax reduction (discretionary reductions and discounts do not qualify on their own);
- income-based jobseeker's allowance;
- income-related employment and support allowance;
- income support;
- child tax credit and your annual income is below £18,660;
- working tax credit and your income is below £18,660.

If you do not meet the criteria, Nest may be able to refer you to alternative schemes. To apply or to get advice, call freephone 0808 808 2244.

Arbed

Arbed is an area-based scheme to retrofit homes with energy efficiency measures and renewable technologies. It includes measures such as new energy-efficient boilers, insulation improvements, solar panels and energy-saving advice.

4. Energy efficiency schemes in Scotland

Home Energy Scotland is a 'one-stop shop' for energy efficiency and advice in Scotland. It is funded by the Scottish government and delivered by the Energy Saving Trust (EST). The service can help you access grants and offers an energy advice service. All households in Scotland can get a home energy check by calling 0808 808 2282.

Home Energy Scotland referral portal

Home Energy Scotland can take referrals from advisers of householders who may be able to benefit from advice and support. Householders can contact Home Energy Scotland on 0808 808 2282 or, with their permission, advisers can refer them through the Home Energy Scotland referral portal. Advisers can refer a householder who answers yes to any of the following questions.
- Do you find your home hard to heat?

- Do you worry about your fuel bills?
- Would you like advice and support to make your home warmer and reduce your fuel bills?

The online portal (hespartnerships.est.org.uk) is secure and works in real time. Once advice has been given to the householder, and referrals made to any of the schemes and partner organisations to help with energy saving or income maximisation, the portal reports the outcomes to the adviser.

For more information, or to register as a portal user, contact your local Home Energy Scotland community liaison officer.

Home Energy Efficiency Programmes for Scotland

The Home Energy Efficiency Programmes for Scotland (HEEPS) is the Scottish government initiative to tackle fuel poverty. It is a cluster of programmes currently including:

- area-based schemes, managed by local authorities (see below);
- Warmer Homes Scotland, managed by Warmworks Scotland (see below);
- a grant and loans scheme, managed by EST, the lead contractor for Home Energy Scotland (see p204).

For all HEEPS schemes, you initially need to call Home Energy Scotland on 0808 808 2282 or via homeenergyscotland.org.

Area-based schemes

HEEPS area-based schemes provide energy efficiency measures in deprived areas. Local authorities choose which areas are eligible and what measures are available. Whether you qualify depends on your postcode. You may qualify whether you own or rent your home.

Warmer Homes Scotland

Warmer Homes Scotland aims to help low-income and vulnerable homeowners and private sector tenants improve the energy efficiency of their homes. Measures available include improvements in central heating systems, insulation improvements, draught proofing and installation of renewable technologies.

If you are a private tenant and your landlord has statutory duties under the statutory Repairing Standard (see p229), you cannot receive measures that your landlord is legally obliged to provide. You are still eligible for other measures available under the scheme if they are recommended for the property – eg, renewables.

To be eligible:

- you must be the homeowner or a private tenant and live in the property as your main residence and have lived there for at least six months (unless you have a BASRiS certificate); *and*

- the property must have an energy rating of 64 or lower and must not be more than 230 square metres in floor size; *and*
- the property must meet the tolerable living standard (see p216) set out in the Housing (Scotland) Act 2006. If it does not, this must not impact on the effectiveness of the measures recommended for installation under the scheme; *and*
- you must not have received support for energy efficiency measures through Warmer Homes Scotland or HEEPS in the last five years.

At least one of the following must also apply:[12]
- you (or a member of your household or your partner) are aged 60 or over and have no working heating system and get a qualifying benefit (also known as a 'passport' benefit – see below);
- you are aged over 75 and get a qualifying benefit;
- you are pregnant or have a child under 16 and get a qualifying benefit;
- you get:
  - personal independence payment (PIP) or adult disability payment (ADP) at any rate; *or*
  - disability living allowance (DLA) or child disability payment (CDP) (care or mobility component) at the highest rate; *or*
  - DLA (care or mobility component) at the lowest/middle rate *and* be in receipt of an income-related benefit;
- you get carer's allowance (CA) or carer support payment (CSP);
- you get armed forces independence payment (AFIP) or war disablement pension;
- you get industrial injuries disablement benefit.

Qualifying benefits

The qualifying benefits for the Warmer Homes Scotland scheme are:
– AFIP;
– attendance allowance;
– CA/CSP;
– council tax reduction;
– DLA/CDP (care or mobility component) at the highest rate or PIP/ADP;
– industrial injuries disablement benefit;
– pension credit guarantee credit;
– universal credit (UC) or a benefit UC is replacing – ie, income support, income-based jobseeker's allowance, income-related employment and support allowance, housing benefit, child tax credit or working tax credit;
– war disablement pension.

To make an application, call Home Energy Scotland on 0808 808 2282 or use the contact form available at homeenergyscotland.org/find-funding-grants-and-loans/warmer-homes-scotland.

Home Energy Scotland grants and loans

The Scottish government introduced grants for the installation of energy efficiency measures and low-carbon heating solutions. You could get grants up to £15,000: up to £7,500 for energy efficiency improvements (eg, insulation) and up to £7,500 for low-carbon heating systems (eg, air source heat pumps). If you live in a rural area, you can get up to an extra £1,500 for energy efficiency improvements and up to £1,500 extra for heating systems.

Interest-free loans are also available under HEEPS for owner-occupiers and private sector landlords to improve their properties. The loans can be used to provide gap funding for measures for households or to support private sector landlords to take forward improvements.

To start an application, call Home Energy Scotland on 0808 808 2282. Once completed, submit your application to the Energy Saving Trust with your chosen quote. You are strongly advised to seek at least three quotes, particularly if you are considering installing more expensive measures.

Your eligibility is assessed, including undertaking credit and affordability checks. If you are successful, you are offered a grant/loan. Work cannot start until you have received a written loan offer. There is an administrative fee of 1.5 per cent of the total loan value up to a maximum of £150 per application.

5. Help from the local authority

Home improvement assistance

Local authorities have discretionary powers to improve living conditions in their areas. You may be able to get a grant or discount to help you improve the energy efficiency of your home. 'Home' means a property, part of a property, boat or caravan that you live in. Your eligibility depends on what is available from your local authority, and in many areas you must be receiving a means-tested benefit. The local authority must publish details of what is available, who is eligible, how to apply and how to complain.

In Wales, the 'Houses into Homes' scheme can provide an interest-free loan to enable an empty property to be made fit to sell or to let. Individuals, charities, companies and businesses can apply. Ask your local authority for its information pack.

Local authorities in Scotland have similar discretionary powers, under the Scheme of Assistance. The scheme also aims to encourage homeowners to take more responsibility for the condition of their homes, to ensure that private housing in Scotland is kept in a decent state of repair.[13] Contact your local authority to apply for the scheme.

See also p226 on local councils' powers in England and Wales to protect occupiers and tenants when an owner or landlord fails to pay fuel or water bills.

Help from social services

Local authorities have duties to provide services to safeguard and promote the welfare of children in need and promote the upbringing of such children by their families.[14] This could include negotiating with a supplier on your behalf.

In exceptional circumstances, this can also include providing assistance in cash; a policy not to provide such assistance in any circumstances at all would almost certainly be unlawful, and could be challenged by judicial review (see Chapter 14). If such payments are available, you can argue that they can be used to meet all or part of a fuel bill, to buy alternative means of cooking or heating, or to provide other aids for keeping warm, such as blankets.

In Scotland, there are also powers to promote social welfare by 'making available advice, guidance and assistance' to people in need aged 18 or over.[15] This can include giving assistance in kind or, in exceptional circumstances, in cash, where giving assistance would avoid you needing greater assistance from the local authority at a future date.

If you are seeking help from social services in an emergency (eg, because the supplier is threatening disconnection), inform your supplier. Suppliers' codes of practice allow for a delay in disconnection, normally for about two weeks, while a local authority investigates whether it can help. This delay will only happen if you ensure the supplier knows of the council's involvement.

Social workers may also have good links with and/or be prepared to make referrals to charities for you.

Local welfare assistance schemes

Each local authority in England and the devolved administrations in Scotland and Wales have local welfare assistance schemes. The schemes can help you if you are in urgent need following an emergency or unforeseen event and have no other source of help. The schemes are run by local councils and they vary. You may be able to get vouchers to pay for fuel or basic living items such as heaters and fridges.

In England, the local scheme is at your local authority's discretion. Check with your local authority to find out what help is available, whether you qualify and how to apply.

In Wales, the Discretionary Assistance Fund offers non-repayable emergency assistance payments and individual assistance payments.

The Scottish Welfare Fund provides community care grants and crisis grants. The basic rules for the scheme are set by the Scottish government, with each local authority having some discretion. You should apply to your local authority. Some Scottish local authority areas may also have access to the Common Good Fund which in many areas can provide funding to help with energy costs.

6. Other sources of help

Energy Saving Trust

The Energy Saving Trust (EST) offers free, impartial advice and information via a range of partnerships. The advice service signposts you to organisations that can help with energy-saving measures and reduce your fuel bills.

The EST has a freephone number (0800 512 012) which can connect you to an adviser in England, Wales or Scotland. Home Energy Scotland can also be contacted directly on freephone 0808 808 2282.

Measures to save energy

EST has produced information on how you can reduce your fuel bills. Some of these cost-saving measures are at energysavingtrust.org.uk/hub/quick-tips-to-save-energy and include:

- draught-proofing gaps;
- insulating your hot water cylinder;
- switching appliances off standby;
- replacing all bulbs with LEDs;
- spending one minute less in the shower each day.

Citizens Advice

Citizens Advice delivers consumer advice services on consumer issues in England, Wales and Scotland. Areas of focus include:

- representing consumers' interests in energy, post and water, working to promote fairer markets and improve customer services in these fields;
- dealing with complex energy cases, or cases received from vulnerable consumers;
- dealing with disconnection or threatened disconnection. The Extra Help Unit (EHU) negotiates with suppliers and offers advice. Citizens Advice Scotland manages the EHU but it helps consumers from anywhere in Great Britain. Most of EHU's cases are referred by the Citizens Advice network, though it may also accept some cases from other sources.

Useful contact numbers
Extra Help Unit: 0345 404 05 06
Adviceline (England): 0800 144 8848
Advicelink (Wales): 0800 702 2020
Ask the Adviser service (Scotland): 0344 980 0041

Energy Advice.Scot

Energy Advice.Scot is a service delivered by Advice Direct Scotland providing free, practical advice and information on energy-related matters to domestic consumers in Scotland. It can help with queries relating to your supplier (no matter how complex) or if you are in difficulty with your energy bills. See energyadvice.scot for more information or call 0808 196 8660.

NI Energy Advice

NI Energy Advice offers free, impartial energy advice to domestic householders in Northern Ireland – including advice about energy grants and other sources of help. For help, in the first instance, contact the advice service via its web form at nidirect.gov.uk/contacts/ni-energy-advice.

Priority Services Register

Energy suppliers are required to keep a register of priority service customers who, by virtue of being of pensionable age, disabled or long-term sick or having a hearing or visual impairment, require information or advice on the special services available. See p98 for more information.

National Energy Action

National Energy Action develops and promotes energy efficiency services to tackle the insulation and heating problems of low-income households. It aims to eradicate fuel poverty and campaigns for greater investment in energy efficiency to help those who are poor or vulnerable. See nea.org.uk for more information.

Energy Action Scotland

Energy Action Scotland campaigns for an end to fuel poverty in Scotland. It seeks to develop and promote effective solutions to the problem of cold, damp and expensive-to-heat homes. It provides information and advice on fuel poverty-related issues. It has a postcode lookup to help people in Scotland find local advice services. See eas.org.uk for more information.

The Energy Ombudsman

The Energy Ombudsman is an independent body that resolves outstanding energy disputes. It is a free service that deals with complaints about energy companies. See Chapter 14 for more information.

Charities

Some charities, particularly charities for ex-service personnel, offer help to meet fuel bills. It is helpful if an advice agency or social worker can write to the charity to explain your circumstances. The *Charities Digest* (available in reference libraries) lists relevant charities. Another useful book is *A Guide to Grants for Individuals in Need*. Your local reference library may also be able to help locate useful local charities.

Turn2us (turn2us.org.uk) is a charitable service that can help you access grants and financial help and has an online benefits calculator.

Some Trussell Trust food banks can also give fuel vouchers to help people in fuel crisis by providing funds to pay for up to two weeks' gas and electricity, alongside emergency food.

However, the demand for charitable payments is high. Many charities will likely refuse to help with fuel debts if Fuel Direct or some other budgeting scheme is available. If you are on a means-tested benefit (eg, universal credit), check that a charitable payment does not affect your benefit.

Trust funds and foundations

Some energy companies have trust funds to help customers who are in debt or may fund projects which provide support for the fuel poor.

British Gas and Scottish Gas

The British Gas Energy Trust Fund is open to customers and non-customers of British Gas and Scottish Gas with current debt. It offers grants to clear arrears of gas/electricity bills and other essential domestic bills or purchase of essential household items.

See britishgasenergytrust.org.uk or telephone 0121 348 7797 for more information.

E.ON

The E.ON Energy Fund assists existing or previous E.ON customers in low-income households. The fund can help pay current or final energy bills arrears, from a previous supplier. It can also help customers buy replacement white goods such as cookers, fridges, freezers and washing machines – and also help to replace and repair gas boilers.

Call 03303 80 10 90 for more information.

ScottishPower

ScottishPower's Hardship Fund can help its customers on a low income or on certain benefits with energy debts. Apply via support.sigmaconnected.com/ scottish-power-hardship-fund or telephone 0121 285 2595. The ScottishPower Foundation also provides funding to registered charities, including those for the prevention or relief of poverty and help for those with a disability or other disadvantage.

Notes

1. National energy efficiency schemes
1 Scottish government, *Draft Fuel Poverty Strategy for Scotland 2018*, June 2018
2 nea.org.uk/energy-crisis/fuel-poverty-statistics-explainer
3 Fuel Poverty (Targets, Definition and Strategy) (Scotland) Act 2019
4 Sch 2 The Electricity and Gas (Energy Company Obligation) Order 2018 No.1183
5 Ofgem, *ECO4 and GBIS Flex Local Authority Guidance*, 10 April 2024
6 Department for Business, Energy and Industrial Strategy, *Energy Company Obligation: ECO3, 2018-22 Flexible Eligibility Guidance*, February 2019
7 Product eligibility list at ofgem.gov.uk/ environmental-and-social-schemes/ domestic-renewable-heat-incentive-domestic-rhi/applicants/eligible-heating-systems
8 Feed-in-tariffs – FAQ Scheme Closure, December 2018, available at ofgem.gov.uk/environmental-and-social-schemes/feed-tariffs-fit
9 ofgem.gov.uk/environmental-programmes/feed-tariff-fit-scheme/ tariff-tables
10 EA 1989; condition 31 SLC

3. Energy efficiency schemes in Wales
11 Reg 2 The Home Energy Efficiency Schemes (Wales) Regulations 2011 No.656

4. Energy efficiency schemes in Scotland
12 Reg 6 The Home Energy Assistance Scheme (Scotland) Regulations 2013 No.148

5. Help from the local authority
13 gov.scot/Topics/Statistics/Browse/ Housing-Regeneration/HSfS/SoA
14 s17 Children Act 1989; s22 Children (Scotland) Act 1995
15 s12 Social Work (Scotland) Act 1968

Chapter 13

....

You, your landlord and fuel

This chapter covers:

1. You and your landlord

Most arrangements for payment of gas or electricity are made directly with the supplier. However, some tenants indirectly pay for fuel or fuel-related services (such as heating, cooking, lighting or hot water) through their landlord – ie, the supplier supplies the fuel to the landlord who resells it to you. Frequently, a landlord will:

- provide gas or electricity, pay the bill and recover charges from tenants by sharing out costs on a fixed or variable basis; *or*
- pay the bill and recover charges from tenants by a separate payment system; *or*
- provide heating from a central boiler and recover charges on a fixed or variable basis.

It can be more economical if your landlord provides fuel-related services – eg, a common boiler in a block of flats may be relatively cheap. However, your landlord's involvement can lead to disputes over the amounts charged or your position if your landlord fails to pay the bills.

Think carefully before beginning a dispute with your landlord. Always consider the strength of your position. As a tenant, this means considering how secure the tenancy is. This depends on your tenancy type (protected, statutory, assured, assured shorthold, secure or none of these). A full discussion of security of tenure is outside the scope of this book, but it is an important issue because, for example, if you have no security and start a dispute with your landlord, you could end up losing your home.

More widely, landlords are responsible for the buildings that they rent out, including maintaining their condition and for insulation and energy efficiency measures.

In England, the Deregulation Act 2015 protects private tenants from eviction in retaliation for requesting repairs or energy efficiency improvements, preventing so-called 'retaliatory evictions'.[1] With council housing, local authorities' housing and evictions policy must comply with this provision and not penalise you for making an application or complaint.[2] You can make reasonable complaints to your landlord about the property (including common shared parts) without fear that you will be evicted. Examples of the repairs covered include a leak or a problem with the heating. You can also complain about issues that might risk the health or safety of you or your family. You must first make a written complaint to your landlord. If you fail to get an adequate response within 14 days, ask the local authority to pursue the complaint. If you do not have a postal or email address for your landlord and you have made reasonable efforts to contact the landlord, you can still contact the local authority.[3]

In some situations, you have a right of appeal to the courts or a tribunal against the decision of a landlord to charge you for the fuel costs for your home or a failure to permit energy efficiency improvement measures being made to the property. The First-tier Tribunal (Property Chamber) hears disputes about rent or payments involving a fuel element, with a further right of appeal to the Upper Tribunal on a point of law.[4] In Scotland, a dispute may go to the First-tier Tribunal for Scotland (Housing and Property Chamber).

If your employer provides accommodation and deducts costs for fuel from your wages, the basic agreement covering such an arrangement is your contract of employment. A written employment contract should set out the terms and conditions.[5] Deductions to cover fuel costs from your wages by your employer may be unlawful if your earnings fall below the minimum wage as a result. The Court of Appeal ruled that deductions made for gas and electricity from wages paid to workers at a holiday resort were unlawful where the wages fell below the minimum wage.[6]

Implied terms

The terms of your tenancy may be contained in a written statement, in which case any terms relating to fuel or fuel-related services will be clear. However, sometimes there is no written agreement, and you have to work out whether your fuel problem is covered by terms implied in your tenancy. An **'implied term'** is one that, although not written down, is considered by the courts to be included automatically in any tenancy.

Every tenancy agreement in England and Wales has an implied term that the landlord will allow a tenant to have 'quiet enjoyment' and that the landlord will not interfere with or interrupt a tenant's ordinary use of the premises. In this case, that would mean not interfering in any way with your use of fuel or fuel-related services. The Scottish equivalent is your right to full possession of your premises, which has the same effect.

In England and Wales, terms are also implied by the Supply of Goods and Services Act 1982. This says that services must be provided with reasonable care and skill within a reasonable time and at a reasonable charge. What is a reasonable time is treated as a question of fact.[7] Problems with fuel supply or fuel-related services can often come within these terms. In Scotland, similar terms may be implied into the contract by common law. Additionally, the Consumer Rights Act 2015 includes local authorities and government departments within the definition of 'businesses' regulated by the Act.[8]

Could you get a discretionary housing payment?

If you get universal credit or housing benefit (and have a shortfall in paying your rent, you may apply for a discretionary housing payment (DHP – see p188). This does not cover heating costs but relates to your overall level of rent. Living costs, including heating, can be a relevant factor the local authority can consider when deciding whether to pay you a DHP.[9] Councils must consider each DHP application on a case-by-case basis having regard to each component of any disability benefit, the purpose of those disability-related benefits and whether the money from those benefits has been committed to other liabilities associated with disability.[10]

2. Rent increases for fuel or fuel-related services

The circumstances in which your landlord can increase your rent because of increases in charges for fuel or fuel-related services depend partly on whether you have a council or non-council tenancy. If you are a non-council tenant, your rights also vary according to whether you took up the tenancy before or after 15 January 1989 (2 January 1989 in Scotland). A landlord's power to increase charges for fuel or fuel-related services can be limited in one of three ways.
- Payments for fuel or fuel-related services are 'service charges', so legislation which affects service charges may be relevant.
- The courts have held that fuel charges are normally part of the rent,[11] so where legislation controls the rent, fuel charges are included.
- A tenancy agreement is a type of contract and may include limits on your landlord's power to increase charges.

If fuel charges are included in your rent, you may be subject to possession proceedings if you fail to pay them in the same way as if you fail to pay your rent.

'Possession proceedings' are where the landlord seeks to regain possession of a rented property – ie, evict you. For charges to be recoverable, they must be agreed by both parties at the beginning of the contract or by you both agreeing during the agreement. If you are subject to possession proceedings, always attend any court hearing as the court may proceed in your absence and automatically grant a possession order against you. A landlord proposing to increase the rent or alter the terms of a tenancy agreement must serve a notice under section 6(2) of the Housing Act 1988 in the prescribed form.[12]

Council tenancies

You have a 'council tenancy' if your landlord is a local authority, unless you have used your 'right to buy' or if, in England and Wales, your tenancy has a fixed term of more than 21 years. Most council tenancies are called 'secure tenancies' – ie, you can usually live in the property for the rest of your life, as long as you do not break the tenancy conditions.

In England and Wales, local authorities are under the general duty to act reasonably in setting levels of service charges or rent for council tenants,[13] and may be subject to judicial review. The Secretary of State has the power to make regulations covering heating charges, including that they are 'reasonable', but this has not been used.[14]

In Scotland, local authorities are limited to making service charges which they think are 'reasonable in all the circumstances'.[15] There is no definition of 'reasonable', but you can apply for judicial review if you think the charges are unreasonable (see Chapter 14).

Some protection may be provided for council tenants by way of contract. If fuel or fuel-related services are provided as part of your tenancy, a failure to provide these is a breach of contract. If there is such a breach, you can go to court to claim damages (ie, compensation) and a court order requiring the council to obey the terms of the tenancy agreement. If a council seeks a possession claim against you, this may be raised as a counterclaim. However, legal aid is unlikely to be available for such claims; increasingly most people have to represent themselves as best they can at any possession hearing. However, with a council tenancy in England and Wales, there is wider scope for a court to decline to grant a possession order than with a private sector tenancy.

Local authority heating systems

All local authorities have the power to produce and sell heat, including electricity which is produced from renewable sources.[16] There is no specific protection about heating charges, but the authority must:
- keep a separate account of them;[17] *and*
- when fixing the charges, act in good faith, not for ulterior or unlawful purposes, and within the reasonable limits of a reasonable local council;[18] *and*
- comply with the law on maximum charges for resale of fuel (see p221).

London boroughs have additional powers to provide heating by hot water or steam.[19] They may prescribe scales of heating charges that apply, unless a specific agreement sets different charges.[20] The charges must be shown separately on rent books, demand notes or receipts, and be differentiated from rent generally. The cost of some ancillary or incidental expenses may be included, such as insurance, and a welfare element may be recognised in this.[21]

London boroughs are not allowed to subsidise heating. They must not show 'undue preference' or exercise 'undue discrimination' when providing heat or setting charges.[22] Some preference or discrimination is inevitable, as not all tenants paying the same charges will be provided with identical heat. To decide if the preference or discrimination is 'undue' consider:

- the cost of providing the heat to you compared with the cost of providing it to other tenants;
- the level and consistency of heat;
- restrictions or terms governing the heat provided – eg, in winter only.

If you can show undue preference or discrimination, you can recover the amount you have been overcharged by taking legal action (see Chapter 14).

In Scotland, local authorities are only entitled to sell electricity produced in association with heat and waste. Scottish local authorities can also sell electricity produced from renewable sources including wind, solar, hydropower and biogas.[23] Scottish local authorities were required to draw up and publish a Local Heat and Energy Efficiency Strategy and Delivery Plan by the end of 2023 and update the Scottish government on a five-year basis. Guidance on what is required to fulfil this duty was published in October 2022.[24]

Do you suspect that the local authority is overcharging for heating?
If you suspect that the local authority is charging more for heat and power than the actual cost to itself, you can make a freedom of information request to obtain the actual costs. The local authority must make the information available within 21 days of a written request, unless the information falls into a restricted category. There is a right of appeal to the Information Commissioner's Office against a refusal to supply information.

Challenging the way heating is provided

If you challenge the legality of how a heating system is being run or charges for heat, complex legal issues arise. As well as the matters mentioned, a court can consider such matters as whether the local authority charges for:

- assumed heat delivery instead of actual heat delivered, if there is a significant difference;
- heating costs that are significantly higher than those of other heating systems;
- amounts unrelated to heat delivered or assumed to be delivered.

When some heating is provided but it is inadequate, it is difficult to prove that there has been a breach of the tenancy agreement unless there is a specific agreement stating how much heating is to be provided and at what times of the year. If nothing is specifically agreed or set out in the tenancy agreement, there is probably an implied term that 'reasonable heat' should be provided, but this is extremely vague. If there is a dispute, keep a detailed diary of when the heating was sufficient, when it was inadequate or off altogether, and even when there was too much.

A failure to consult adequately on local authority changes to district heating schemes is potentially open to judicial review.[25] In respect to specific groups of dwellings, the local authority or landlord may apply to the First-tier Tribunal (Property Chamber) for a dispensation from the duty to consult – eg, when replacing boilers on an estate. If a landlord seeks a dispensation, you may challenge it by showing that you will be financially or otherwise prejudiced.[26] Once you – and other leaseholders – have shown a credible case for prejudice, the landlord should rebut it, and the tribunal should regard the leaseholders' arguments sympathetically. The duty to consult is important and good practice would dictate that it occurs even in emergencies. Failures to consult and delays in doing so will count against a landlord.

Pressure by tenants' groups

It may be more effective for tenants' associations to pressure a local authority to change how it manages the heating system or the charges for it. In challenging high heating charges, tenants' groups can look at:

– copies of local council committee reports on heating systems and charging policies;
– a comparison of income from, and expenditure on, individual estate systems and across a local council area;
– expenditure charged to the heating account: does it include all fuel expenditure, maintenance, insurance, caretakers' wages, interest on the cost of the system; is this consistent with other public landlords?;
– district heating systems: the number of dwellings supplied, the costs and type of fuel;
– level of service: heating and hot water, hours per day, winter and summer, temperature standards assumed and achieved;
– method of calculation of charges: pooling of costs, property by property, flat charge, charges related to size and number of bedrooms;
– energy efficiency of dwellings: insulation quality, double-glazing;
– arranging a temperature survey to find out what heat is being delivered. Temperatures in all rooms at different times of the day can be measured simultaneously in a number of dwellings.

Requests made under the Freedom of Information Act 2000 may assist in obtaining relevant information from local authorities (see p214). Media interest is also high in energy supply issues.

Council tenancies: heating standards

In England and Wales, to be 'fit for human habitation', your home must have adequate provision of heating. Public Health England recommends that heating homes to at least 18°C (65F) in winter poses minimal risks to the health of a sedentary person, wearing suitable clothing and is also important for people over 65 years or with pre-existing medical conditions.[27] Having temperatures slightly above this threshold may be beneficial for health. Maintaining the 18°C (65F) threshold overnight may protect the health of those over 65 or with pre-existing medical conditions. They should also continue using sufficient bedding, clothing, thermal blankets or heating aids as appropriate.

However, a local authority may provide heating to another standard which it has set for itself. Some landlords use their own standards. Ask your local authority what standards it uses, as these are probably used in setting the charges.

In Scotland, a property is considered uninhabitable if it is deemed '**below tolerable standard**', which may include lacking in satisfactory provision for heating. Local authorities may take action against properties that fall below this standard under powers contained in the Housing (Scotland) Act 2006.

In Wales, accommodation for homeless people and families (eg, B&B accommodation) must be adequately heated. All habitable rooms must maintain a minimum temperature of 18°C when the outside temperature is -1°C.[28]

Non-council tenancies

If your landlord is not a local authority, legislation on variable service charges and rent control applies. The legislation on variable service charges does not apply in Scotland (see p220), but there are some court cases which give rights to tenants in this area. The rent control provisions are different for all tenancies granted before 15 January 1989 compared with most of those granted after 15 January 1989 (2 January 1989 in Scotland).

Variable service charges in England and Wales

In England and Wales, variable service charges are covered by the Landlord and Tenant Act 1985.[29] The Act applies to both private, public and social sector landlords. If your landlord used to be a council but it sold the property to a private landlord, you have similar rights under the Housing Act 1985.[30]

Variable service charge
An amount payable directly or indirectly by a tenant as part of, or in addition to, rent for services, repairs, maintenance, improvements, insurance, or management costs, the whole or part of which varies according to the landlord's costs or estimated costs.[31]

This broad definition includes payments for fuel, whether made directly to the landlord or indirectly through a landlord's meter. These provisions apply to all tenants unless you are:

- a tenant of a local council or any other public authority, unless your lease is for over 21 years or was granted under the 'right to buy' legislation;[32] *or*
- a tenant whose rent has been registered with a service charge as a fixed sum.[33]

Your landlord can recover the costs of the services they provide (eg, heating, lighting or cooking facilities) only if the service is of a 'reasonable' standard and the costs are 'reasonably' incurred.[34] There is no one definition of 'unreasonable', but it includes something which can be proved to be excessive. What is reasonable is a question of fact and degree.[35]

When it comes to discharging duties, a change of landlord does not affect the position, with either the previous landlord being liable or a successor in title.[36] If the charges are based on an estimate in advance, the estimate must be reasonable and, after the costs have actually been incurred, the charges must be adjusted by repayment, reduction of future charges or additional charges. The question of the reasonableness of an advance payment includes:[37]

- the time at which the landlord became (or is likely to become) liable for the costs; *and*
- the certainty of the costs; *and*
- the certainty that the works would be carried out and paid for during the period covered by the advance payment.

If paid in arrears, most charges cannot relate to periods of more than 18 months before.[38] Similarly, charges may not be reasonable to impose where major works are undertaken and charged to an individual tenant or leaseholder who may only have a short period left in occupation of the property.

You are not liable for any costs included for any service charge incurred more than 18 months before a demand for payment of the service charge is served. Only if you are served with a notice in writing during the 18 months that the costs have been incurred, and you are required to meet them, does a right to recover the charges arise.[39] This is to prevent you from being surprised by an unexpected bill for services or works carried out in earlier years.[40]

Application to energy bills

In the context of energy bills, this is likely to be the point at which the charges are identified as becoming payable, not necessarily when all the services were provided or used. For example, in one case, the management of an estate received and paid gas bills from the wrong energy company.[41] The mistake was found some years later, and a higher bill had to be paid to the actual gas supplier, with costs passed on in the service charges. The Court of Appeal ruled that, although parliament intended to protect tenants against stale claims, the court rejected the argument that costs recoverable as a service charge are incurred when services are used. A liability did not become a recoverable cost until it was established, either by being met or paid or possibly by being set down in an invoice or certificate under a building contract. The court also noted that estimated costs could be legitimately included in a service charge.

In a case where a leaseholder had disconnected his flat from the landlord's heating system, the Upper Tribunal ruled that, in the absence of any express obligation in a lease to contribute to the costs of communal heating, liability to pay a service charge in respect of ongoing heating ceased when the appellant disconnected the communal heating system and removed radiators from it.[42] The tribunal also considered that the question of whether heating had been provided to the flat to a reasonable standard was a relevant one.

In a case involving the recouping of energy costs (including the cost of reading meters, a standing charge and preparing energy bills) through a service charge, the Upper Tribunal found the landlord was not entitled to demand such associated costs as part of a contractual clause concerning the basic cost of the utility supply alone.[43]

Any obligation to pay a service charge must be founded on the terms the parties have expressly agreed to and recorded in writing. Agreements must be read and understood in their proper context, as they would be understood by any objective reader of the lease who was aware of the circumstances when the lease was entered into.[44] The cost of providing services may include the cost of administration and overheads, but the lease must be worded appropriately to allow this.[45] The fact that a management company undertakes administrative work in paying an electricity bill for common parts does not mean a management fee is recoverable unless management fees are expressly stated as recoverable in the lease.

Ofgem guidance on resale may be considered in proceedings. The effect of Ofgem guidance is that the unit rate payable may not exceed the rate paid by the reseller. In a dispute over the rate of consumption, the Leasehold Valuation Tribunal may determine the figure to be applied.[46]

In England, it may be worth investigating if the management company or person exercising management functions in respect of residential property adheres to the standards set out in the Service Charge Residential Management Code published by the Royal Institution of Chartered Surveyors.[47] Failure to comply with any provision of any approved code does not of itself render any person liable to any proceedings, but in any proceedings, the codes of practice shall be admissible as evidence and any provision that appears to be relevant to any question arising in the proceedings is taken into account.

In the case of service charges applied for caravan pitches, electricity charges are not recoverable unless expressly mentioned in the agreement for the pitch.[48] Costs incurred in maintaining energy supplies and other utilities may be restricted and recoverable only as part of a basic pitch fee.[49]

Changes in heating systems and buildings

Service charges should relate to the services actually provided. Where there has been a radical change or alteration in the heating system (eg, a new system or a change in the building), the court or tribunal may intervene and determine whether an original term in a lease requiring payment of a service should still apply. Where there has been a substantial change, the court or tribunal may require a different method of calculation once the change has taken place. Among the factors considered are the circumstances in which the contract was made, whether it applies to the new situation and what is 'fair and reasonable' in the new situation.[50]

Costs incurred in installing energy efficiency or carbon reduction measures paid or contributed to by the energy efficiency schemes or obtained from power companies should not be recoverable as part of service charges. Where a third party pays the costs, the rule against double recovery of sums from tenants should be applied.[51]

Where only some properties benefit from measures, service charge costs should not be apportioned to those tenants not affected.[52] Where a third party has paid a landlord (eg, by way of insurance payment or compensation for damages),[53] it may be possible to argue that a credit on a service charge should be made to you. Get specialist advice if you think this applies to you.

A landlord's costs for employing solicitors to recover arrears for fuel or service charges from other lessees are not recoverable unless there is a clear and unambiguous clause allowing this.[54]

Access to information

You have the right to require your landlord to provide information; your request must be in writing. Your landlord must provide a written summary of costs incurred over 12-month periods and must comply within six months of your request.[55]

If the service charges are payable by tenants of more than four dwellings together, a qualified accountant must provide a summary of costs.[56] This is aimed mostly at tenants such as those in mansion blocks, but it also applies if you live in a house in multiple occupation.[57]

Within six months of receiving the summary of costs, you can require your landlord to allow you to inspect accounts and receipts. You can also make copies of any documents at a reasonable charge.[58] This is particularly useful if you suspect you are being overcharged.

Exercising these rights through a tenants' association may be more effective. If members' tenancies require them to contribute to the same costs, a tenants' association can apply to the landlord to become a 'recognised tenants' association'.[59] If the landlord disagrees, the association can apply to the local rent assessment committee for a certificate requiring the landlord to recognise it. It can then exercise the rights to information on behalf of its members.

Challenging a service charge

Your right to challenge should be included with the notice of your service charge.[60]

An application may be made for a determination whether a service charge is payable and, if it is, as to:[61]

- the person who should pay it; *and*
- the person to whom it should be paid; *and*
- the amount which is payable; *and*
- the date at or by which it should be paid; *and*
- how it is paid.

If you think service charges should not be payable, apply to the First-tier Tribunal (Property Chamber) in England or Residential Property Tribunal Wales to rule on these questions.[62] You must complete an application form and send it to the tribunal with the relevant fee and a copy of the lease. The tribunal may transfer the case to the court if it involves complex matters of law.

For more details and how to apply:

- in England, refer to guidance leaflet T541 available at gov.uk;
- in Wales, refer to guidance leaflet LVT-G2 available from residentialproperty-tribunal.gov.wales/leasehold-disputes.

It is best to get advice before starting an application. There are fees involved in some, but not all, applications. If you get certain means-tested benefits, you can apply to have the fees waived using Form EX160.[63]

It may be possible to negotiate with the landlord after making an application. A landlord may agree to reduce the charges before going as far as the tribunal hearing. However, a tenant who has paid a service charge without receiving a proper demand cannot claim a right to require repayment for previous years simply because no notice was given.[64]

County court proceedings

The county court has the power to make declarations,[65] but you are normally expected to use the First-tier Tribunal. Orders of the tribunal can be enforced through the county court, which also has the power to transfer proceedings to the First-tier Tribunal where a question within the jurisdiction of the tribunal arises.[66] Both the court and the First-tier Tribunal have powers to deal with litigation costs incurred in proceedings or after the transfer, but only the county court can reduce or extinguish costs incurred in the county court.[67] This is a matter that the court should consider when deciding whether to ask for or agree a transfer.

Variable service charges in Scotland

The legislation mentioned above for variable service charges does not apply in Scotland. To find out if there is any limit on your landlord's discretion to increase charges for fuel or fuel-related services, look at your written tenancy agreement if you have one. If a term covers how service charges can be increased, that applies.

If there is no such term or it is unclear, the courts may be prepared to introduce an 'implied term' (see p211) into the tenancy agreement. In one case,[68] the court introduced an implied term that any service charge had to be 'fair and reasonable'.

Rent control

Rent control is relevant to payments made to a landlord for fuel and fuel-related services because such payments are normally part of the rent. Therefore, the payments can be increased only if the rent can be increased. If it is unclear what kind of tenancy you have, refer to any standard text on landlord and tenant law.

The Rent Act 1977 and the Rent (Scotland) Act 1984 used to provide a comprehensive system of rent control. However, they do not apply to most tenancies that started after 15 January 1989 in England and Wales, or 2 January 1989 in Scotland, as these are covered by the Housing Act 1988 or the Housing (Scotland) Act 1988. The system of rent control under these later Acts is so loose that it is virtually useless as a tool for limiting rises in charges for fuel or fuel-related services and is not therefore covered in this book. However, from 2017 a degree of rent control is being reintroduced in Scotland following the Private Housing (Tenancies) (Scotland) Act 2016 with a tenant having the right to refer any increase to a rent officer.[69]

Between 6 September 2022 and 31 March 2024, a rent cap applied in Scotland limiting rent increases to 3 per cent. A landlord could apply to increase the rent in this period to a maximum 6 per cent of the rent or 50 per cent of the costs (whichever is lower) to cover certain costs, including service charges.[70]

If you have one of these tenancies, see the 18th edition of this *Handbook*.

---

3. **Resale of fuel by a landlord**

The basis on which your landlord sells you fuel is a term of your tenancy agreement. In practice, this is not normally set out in writing. However, it is subject to an upper limit – a landlord reselling fuel cannot recover more than the maximum charge.

Maximum permitted charges

Landlords who resell energy obtained from licensed suppliers are generally exempt from licensing conditions imposed by Ofgem.[71] However, Ofgem has the power to fix maximum charges for the resale of gas and electricity.[72] Ofgem's *The Resale of Gas and Electricity: guidance for resellers* sets out the maximum resale price and guidance.[73] The maximum amount should be no more than the price the landlord pays for the supply, including any standing charges. Charges have two elements: a charge for each unit of electricity or therm of gas consumed and a 'daily availability charge' to cover the standing charge.

If your landlord overcharges for gas or electricity, you can recover the excess through legal action through the civil courts in a claim for the amount overcharged and interest if so directed by Ofgem. In England and Wales, this would be through the small claims court jurisdiction of the county court (see Chapter 14).[74] In Scotland, equivalent procedures apply in the sheriff court. If you are overcharged, refer to *The Resale of Gas and Electricity: guidance for resellers*.

If your landlord undercharges, you may have to make an additional payment, but this depends on your tenancy agreement. There is no implied term (see p211) that you should pay the maximum charge.

Approval of meters

Electricity meters cannot be used unless the pattern and installation method are approved by regulations.[75] The meter must be tested and approved by a meter examiner appointed by Ofgem. Ofgem has the power to carry out examinations[76] and prosecute and fine your landlord for failure to comply with these provisions.

Gas meters must be of a pattern approved by the Gas and Electricity Markets Authority and stamped by, or on behalf of, a meter examiner appointed by the Authority.[77] Meters are tested in a laboratory by SGS (sgs.co.uk), although test reports from other accredited laboratories may be accepted in some circumstances. SGS provides a report detailing its findings to you, the meter owner and Ofgem. Ofgem analyses the report and makes the final decision on approving a specific meter type.

If your meter works within the legal limits, the report will say it is accurate. If your meter is faulty, the report will say it is inaccurate, stating how far it is outside the legal limits and, if possible, estimating how long this has been the case. You may be able to claim compensation from your landlord for over-billing or agree a payment plan for under-billing.

A supply of gas through an unstamped meter is an offence subject to a fine. The Gas Act 1986 does not state who would prosecute, but presumably, it would be Ofgem or by way of a private prosecution in England and Wales.[78]

Obtaining a meter directly from a supplier

If you encounter continual problems with your landlord's approach to reselling fuel, you could get your own supply directly from a supplier. Both gas and electricity suppliers are obligated to provide a supply, with your own meter, if requested, although you may have to pay connection charges. If you are doing this because of persistent breaches of the tenancy agreement by your landlord, you may be able to recover the charges from the landlord as compensation for the breaches.

If you have a meter installed, this would be a tenant's **'improvement'** – ie, an 'alteration connected with the provision of services to a dwelling house'. A tenant of a secure or regulated tenancy is not allowed to make any improvement without the landlord's consent.[79] Landlords cannot withhold their consent unreasonably. If it is unreasonably withheld, it is treated as given. If suppliers are reluctant to co-operate with you, remind them you have these rights.

The landlord fails to pay bills

If you pay for fuel with your rent, you can be disconnected if your landlord does not pay the bill. The supplier's codes of practice should lay down a period during which disconnection action will not proceed in such circumstances. There are legal remedies to deal with conflicts in this area (see Chapter 14).

Transferring the account

If your landlord consistently fails to pay bills, the simplest solution may be for you to open an account and get the supply in your own name (see Chapter 3).

Rewiring work might be necessary if a meter is moved or a new one is installed. For example, in houses in multiple occupation, considerable work is needed to replace one main meter with separate meters for each tenant – in most cases, you would only have to pay for the costs of work to the premises you occupy.

If a supply is being transferred because of a breach of the tenancy terms, you can claim the costs of the work as damages in a court action. Otherwise, this work is an 'improvement' (see p231).

The landlord is disconnected

Gas can only be disconnected at the premises for which there are arrears.[80] However, electricity can be disconnected at any premises your landlord occupies and for which they are registered as the consumer (eg, at the landlord's home or workplace) for failure to pay a bill incurred at other premises.[81] Your electricity supply may therefore be at risk of disconnection if your landlord has arrears elsewhere. This provision is more difficult to use if different companies supply the two premises. Remember that the supplier may not be aware that your landlord is not the occupier unless you, as the tenant, provide this information. Inform the supplier of the situation. Always press for disconnection of your landlord rather than you, if disconnection cannot be avoided, and attend any proceeding that comes to your attention to make representations.

Breach of quiet enjoyment

If you pay for fuel with rent, it is a term of your tenancy – implied (see p211), if not written down – that your landlord maintains the supply. If your landlord fails to pay a bill and the supply is threatened or cut off, you could seek a court order by way of an injunction to restore the supply and for damages for loss and suffering (see Chapter 14). Where action or inaction (such as failing to pay a bill) by a landlord results in disconnection, the landlord is in breach of an implied covenant to ensure a supply of gas and electricity and for breach of the implied covenant for 'quiet enjoyment'[82] (in Scotland, for having been deprived of full possession).

The covenant of quiet enjoyment protects you against both wrongful acts by a landlord and also lawful acts of other persons claiming under the landlord, by way of entry, eviction or disruption of your peaceful enjoyment of the land. Interventions by fuel suppliers which have been caused by the landlord's wrongful act or omission may count as breaches of quiet enjoyment or an easement in terms of the uninterrupted supply of electricity to the land.[83] You can sue the landlord for breach of the implied contract term that it would supply the fuel through the meters so long as the tenancy continued, and also for breach of the covenant of quiet enjoyment. This covenant is 'not confined to direct physical interference by the landlord but extends to any conduct of the landlord or his agents which interferes with the tenant's freedom of action in exercising his rights as tenant'. For example, if a supplier takes lawful action to disconnect because of a bill that a landlord has failed to pay, a claim for breach of quiet enjoyment is sustainable against the landlord for allowing the situation to arise. A claim for distress arising from disconnection may be included.[84] Removing a gas ring which provides the only heating for a tenant is an example of a criminal act if the other elements of the offence are proved.[85] Such a claim may cover physical inconvenience and discomfort caused by the breach and mental distress directly related to that inconvenience and discomfort[86] and, if the disconnection is deliberate, a harassment claim may also be added. Failure to rectify a wrongful act may be treated as a positive act rather than an omission.[87] However, a claim for distress will not extend to periods where you are not in actual occupation or when third parties (eg, family members or friends) are in occupation instead of you.[88]

Protection of supply where a landlord is insolvent

If your landlord becomes bankrupt, the official receiver (or an insolvency practitioner) automatically becomes landlord of the property upon their appointment as trustee of your landlord's estate. You must be notified of this in writing. Questions about the supply should be directed to the trustee.[89] Your fuel supply should be protected under special rules.[90] Where you have an agreement on something such as the heating system, the official receiver should obtain all documents relating to that agreement and consider continuing the agreement if the cost of doing so is not prohibitive.

Where you have a long lease, the 'leaseholders' collective right of first refusal' may arise.[91] This means you have the right of first refusal and are given a chance to buy the property before it can be sold to a third party. This minimises the consequences of the landlord's situation on you. Where the property contains two or more flats and you have a long lease, you have the power to serve notices on the official receiver requiring that certain actions are carried out.

The right of collective enfranchisement and the right to obtain a new lease are not exercisable by tenants with assured shorthold tenancies, but, usually, you are entitled to remain in the property if the fixed term has not yet expired. The trustee cannot force you out and a supplier should not disconnect supplies. However, a secured creditor (eg, a bank or lender who is a mortgagee) may take its own possession action against you, and the court may grant a possession order independently of the bankruptcy.

In Scotland, provision is made for the winding up of companies and registered social landlords under the Housing (Scotland) Act 2010 as amended by the Housing Amendment Scotland Act 2018.

Breach of trust

If two or more tenants contribute to the same costs by paying a variable service charge, the sums paid to the landlord are held 'on trust' by them. This imposes strict obligations on the landlord as 'trustee'. Failure to pay fuel bills with this money is a 'breach of trust'.

Harassment

If your landlord removes or restricts essential services such as electricity, hot water or heating, or fails to pay bills so that these services are cut off, they could be committing the criminal offence of harassment. '**Harassment**' means action likely to interfere with your peace or comfort, including the withdrawal of services that are reasonably required at the premises such as the supply of gas or electricity.[92] The offence may be committed by the landlord of a residential occupier (which is wider in meaning than a tenant) or by an agent of the landlord.

The landlord must persistently withdraw the services that you reasonably require for peaceful occupation. To be considered to be 'persistent', there must be some element of 'deliberate continuity'.[93] However, a single act that affects you over a period of time (eg, leaving an electricity bill unpaid for an extended period) should be regarded as persistent withdrawal.

A person convicted of harassment in the magistrates' court may be jailed for up to six months or fined up to £5,000; if convicted in the Crown Court, the prison sentence may be up to two years and the fine at whatever level the court sees fit. Where you are the victim of unlawful harassment, you can also sue for damages, which can be very large if you have to give up your home.[94] You may be able to obtain advice and assistance from the tenancy relations section of the local authority.

Proceedings may be taken in the county court or High Court. An injunction may be obtained from the court, ordering a landlord to restore fuel supply (see p265). In emergency cases, the injunction may be obtained outside normal court hours by telephoning the court. Damages are also available for breach of contract and for harm caused by acts of harassment, of which the cutting off or disruption of fuel supplies may be just a part. This area of law is governed by the law of tort which covers civil harms, wrongs and injuries. Four different types of damages may be available in a case of harassment or unlawful eviction, depending on the facts of the case. Potential claims may include:

- special damages, representing financial loss that can be identified – eg, cost of alternative accommodation;
- general damages, to put you back in the position you would have been in if the harassment or eviction had never happened. These include damages for pain, distress and nuisance;
- aggravated damages, which are awarded for especially severe harm and demonstrate the outrage and indignation of the court at the conduct of the landlord;
- exemplary damages, awarded where a landlord has acted with a deliberate disregard for your rights and their behaviour is calculated to make a profit. Exemplary damages are awarded where it is necessary to 'teach a wrongdoer that tort does not pay'.[95] To sustain an action for exemplary damages, other torts such as trespass, assault and nuisance would have to be shown in addition to action for breach of quiet enjoyment.[96]

Your landlord has a defence if they can show reasonable grounds for interfering with your peace or comfort, or for withdrawing services – eg, the gas was turned off because of an emergency such as a nearby fire.

Local authorities are often prepared to prosecute landlords for harassment. You can ask the tenancy relations officer to intervene.

Local authorities' powers in England and Wales

Local authorities have powers to help tenants whose landlords are endangering their gas or electricity supply through non-payment of charges. If you are seeking the help of the local authority in an emergency (eg, the supplier is threatening disconnection), tell the supplier – its code of practice may allow for a delay in disconnecting while the council investigates whether it can help, but the delay will only come into effect if the supplier knows that the council is involved.

Note: although the following section on local authorities' powers has been written for landlords and tenants, it applies where any 'occupier' has been affected by the failure of an 'owner' to pay a bill. 'Owner' has a wide definition,[97] and might cover the position where one of a number of flat-sharers is both tenant and the person responsible for paying the fuel bills.

Outside London

Local authorities outside London have the power to protect occupiers if the supply is threatened or cut off due to an owner's failure to pay fuel charges.[98] Once a request is made in writing, the council can make arrangements with the supplier to reconnect the supply; such arrangements can include payment of arrears and disconnection or reconnection charges.

Having arranged reconnection, the council can recover expenses plus interest from the person who should have paid in the first place. If you have an arrangement where the owner, your landlord, pays the fuel bills, the local authority can also serve notice on you to pay your rent directly to set off against its expenses.

Within London

London boroughs have powers to protect you if an owner, usually a landlord, fails to pay a bill.[99] They can make arrangements with suppliers, including paying the expenses of reconnecting the fuel supply. After reconnection, they have a duty, as long as they think it is necessary, to pay the supplier's charges for future consumption.

However, the boroughs have no power to pay arrears – ie, for past consumption. This can be a stumbling block, as suppliers are not obliged to reconnect the supply while money is owed. The supplier cannot chase you for the arrears because your landlord is the customer, not you. While such arrears are outstanding, a supplier may be reluctant to reconnect a supply.

You can get around this by getting the borough to recover the arrears. The borough has the power to take proceedings to recover money owing at the time fuel was reconnected,[100] and these proceedings can be taken against either you or the defaulting owner. If you pay your rent to the borough under these provisions, you are treated as meeting your obligation to pay rent to the owner. You cannot be required to pay more than the rent you would otherwise pay your landlord.

Suppliers should be keen on this kind of arrangement and prepared to reconnect, as it means the borough does the supplier's debt-collecting and, provided you pay your rent to the borough, payment is guaranteed. Boroughs can protect themselves by 'registering a charge'[101] on the affected property to recover their expenses (including administrative costs). Local authorities usually appoint a particular officer – such as a tenancy relations officer – to deal with these matters. If they are reluctant to become involved, you can point out that they can put a charge on the property to cover their expenses and protect themselves. It is unlawful to have a blanket policy not to exercise these powers; they must consider each case individually. If you are told, 'we don't do that', you can consider judicial review (see Chapter 14).

Local authorities' powers in Scotland

There are no powers in Scotland equivalent to those in England and Wales. However, local authorities throughout Great Britain do have powers to make 'control orders' in extreme cases.[102] This means that the council can take over a house in multiple occupation from a landlord and collect the rent to pay for any necessary repairs and to pay bills such as fuel bills. Unfortunately, it is unlikely that a control order would be made on the basis of unpaid fuel bills alone; these powers are more typically used if there is substantial disrepair.

4. Defective housing and heating systems

A full discussion of legal remedies for defective housing is outside the scope of this book. However, defective heating systems and appliances, structural disrepair, use of poor materials, and inadequate insulation and draught proofing can all contribute to high heating bills. Tackling these problems can be expensive and is rarely a tenant's responsibility. This section looks briefly at the legal remedies available to a tenant: repairing obligations (see p229), negligence (see p232), premises prejudicial to health (see p233) and other local authority powers (see p235).

There are also regulations covering the maintenance of gas appliances by landlords (see p236).

There are different forms of action which can be taken against a landlord, but the purpose is always to get work carried out and/or to get compensation. Good records are important evidence and can make a big difference to the level of any compensation. Keep proper records (and take photographs) of what is in disrepair and, for instance, note:

- when the problems started;
- when your landlord was first told of the disrepair;
- all other occasions on which your landlord has been told about the disrepair;
- what has been done, if anything, to put things right.

If you incur extra expenses (eg, to keep warm, eat out or for replacement heaters), make notes and keep receipts. If heating bills are higher than normal, also keep these. The sums can be recoverable.

Always inform your landlord in writing (by post or email) of the problem as soon as possible. If your landlord has a complaints procedure, you should use this. Keep a copy of the correspondence you send with details of the disrepair. If the landlord does not act, you should inform your local council.

Protection under the Deregulation Act 2015

The Deregulation Act 2015 protects tenants in England and Wales against unfair eviction.[103] Where your landlord fails to address a genuine complaint you have made about the property's condition, and the complaint has been verified by a local authority inspection, your landlord cannot evict you using the 'no fault' eviction procedure known a section 21 eviction.[104] A 'no fault' eviction is one where you do not have to have done anything wrong. After you have served a repair notice, if the landlord serves a section 21 notice in response, the section 21 notice is deemed to be invalid.

The landlord is also required to ensure that the repairs are completed, and you may also have a counter claim for damages arising from the failure to undertake repairs.

Repairing obligations

Your landlord's repairing obligations may be set out in a written tenancy agreement; for most private tenancies entered into since 1989 in England and Wales, this is an 'assured shorthold' tenancy or, more rarely, an assured tenancy. Tenants of councils and housing associations in Scotland have a right to a formal written lease.[105] Whether or not you have a written agreement and whatever is stated in any such written agreement, there is legislation which puts a wide range of obligations on landlords.[106]

Repairing obligations can be enforced through the county court and applied against public and private sector landlords. For claims of up to £10,000, the arbitration or small claims procedure is used. As well as compensation, remedies by way of specific performance or an injunction are available to compel a landlord to fulfil obligations or take steps to remedy harm with decisions of tribunals being enforceable by the courts.[107] Under the rules of court, you are expected to take certain steps before commencing a claim. A 'pre-action disrepair protocol' applies, setting out procedures for both parties to follow in a disrepair claim, encouraging the exchange of information and settlement without recourse to litigation. Details and guidance notes are available on the Ministry of Justice website (justice.gov.uk).

Scotland

The landlord's obligation is to make sure that any property rented out is in a 'tenantable and habitable condition',[108] or 'reasonably fit for human habitation'.[109] These two phrases almost certainly mean the same thing – the property must be safe, free from damp and generally in a suitable condition for you and your family to live in. Local authorities may act where properties are 'below tolerable standard'. Private landlords in Scotland have a duty to ensure that rented accommodation meets a basic standard of repair called the **'Repairing Standard'** under the Housing (Scotland) Act 2006.[110] This covers the legal and contractual obligations of private landlords to ensure that a property meets a minimum physical standard. It must have 'satisfactory thermal insulation' and an electricity supply which complies with the requirements for the electrical installations in the property.[111]

Your landlord must carry out a pre-tenancy check of the property to identify work required to meet the Repairing Standard and notify you of any such work. Your landlord has a legal obligation to provide you with written information about the effect of the Repairing Standard provisions on the tenancy. A home meets the Standard if:

- it is wind- and water-tight and in all other respects reasonably fit for human habitation;
- its structure and exterior (including external pipes) are in a reasonable state of repair and in proper working order;
- its installations for the supply of water, gas and electricity and for sanitation, space heating and heating water are in a reasonable state of repair and in proper working order;
- any fixtures, fittings and appliances provided by the landlord under the tenancy are in a reasonable state of repair and in proper working order.

It is the landlord's duty to repair and maintain the property from the tenancy start date and throughout the tenancy. On becoming aware of a defect, the landlord must complete the work within a reasonable time.

The repairing obligation applies to all tenancies except Scottish secure tenancies and short Scottish secure tenancies with various social landlords and certain agricultural tenancies.[112] The landlord should inspect the property and bring it up to standard before any tenancy starts. If this is not done, you can sue for damages and/or an order of 'specific implement' to force the landlord to carry out any necessary works. The landlord's duty may include carrying out works to improve the property, rather than merely repairing it, if that is necessary to comply with the duty. However, it is much more difficult in Scotland to get an order ('specific implement') that enforces that duty.

If problems arise after the tenancy starts, your landlord is only obliged to deal with them if they know, or should know, about them. If you believe your home falls short of the Standard, you should report any problems as soon as they arise, preferably in writing.

If you cannot agree with your landlord about whether or not the Standard is being met, you can take your case to the First-tier Tribunal for Scotland (Housing and Property Chamber).[113] This tribunal is an independent body that provides mediation services in repairing obligation cases. If mediation is unsuccessful, an inspection of your home may take place and a hearing held before the tribunal.[114] It may decide:

- whether your landlord has failed to comply with the Repairing Standard or not;
- to issue an enforcement order if your landlord has failed to comply, setting out the work to be completed;
- to reduce your rent during some of the enforcement order period.

If an enforcement notice is issued, it sets out the repair work required, and when it must be completed (this will be at least 21 days). If your landlord fails to comply with the notice, the local authority may undertake the work (and charge the landlord).

Repairs and improvements

For England and Wales generally, and in Scotland in connection with the following rights, it is important to distinguish between 'repairs' and 'improvements'. If the works which are needed constitute improvements, rather than just repairs (and the case cannot be brought under the headings of 'negligence' or 'premises prejudicial to health' – see p232 and p233), a landlord has no obligation to improve a home, and you have no rights.[115]

Local authorities have a duty to control premises prejudicial to health under public health legislation.[116] Report your situation to your local authority's environmental health department, which can give you advice and take enforcement action if necessary.

You may also take legal action against your landlord for disrepair only if they know about it or should have known about it.[117] It is best to tell your landlord in writing (keeping copies) about the disrepair so there can be no dispute about whether notice has been given.

Your rights are set out in the Landlord and Tenant Act 1985, the Housing (Scotland) Act 1987 and the Housing (Scotland) Act 2006 as amended. (These provisions do not apply to tenancies for a fixed period of seven years or more.)

Structure and exterior

Your landlord must keep in repair 'the structure and exterior of the dwelling-house (including drains, gutters and external pipes)'.[118] This includes walls, roofs, windows and doors. If these are not kept in good repair, a house can become damp and hard to heat. In Scotland, the property must not be 'below tolerable standard' (see p216).

Installations for heating and for the supply of gas and electricity

Your landlord must keep in repair and proper working order – directly or indirectly[119] – installations for space heating (ie, central heating, gas and electric fires), for heating water and for the supply of gas and electricity.[120] This does not include fittings or appliances making use of the supply – ie, wiring and pipes are included but not cookers or refrigerators. For tenancies that started after 15 January 1989 (2 January 1989 in Scotland), a central heating boiler in the basement of a block of flats would normally be within the repairing obligation.[121] For the supply of gas and electricity, an installation is considered in proper working order if it is able to function under the conditions of supply which are reasonable to anticipate.[122]

What can you do if your landlord does not keep the property in good repair?
You have two options if your landlord does not keep the structure, etc in good repair.
1. You can bring an action for damages and for a court order requiring your landlord to carry out the repair. Damages are calculated by assessing how much the value of the premises to you has been reduced so as to put you, as far as possible, in the same position

as if there had been no breach.[123] This may involve calculating the costs of alternative accommodation, redecoration, eating out, using public baths or launderettes, together with an amount for discomfort and inconvenience arising from the disrepair. Keep a record, as far as possible, of all expenses. Most claims are made in the county court or, in Scotland, the sheriff court. You will need the help of a solicitor. In Scotland, you can take your case to the Housing and Property Chamber.

2. In some cases, it is easier to do the repair work yourself and recover the costs by withholding rent to the same value. Always write to your landlord to warn them of what you are doing. You cannot recover the costs unless the works fall within your landlord's repairing obligations, so you must give them an opportunity to object or comment. Send estimates for the cost of the work to your landlord and give them time to comment on what is being suggested – eg, 21 days. After the work has been done, write to your landlord to warn that, unless they pay the costs, rent to the same value will be withheld. These costs are a 'set-off' against rent due and are not treated by a court as rent arrears, provided the court agrees that the costs were reasonable.[124] The consequences of getting this procedure wrong can be serious, so get legal advice. Note that in Scotland, this way of retaining your rent is not available if you are a statutory tenant.

Negligence

As a tenant, you can hold builders,[125] developers,[126] architects and engineers[127] liable for their work in building or developing your home if that work was carried out negligently[128] and it caused damage to you or your property or belongings.[129] Local authorities may also be liable for negligence if they fail to inspect properly the plans for, or the site of, your home or to enforce the appropriate building regulations.[130]

From 1 April 2024, new standards are being phased in for Scotland in relation to heating and water systems and energy efficiency.[131] If a landlord has repairing obligations, they are also under a duty to make sure that anyone else who could be expected to be in the premises will not suffer harm from any disrepair.[132] Effectively, this extends the repairing obligations to your guests and family members, such as your children, even though they are not parties to the tenancy itself. In England and Wales, this duty is specifically extended to situations where the works are carried out before a tenancy is granted.[133] Your landlord is treated as having such repairing obligations if they have reserved the right to enter your home to carry out any maintenance or works of repair.[134] Unlike the repairing obligations set out in the previous section, your landlord can be liable under this duty in England and Wales not only if you have given them notice of any problem, but also if they ought to have known about it.[135]

Electricity and gas can be dangerous. You are protected by safety regulations which prescribe standards and methods of installation of meters and other equipment for the supply of gas or electricity.[136] A landlord carrying out work on the premises must comply with such standards and is also under a duty to use reasonable care to ensure the safety of those who might be affected by the work.[137]

Failure to meet the appropriate standards may be negligence. The main remedy for negligence is to claim damages in a court action. These are assessed to put you, as far as possible, in the position you would have been in had there been no negligence. Legal advice is essential.

Landlords are bound by the Gas Safety (Installation and Use) Regulations 1998 to maintain in a safe condition gas fittings and flues which serve any relevant gas fitting[138] and keep records for two years. A landlord must supply a copy of any gas safety record, which may be required by the Gas Safety (Installation and Use) Regulations 1998, with the tenancy details and agreement.[139]

Premises prejudicial to health

The Environmental Protection Act 1990 gives a remedy to any person 'aggrieved' by a 'statutory nuisance'. The Act defines 'statutory nuisance' to cover a range of matters. For people who live in defective premises, the most relevant is 'any premises in such a state as to be prejudicial to health or a nuisance'.[140] Whether you qualify as a 'person aggrieved' is a question of fact and degree.

Severe damp, including condensation, is generally accepted as being prejudicial to health for the purposes of the Act. Loose or exposed wiring and draughty windows and doors are other examples.[141] Health is distinguished from accidental physical injury and would cover, for instance, health problems triggered by gas leakage. There may be grey areas such as cracked electrical fittings which might result in electric shocks.

A **'nuisance'** is anything coming from neighbouring property which causes substantial interference with your use and enjoyment of your home.[142]

Local authorities have a duty to investigate complaints of statutory nuisance. The local authority may serve a notice requiring any 'nuisance' to be 'abated' – ie, put right. If the notice is not appealed against or complied with, the local authority can prosecute the person who was sent the notice and/or do the works itself. Where the offending landlord is the council itself, it may also be prosecuted under these provisions by you taking a private prosecution.

You can take your landlord to the magistrates' court or, in Scotland, the sheriff court.[143] Legal advice should be obtained. You must give 21 days' written warning to your landlord that you are going to take proceedings. You then 'lay an information' at your local magistrates' court giving details of the defective premises and why they are prejudicial to your health and/or that of any other occupier of the premises. In Scotland, the procedure is by 'summary application' at the local sheriff court.[144] At the subsequent hearing, you must prove the existence of the statutory nuisance and that your landlord is responsible. Environmental health officers can give evidence of the existence of a statutory nuisance. Expert evidence on the state of premises is sufficient to find that premises are prejudicial to health, without having to prove that you are suffering from a condition. A doctor's report explaining the danger to health may be used, and in some cases it may be useful to call the medical practitioner or other expert as a witness.

The proceedings in the magistrates' court follow the rules for criminal procedure, and a finding that a statutory nuisance exists ranks as a criminal conviction[145] – an outcome that most landlords will wish to avoid.

The court can make an order that your landlord must 'abate' the nuisance. The court has wide discretion over what work it may order a landlord to do,[146] although it must be for abating the nuisance. As explained above, repairing obligations can be limited, so this kind of action can be useful if something additional, including improvements, is needed – in some cases, courts have ordered the installation of central heating, double glazing and mechanical ventilators. Where a person contravenes any requirement or prohibition imposed by an order, a fine of up to £5,000 may be imposed, together with a fine at a rate of £200 a day for each day on which the offence continues after conviction.[147]

In England and Wales, the magistrates' court can make a compensation order.[148] The order can be for up to £5,000 for things such as damaged belongings, discomfort and inconvenience, although only if the loss was suffered after you sent the 21-day notice.[149] If a court refuses to make a compensation order, it must give reasons. In Scotland, the proceedings are civil, not criminal, and the court cannot award compensation.

There is a small risk that you might have to pay the defendant's legal costs if you lose,[150] so take legal advice before starting a prosecution. However, so long as the statutory nuisance existed at the time you started the court proceedings, you can ask for your reasonable costs to be paid by your landlord.[151] Also, lawyers can represent you in court on the basis that they will only be paid if the case is successful.[152] Therefore, although financial assistance is not available, if you can find a lawyer who will take the case on such a 'no win, no fee' basis, it will not cost you anything. Costs are at the discretion of the court.[153]

Condensation

Condensation dampness causes severe problems for many people. The dampness and consequent mould growth can damage health and can destroy clothing and furnishings. Attempts to heat damp premises can lead to high fuel bills. The causes of, and remedies for, condensation are complex. Most remedies are beyond the means or control of tenants, involving substantial expenditure on, for example, structure and heating systems.

Legal remedies for condensation

In Scotland, the obligations on a landlord under the Repairing Standard (see p229) are wide enough to cover condensation. This means your landlord has to ensure that there is no condensation problem when your tenancy starts and, if it arises during the tenancy and you report it, they must carry out whatever works are necessary to solve the problem. Condensation and dampness are not limited to physical dangers, regard should also be given to your comfort.[154]

In England and Wales, for condensation to come within a landlord's repairing obligations you must show that there has been 'damage to the structure and exterior which requires to be made good'.[155] This has to relate to the physical condition of the structure or exterior. Unless condensation has occurred over a long time and plaster has perished or window frames are rotten as a result, it may be hard to show this.

If the condensation damage is caused by inherent defects in the building (eg, because of defective materials) and if the only way to correct this is to carry out improvements, the court can order this. A landlord will not, however, be ordered to renew a building completely or to change it substantially – what will be required is a question of degree.[156] It is very unlikely that a court would order the installation of a different heating system or the full range of works necessary to remedy condensation.

Therefore, in England and Wales, it is normally more effective to prosecute under the Environmental Protection Act 1990 for a 'statutory nuisance' (see p233). It is not necessary to prove a breach of any contractual or statutory duty to use this remedy. This means that a court can hold a landlord liable even if they are not in breach of their responsibilities for repairs. A court can also order works of improvement if these are necessary to abate a nuisance.[157]

Landlords sometimes argue that tenants could avoid the nuisance by changing their lifestyle or heating premises properly. This is rarely correct. If your landlord provides ventilation or a heating system, you are expected to use it,[158] but you are not required to use 'wholly abnormal quantities of fuel'.[159]

In a private civil claim arising from nuisance caused by another tenant rather than the premises, the landlord is only liable to the extent that they 'must either participate directly in the commission of the nuisance' or they have 'authorised it by letting the property'. Merely being aware of a tenant creating a nuisance is not sufficient to ground a claim.[160]

Other local authority powers

Local authorities have powers to bring unfit properties up to certain minimum standards. Compared with your rights, these powers are more detailed and wide-ranging. However, the disadvantage is that you have to rely on a local authority's willingness to use its powers, which can be limited, mainly due to budget restrictions. Such financial limitations are particularly relevant where mandatory grants are available to bring homes up to the relevant standard (see Chapter 12).

In England and Wales, the relevant standard is prescribed by the Housing Health and Safety Rating System under Part I of the Housing Act 2004. Exactly what satisfies each of these standards is further defined in government guidance (see p216).

In Scotland, the relevant standard is the 'tolerable standard', which is less comprehensive.[161]

Once a property has been identified as falling below the relevant standard, local councils have duties to inspect and make arrangements for dealing with it.

If you feel that your home falls below the relevant standard, contact your local authority.

Do you live in a house of multiple occupation?

In a house of multiple occupation (HMO), the manager should ensure that every fixed electrical installation is inspected and tested by a qualified person at intervals not exceeding five years. A certificate of such inspection is produced to the local housing authority within seven days of a request. [162]

Maintenance of gas appliances

Landlords often provide gas fires and other gas-fired appliances. Your landlord must maintain any such appliance or installation pipework owned by them in a safe condition to prevent the risk of injury to any person.[163] Your landlord must also ensure that each appliance is checked at least every 12 months by a registered gas engineer.[164] Your landlord must give you a copy of the gas safety record within 28 days of it being carried out or before you move in. If you have a social landlord, it is a term of your tenancy that you allow the landlord access to perform necessary safety checks and you risk court action if you prevent or obstruct entry.

Gas Safe Register is the statutory gas registration body in Great Britain. By law, all qualified gas engineers must be on the Gas Safe Register and carry a photo ID card with their licence number and the type of work they are qualified to do. The register is at gassaferegister.co.uk or you can call 0800 408 5500.

5. Energy efficiency matters

Energy performance certificate

An energy performance certificate (EPC) gives you an idea of the amount of energy and cost needed to heat the property. An EPC contains:
- information about a property's energy use and typical energy costs using an energy efficiency rating from A (most efficient) to G (least efficient); *and*
- recommendations about how to reduce energy use and save money.

An EPC is valid for 10 years. Landlords must make valid EPCs available, free of charge, to prospective tenants at the earliest opportunity or wherever information in writing about the property is supplied or a viewing takes place (whichever is the sooner).[165] Where appropriate, the property's rating must be stated in any advertisement.[166] An EPC must be accompanied by a recommendation report indicating how the property's energy efficiency can cost-effectively be improved.[167] You can check a property's EPC at gov.uk/find-energy-certificate.

If you want to make any of the improvements listed in the EPC, your landlord must consent to certain energy efficiency measures being made.

In Scotland, the EPC must be displayed somewhere in the property – eg, in the meter cupboard.[168] It should be included in a Tenant Information Pack, along with a copy of any gas certificate and electrical inspection.[169]

Subject to certain exceptions, a landlord must not renew or grant a new tenancy after 1 April 2018, and must not continue to let the property after 1 April 2020, where the energy performance of the property is below the minimum energy performance rating of E (see below).[170]

In England, if you are a private tenant, you must also be given a copy of the government booklet *How to Rent: the checklist for renting in England,* available at gov.uk/government/publications/how-to-rent.[171]

The duty to supply a certificate does not apply if the landlord reasonably believes that you do not have the means to rent, or are not genuinely interested in renting, the property. Similarly, if you are not a person to whom the landlord would decide to rent, the duty does not apply, providing this is not a form of unlawful discrimination.[172]

Failure to supply an EPC or a Gas Safety Certificate affects the landlord's 'no fault' right to recover possession of the property at the county court.

Future changes

The Minimum Energy Performance of Buildings Bill proposes all new tenancies must have an EPC of at least Band C from 31 December 2025 and all existing tenancies must be at least Band C from 31 December 2028 where practical, cost-effective and affordable. Social landlords have until 2035 to ensure that a significant amount of their residential properties are at least Band C.

Minimum Energy Efficiency Standard

From April 2020, in England and Wales, private rented properties must normally have a minimum energy performance rating of E on an EPC. If this is not the case, the property is likely failing to meet the Minimum Energy Efficiency Standard requirements set by the government.

Properties not meeting the minimum E rating are called 'sub-standard properties'. The landlord is then registered and obliged to bring the property up to the required standard (unless an exemption applies). The property cannot be let unless the work is done.

Local authorities enforce compliance with the regulations.[173] A financial penalty and/or a publication penalty (recorded on the private rented sector exemptions penalty register) may be imposed on a landlord who breaches these obligations.[174]

Private rented tenants in England and Wales

If you are a private renter, you usually require your landlord's consent to carry out energy-efficiency improvements. Measures you can request are from a prescribed list, including boilers, hot water and heating systems, draught proofing, wall insulation and solar panels. It can also include installing pipes to connect to the gas grid if the property is within 23 metres of a relevant gas main.[175] The Energy Efficiency (Private Rented Property) (England and Wales) Regulations 2015 set out a statutory scheme to make it easier to obtain the required permission from your landlord for specified improvements.

Your landlord, and any superior landlord whose consent is required, must not unreasonably refuse consent to the improvements unless an exemption applies, or the landlord proposes alternative energy efficiency measures.[176]

Arranging the funding is your responsibility. See Chapter 12 for funding sources if you cannot pay for the work yourself. You must ensure that there are no upfront costs to the landlord, unless the landlord agrees to contribute.

You are entitled to apply if you rent your home under:[177]

- an assured tenancy under the Housing Act 1988;
- a regulated tenancy defined under the Rent Act 1977;
- certain agricultural tenancies.

Tenants' energy efficiency improvements request process

Step 1: consider the energy efficiency measure you would like installed and how you would fund the cost of the measure and installation. Check if you can get help from the schemes detailed in Chapter 12.

Step 2: make a formal written request to your landlord or their agent to ask for permission for the measure. You must state:[178]

– the measure you wish to install;

– the works you will carry out (eg, redecoration) to ensure the property is returned to its original condition after the installation;

– details of a funding plan, if relevant.

You must include relevant documents about the measure (eg, an EPC) and evidence of funding or details of how it may be achieved free of charge. Where the consent of another tenant or third party in the property is needed, a copy of that consent should be included. Two or more tenants in the same premises can serve a joint written request.[179]

Step 3: your landlord must consider the request and obtain any further advice, evidence or consents needed. They should respond to you within one month to consent, refuse or offer a counterproposal.[180]

Step 4: consider your landlord's response, whether you wish to accept it or whether you wish to renegotiate. You can appeal to the First-tier Tribunal if you think the landlord has not complied with the regulations (see below).

Once the measure is installed, it becomes part of the property's fixtures and fittings and so you cannot remove it at the end of your tenancy unless this is agreed with the landlord when the consent is granted.

You cannot make a request in certain circumstances,[181] including where you have arranged Green Deal improvements within the previous six months or where you have served notice to end the tenancy.

If preferred, it remains open to you and your landlord to make more informal energy efficiency arrangements.

Challenging a decision

If you are not satisfied that your landlord has complied with the regulations, there is a right to appeal to the First-tier Tribunal (General Regulatory Chamber).[182] It is recommended that you initially try to resolve the matter direct with your landlord and get advice before progressing to the tribunal.

You can apply to the First-tier Tribunal within 28 days from the date of your landlord's response. If your landlord has not responded, this is 28 days from the last date they should have replied. Note that there is a charge of £100 to appeal.

Notes

1. You and your landlord

1   s33 DA 2015 amending s215 Housing Act 2004 (tenancy deposit schemes)
2   *Humber Landlords Association v Hull City Council* [2019] All ER (D) 62
3   s33(4) DA 2015
4   See Explanatory Leaflet T605, available at assets.publishing.service.gov.uk/government/uploads/system/uploads/attachment_data/file/718600/t605-eng.pdf
5   s1 Employment Rights Act 1996
6   *Leisure Employment Services Ltd v Revenue and Customs Commissioners* [2007] EWCA Civ 92
7   s14(2) Supply of Goods and Services Act 1982
8   s2(7) CRA 2015
9   DWP, *Discretionary Housing Payments Guidance Manual*, 31 May 2022, available at gov.uk/government/publications/discretionary-housing-payments-guidance-manual/discretionary-housing-payments-guidance-manual; Scottish government, *Scottish Discretionary Housing Payment: guidance manual*, 27 March 2024, available at gov.scot/publications/scottish-discretionary-housing-payment-guidance-manual

10 *R v Sandwell MBC ex parte Hardy* [2015] EWHC 890

2. Rent increases for fuel or fuel-related services

11 *Montague v Browning* [1954] 2 All ER 601

12 Part 1 and Sch 1 HA 1988; Form 1 Assured Tenancies and Agricultural Occupancies (Forms) (England) Regulations 2015 No.620 as amended by 2021 No. 994

13 *Associated Provincial Picture Houses v Wednesbury Corporation* [1948] 1 KB 223

14 s108 HA 1985

15 s211 H(S)A 1987

16 s11 LG(MP)A 1976; Sale of Electricity by Local Authorities (England and Wales) Regulations 2010 No.1910; ss170A and 170B Local Government Scotland Act 1975 as inserted by s102 and Sch 13 EA 1989; Sale of Electricity by Local Authorities (Scotland) Regulations 2010 No.1908

17 s12(4) LG(MP)A 1976

18 *Bromley LBC v GLC* [1982] 1 All ER 129

19 Part III London County Council (General Powers) Act 1949

20 s22 London County Council (General Powers) Act 1949

21 *Attorney General v Crayford Urban District Council* [1962] Ch 246 per Lord Evershed

22 s20(3) London County Council (General Powers) Act 1949

23 s170A Local Government Scotland Act 1973; reg 2 Sale of Electricity by Local Authorities (Scotland) Regulations 2010 No.1908

24 Scottish government, *Local Heat and Energy Efficiency Strategies and Delivery Plans: guidance,* 20 Oct 2022; see also The Fuel Poverty (Enhanced Heating) (Scotland) Regulations 2020 No.58

25 *R (on the application of Ofogba) v Secretary of State for Energy and Climate Change* [2014] EWHC 2665 (Admin)

26 *Camden LBC v Leaseholders of 46 Flats in Harben Road Estate* [2015] LON/00AG/ LDC/2014/0123, 27 April 2015

27 Public Health England, *Minimum Home Temperature Thresholds for Health in Winter: a systematic literature review,* 2014

28 Sch 1 para 2(2) Homelessness (Suitability of Accommodation) (Wales) Order 2015 No.1268

29 ss18-30 LTA 1985

30 ss47-51 HA 1985

31 s18 LTA 1985

32 s26 LTA 1985

33 s27 LTA 1985

34 s19 LTA 1985

35 See *Russell v Laimond Properties Ltd* (1983) 269 EG 947; *Levitt and Another v Camden LBC* [2011] UKUT 366 (LC)

36 s23 LTA 1985 as inserted by s157 Sch 10 Commonhold and Leasehold Reform Act 2002

37 *Avon Ground Rents Ltd v Cowley and Others* [2018] UKUT 92 (LC)

38 s20B LTA 1985

39 s20B(1) and (2) LTA 1985; *Brent LBC v Shulem B Association Ltd* [2011] EWHC 1663 (Ch); *Gilje v Charlgrove Securities* [2004] 1 All ER 91

40 As Etherton J explained in *Gilje v Charlegrove Securities Ltd* [2003] EWHC 1284 (Ch) at (27)

41 *OM Property Management Ltd v Burr* [2013] EWCA Civ 479

42 *Saunderson v Cambridge Park Court Residents Association Ltd* [2018] UKUT 182 (LC)

43 *No.1 West India Quay (Residential) Ltd v East Tower Apartments Ltd* [2020]; All ER (D) 21 (Jun) [2020] UKUT 163 (LC)

44 *Westleigh Properties v Grimes* [2014] UKUT 213 (LC)

45 *Waverley BC v Arya* [2013] UKUT 501 (LC)

46 *No.1 West India Quay (Residential) Ltd v East Tower Apartments Ltd* [2020] All ER (D) 21 (Jun)

47 Royal Institution of Chartered Surveyors, *Service Charge Residential Management Code 2016,* 3rd Edition, available at rics.org/uk/upholding-professional-standards/sector-standards/real-estate/ service-charge-residential-management-code

48 Sch 1 para 29 Mobile Homes Act 1983; *Britannia Crest v Bamborough and Another* [2016] UKUT 144

49 *Greenwood and Another v Hardman and Partners* [2017] EWCA Civ 57

50 *Pole Properties v Feinberg* (1981) 43 P&CR 121 CA applying *Staffordshire Area Health Authority v South Staffordshire Waterworks Co* [1978] 1 WLR 1387

51 s20A LTA 1985

52 *Sheffield City Council v Oliver* [2017] EWCA Civ 225

53 *Craighead v Homes for Islington* [2010]
UKUT 47 (LC); *Edozie v Barnet Homes*
[2015] UKUT 348 (LC)
54 *Sella House Ltd v Mears* (1989) 21 HLR
147; [1989] EGLR 65 (CA)
55 s21 LTA 1985 as amended by Sch 12
Housing and Regeneration Act 2008;
Housing and Regeneration Act 2008
(Commencement No 2 and Transitory
Provisions) Order 2008 No.3068
56 s21(6) LTA 1985
57 s38 LTA 1985; 'dwelling' is defined as a
building or part of a building occupied
as a separate dwelling. Provided the
occupants of a house in multiple
occupation are tenants with exclusive
occupation of at least a room, their
landlord would have to provide certified
accounts
58 s22 LTA 1985
59 s29 LTA 1985
60 ss21A and 21B(1) LTA 1985
61 s27A LTA 1985
62 s19(2A) and (2B) LTA 1985
63 gov.uk/help-with-court-fees
64 *Middleton and Another v Karbon Homes*
[2023] UKUT 206 (LC)
65 s19(4) LTA 1985
66 ss112 and 176 Commonhold and
Leasehold Reform Act 2002
67 Sch 11 para 5A Commonhold and
Leasehold Reform Act 2002
68 *Finchbourne Ltd v Rodrigues* [1976] 3 All
ER 581
69 See ss18-24 Private Housing (Tenancies)
(Scotland) Act 2016
70 Cost of Living (Tenant Protection) Act
2022

3. Resale of fuel by a landlord
71 Sch 4 Electricity (Class Exemptions from
the Requirement for a Licence) Order
2001 No.3270
72 s44 EA 1989
73 Ofgem, *The Resale of Gas and Electricity:
guidance for resellers*, October 2005
74 s44 EA 1989
75 Meters (Approval of Pattern or
Construction and Manner of
Installation) Regulations 1998 No.1565;
Meters (Certification) Regulations 1998
No.1566
76 Sch 7 EA 1989; s17 GA 1986
77 s17 GA 1986
78 *R v Stewart* [1896] 1 QB 300
79 s97 HA 1985; s57 H(S)A 1987; s81 HA
1980; s101 R(S)A 1984
80 Sch 2B para 7(3) GA 1986

81 Sch 6 para 1(6) EA 1989
82 See *Perera v Vandiyar* [1953] 1 All ER
1109; *McCall v Abelesz* [1976] 1 QB 585
(CA)
83 *Cardwell and Others v Walker and another*
[2003] All ER (D) 395 (Dec)
84 Per Lord Denning in *McCall v Abelesz*
[1986] 1 QB 585
85 *Wu v Chelmsford City Council* [2023] All
ER(D) 41
86 *Watts v Morrow* [1991] 4 All ER 937;
Halcyon House v Baines and others [2014]
EWHC 2216 (QB)
87 *Wu v Chelmsford City Council* [2023] ALL
ER(D) 41, para 71
88 *Moorjani v Durban Estates Ltd* [2015]
EWCA Civ 1252
89 Insolvency Service, *Technical Manual*,
Chapter 33, Part 11
90 ss233, 233A, 372 and 372A IA 1986;
Sch 2 GA 1986; Insolvency (Protection
of Essential Supplies) Order 2015
No.989
91 Chapter 1 Part 1 Leasehold Reform,
Housing and Urban Development Act
1993
92 ss1 and 3 Protection from Eviction Act
1977; R(S)A 1984 as amended by s38
H(S)A 1988; see also *R v Sakaut (Sajeed)*
[2014] 0548/B4
93 *R v Abrol* [1972] Crim LR 318 (CA)
94 s27 HA 1988; s36 H(S)A 1988
95 *Rookes v Barnard* [1964] AC 1129 at
1227; *Stratton and Anr v Patel and
Another* [2014] EWHC 2677 (TCC)
96 *Kenny v Preen* [1963] 1 QB 499 at 512
(CA)
97 s19(8) Greater London Council (General
Powers) Act 1972; s33(5) LG(MP)A
1976
98 s33 LG(MP)A 1976
99 s19 Greater London Council (General
Powers) Act 1972 as amended by s42
London Local Authorities Act 1990
100 s19(3)(b) Greater London Council
(General Powers) Act 1972
101 Registering a charge means to attach a
charge to the title of the property at the
Land Registry so that the owner cannot
sell the property without paying off the
charge.
102 HA 1985; H(S)A 1987

4. Defective housing and heating systems
103 ss33-34 DA 2015
104 s21 HA 1988
105 ss53 and 54 H(S)A 1987
106 For example, s11 LTA 1985

107 *Joyce v Liverpool City Council; Wynne v Liverpool City Council* [1995] 3 All ER 110
108 Erskine's Institutes II/4/63
109 s27 H(S)A 2001
110 s13 H(S)A 2006
111 ss861(ca) and (ga) H(S)A 1987 as amended by s11 H(S)A 2006
112 s12 H(S)A 2006
113 First Tier Tribunal for Scotland (Transfer of Functions of the Private Rented Housing Panel) Regulations 2016 No.338
114 First Tier Tribunal for Scotland Housing and Property Chamber (Procedure) Regulations 2016 No.339
115 *Ravenseft Properties Ltd v Davstone Holdings Ltd* [1979] 1 All ER 929
116 See Environmental Protection Act 1990; Public Health Act 1936
117 *O'Brien v Robinson* [1973] AC 912
118 s11(1)(a) LTA 1985; Sch 10 para 3(1)(a) H(S)A 1987
119 *Niazi Services Ltd v Van der Loo* [2004] All ER (D) 139 (CA)
120 s11(1)(b) and (c) LTA 1985; Sch 10 para 3(1)(b) H(S)A 1987; *Niazi Services Ltd v Van der Loo* [2004] All ER (D) 139 (CA)
121 s11(1A) LTA 1985; Sch 10 para 3(1A) H(S)A 1987
122 *O'Connor v Old Etonians Housing Association Ltd* [2002] EWCA Civ 150
123 *Calabar Properties v Stitcher* [1984] 1 WLR 287
124 *Lee-Parker v Izzett* [1971] 1 WLR 1688; *British Anzani (Felixstowe) Ltd v International Marine Management (UK) Ltd* [1980] QB 137
125 *Gallagher v McDowell Ltd* [1961] NI 26
126 *Batty v Metropolitan Property Realisations* [1978] QB 554
127 *Cedar Transport Group v First Wyvern Property Trustees Co* [1981] EG 1077
128 s1 DPA 1972
129 *Murphy v Brentwood DC* [1990] 3 WLR 414
130 *Murphy v Brentwood DC* [1990] 3 WLR 414
131 The Building (Scotland) (Amendment) Regulations 2023 No.177
132 s4 DPA 1972; s3 Occupiers' Liability (Scotland) Act 1960
133 s3 DPA 1972
134 s4(4) DPA 1972
135 s4(2) DPA 1972

136 GS(IU) Regs; Meters (Approval of Pattern or Construction and Manner of Installation) Regulations 1998 No.1565; Meters (Certification) Regulations 1998 No.1566 as amended by 2002 No.3129
137 *AC Billings & Son v Riden* [1957] 3 All ER 1
138 s30A HA 1988
139 Reg 36(2) GS(IU) Regs
140 s79(1)(a) EPA 1990
141 But see *R v Bristol City Council ex parte Everett* 13 May 1998 – a dangerous staircase is not a statutory nuisance
142 *National Coal Board v Neath BC* [1976] 1 WLR 543
143 s82 EPA1990
144 r4 Sheriff Court Summary Application Rules 1993 No.3240
145 *Herbert v Lambeth LBC, The Times*, 21 November 1991
146 *Whittaker v Derby Urban Sanitary Authority* [1885] LJMC 8
147 s82(8) EPA1990
148 s35 Powers of Criminal Courts Act 1973
149 *R v Liverpool Crown Court ex parte Cooke* [1996] 4 All ER 589
150 s18 Prosecution of Offences Act 1985
151 s82(12) EPA 1990
152 *Thai Trading v Taylor, The Times*, 6 March 1998
153 *Southampton City Council v Oddysseas (Op Co) Ltd* [2017] EWHC 2783 (Admin)
154 *Agnes Fife Pursuer v Scottish Home Defenders* (1995) SCLR 209, 26 January 1994
155 Dillon LJ in *Quick v Taff Ely BC* [1985] 18 HLR 66
156 *Ravenseft Properties Ltd v Davstone Holdings Ltd* [1979] 1 All ER 929
157 *Birmingham DC v Kelly* [1985] 17 HLR 572
158 *Dover DC v Farrar* [1980] 2 HLR 32
159 *GLC v LB Tower Hamlets* [1983] 15 HLR 54
160 *Southwark LBC v Mills* [2001] 1 AC 1; *Lawrence and Another v Fen Tigers Ltd and Others* [2014] 2 All ER 622
161 s14 H(S)A 1987
162 Reg 7(3) Licensing and Management of Houses in Multiple Occupation (Additional Provisions) (England) Regulations 2007 No.1903; *Sutton and Another v Norwich City Council* [2020] LLR 656
163 Reg 36(2) GS(IU) Regs
164 Reg 36(3)(a) GS(IU) Regs

5. **Energy efficiency matters**
165 **EW** Reg 6 EPB(EW) Regs
 S Reg 5 EPB(S) Regs
166 Reg 6(2) EPB(EW) Regs
167 **EW** Reg 4 EPB(EW) Regs
 S Reg 6 EPB(S) Regs
168 Reg 9 EPB(S) Regs
169 Tenant Information Packs (Assured
 Tenancies) (Scotland) Order 2013
 No.20
170 EE(PRP)(EW) Regs
171 Reg 3 The Assured Shorthold Tenancy
 Notices and Prescribed Requirements
 (England) Regulations 2015 No.1646
172 Reg 6(2)(an) and (b) EPB(EW) Regs
173 Reg 34 EE(PRP)(E&W) Regs
174 Reg 38 EE(PRP)(E&W) Regs
175 Reg 2(1) EE(PRP)(E&W) Regs
176 Reg 10(1) EE(PRP)(EW) Regs
177 Under reg 2 Energy Efficiency (Domestic
 Private Rented Property) Order 2015
 No.799 applying s42(1) Energy Act
 2011
178 Regs 3 and 8 EE(PRP)(EW) Regs
179 Reg 8(3) EE(PRP)(EW) Regs
180 Reg 12 EE(PRP)(EW) Regs
181 Reg 9 EE(PRP)(EW) Regs
182 Reg 17 EE(PRP)(EW) Regs

Chapter 14

Remedies

This chapter covers:
1. Available remedies (below)
2. Negotiations (p245)
3. Action by Ofgem (p249)
4. Unfair terms (p255)
5. Using the civil courts (p258)
6. The Energy Ombudsman (p270)

---

1. **Available remedies**

This chapter rounds up the remedies available if you are in dispute with a supplier of electricity, or a supplier or transporter of gas. The ultimate arbiters of such disputes are Ofgem and the Energy Ombudsman or the civil courts, which determine and enforce the standards and protections given by law. The courts may be used by both official bodies and individual consumers.

Originally, under European law the UK was required to ensure the integrity and transparency of the energy market[1] and have national authorities with investigatory and regulatory enforcement powers. The responsible regulatory authority was, and remains, Ofgem, with other functions exercised by other state bodies or state-supported organisations. Ofgem is an independent regulator, not acting on behalf of you or the supplier, so you cannot instruct it what to do.

This structure is preserved under the European Union (Withdrawal) Act 2018 and the Consumer Protection (Amendment etc.) (EU Exit) Regulations 2018.[2] These expressly preserve certain European Union rules and domestic legislation (ie, UK law) which is deemed to be 'transposed' into UK law and will remain in force for the time being.[3]

The statutory remedies described in this chapter have limitations. For all practical purposes, taking your own legal action is sometimes a better way of asserting your rights. However, it costs time and money and, because of restrictions in legal aid, there may be no realistic prospect of receiving help with any civil claim beyond £10,000, except in a small number of cases.

The first step in any dispute is approaching the supplier or transporter and attempting to negotiate with it, being prepared to make a complaint if necessary. If you remain dissatisfied, you may take the complaint to the Energy Ombudsman.

Although not strictly a remedy, the possibility of media attention and publicity in the press, on television or via social media should not be overlooked.

2. **Negotiations**

Negotiating with the supplier or transporter can be the most appropriate way of resolving a problem or dispute, with the backup of a civil claim through the courts if it is not resolved. To negotiate effectively, you need to rely on a range of documents which, in their different ways, provide 'rules' about how suppliers and transporters should behave. Chapter 1 gives background information on sources of law and it may be useful to read it first.

If you contact the supplier, keep a record of the person/section you contacted. Putting your complaint in writing is preferable (although suppliers appear increasingly less equipped to deal with correspondence) and essential if you wish to pursue a complaint. It is important to keep a copy of all correspondence should you decide to pursue a civil claim through the courts.

Using codes of practice and policy statements

Suppliers are subject to regulations which govern how they handle a complaint. The Gas and Electricity (Consumer Complaints Handling Standards) Regulations 2008 set down standards for handling complaints and supplying information to consumers. All suppliers must conform to the regulations; they should have a code of practice based on the regulations for handling complaints. A supplier must provide a copy of its complaints-handling procedure, free of charge, to any person who requests a copy and must have its complaints procedure in a prominent position on its website.[4] Ofgem reviews the complaints system every two years. Suppliers which breach these regulations may be issued with a penalty notice requiring them to pay compensation. For example, in August 2014, EDF Energy was required to pay £3 million in compensation to vulnerable customers for breaching regulations in the way it dealt with customer complaints, arising from long waiting times when customers attempted to contact the company.[5]

Suppliers have also produced other codes of practice, as required by their licences, and staff may be more familiar with these than with the precise provisions of the law. So long as the provisions of a code of practice support your case, it may be easier and more effective to quote these; alternatively, extracts from the Standard Licence Conditions may be quoted where appropriate. Each code of practice has to be approved by Ofgem before being used.[6]

Each supplier should have codes of practice on:

- payment of bills;
- services for elderly or disabled people;
- using fuel efficiently;
- complaints procedures;
- prepayment meters and site access.

Each supplier also produces various documents on its policies and other useful information. It is obliged to publish information regularly about its performance compared with targets set by Ofgem and by itself. Use these if they support your case, but always be cautious – as a summary of the law, they will not always be accurate.

Also, as the supply of fuel is carried out by contract, not by statutory duty, provisions as to unfair contract terms apply. If you believe that a term in your contract is unfair, you can use this to support any negotiations (see p255).

Failure to follow a code of practice or an inadequate code of practice is not automatically negligence or a civil wrong in itself, but it can be evidence in support of such a claim.[7]

Your supplier should send you an annual written notification about the existence of its complaints-handling procedure and how you can obtain a copy of it.[8] This obligation does not apply to gas transporters or electricity distributors.[9]

Making a complaint

Where you have a problem with the conduct of an energy company, and you cannot get it resolved or correspondence is ignored, make a complaint. This is important as both Ofgem and the Energy Ombudsman expect you to use the complaints service, if you are capable, before contacting them.

If you have asked an adviser or another person to make the complaint for you, give them a signed authority to act for you, allowing information about you to be released.

Regulations lay down minimum standards for how suppliers deal with complaints.[10] If making a complaint, you should request a copy of the company complaints policy.

Definition of a complaint

A complaint is any expression of dissatisfaction made to an organisation, related to any one of its products, its services or how it has dealt with any such expression of dissatisfaction, where a response is either provided by or on behalf of that organisation at the point at which contact is made or a response is explicitly or implicitly required or expected to be provided thereafter.[11]

This definition is wide enough to include an independent subcontractor used by an energy supplier to carry out certain tasks – eg, the enforcement of warrants of entry and the fitting of prepayment meters. If a subcontractor behaves wrongly, a complaint can be made under the regulations to the supplier who appointed them.

A complaint may be made about any of the following:

- billing – including the accuracy of bills, frequency of billing, estimated bills, sending bills to the wrong address and issuing bills to the wrong person;
- sales – including misleading sales information and behaviour of sales staff;
- transfers – problems that occur when switching suppliers;
- meters – including faulty meters, inaccurate meter readings and problems with fitting and changing meters;
- prices – increase of prices on agreed contracts, misleading price information, problems with direct debits and credits, payment schemes and lack of notification of increases;
- access – problems with access to low-income schemes, special tariffs and government schemes;
- debt – problems with debt, disconnection and payment of arrears and failure to apply for Fuel Direct where available;
- customer service – inconsistent or inaccurate information, failures by staff, delay in responding to enquiries and problems with prepayment cards.

A supplier is required to have a complaints procedure in place and must comply with it in relation to each complaint it receives.[12] The procedure must:[13]

- be in plain and intelligible language;
- allow for complaints to be made and progressed orally (by phone or in person) or in writing (including email);
- describe the steps it will take to investigate and resolve your complaint and the likely time this will take;
- provide an internal review of your complaint if you are dissatisfied with the response.

The supplier must provide details of sources of independent help, advice and information. To be independent, the advisers must not be connected with the energy company.

It is possible for many complaints to be resolved at the initial contact or within a couple of days. The complaints that suppliers cannot resolve so quickly are more likely to be recorded by the supplier as a complaint. Ofgem focuses on those complaints that remain unresolved by the end of the working day after the complaint has been recorded. Complaint data on companies is available from the 'big six' suppliers since October 2012 and on most of the medium and smaller energy companies since 1 April 2013.[14] This information provides data for potential enforcement action and the imposition of penalties. Ofgem has already taken action over suppliers' complaint handling. In December 2015, Npower had a £26 million penalty imposed due to billing and complaint handling failings and in April 2016 Scottish Power had to pay out £18 million for similar failures.

Your right to refer your complaint to a qualifying redress scheme (eg, the Energy Ombudsman) from the point at which the supplier notifies you in writing that it is unable to resolve your complaint to your satisfaction should be explained. Your supplier should send information on potential redress schemes when this point is reached.[15] It must notify you:

- of your right to refer your complaint to a free redress scheme which is independent from your supplier;
- of the types of redress;
- that any outcome of the redress scheme process is binding upon the regulated provider but not upon you.

Recording a complaint

On receiving your complaint, a supplier must electronically record the date, whether the complaint was made orally or in writing and your name and contact details or those of the person making the complaint for you.[16]

Where the supplier is licensed by Ofgem, details of the complaint must be recorded along with details of you and your account, together with a summary of any advice given and any agreement on future communication.[17]

Where you have made a complaint, but the supplier cannot find it, the supplier must record the fact that it cannot trace your complaint.[18]

Where a supplier has recorded that your complaint is resolved but subsequent contact from you contradicts this, the supplier must not treat your complaint as a resolved complaint until it is demonstrably resolved.[19]

If you reach the position where the complaint is not resolved, the supplier must issue a letter saying this. This is known as a 'deadlock letter'. However, in reaching this point, the supplier must also set out the different remedies available to you under the complaints-handling procedure, which must include:

- an apology; *and*
- an explanation; *and*
- the taking of appropriate remedial action by the regulated provider; *and*
- the award of compensation in appropriate circumstances.

When a complaint is treated as received

Your complaint and any subsequent communication must be treated as having been received:[20]

- where contact is made orally (by phone or in person), at the time it is received by that regulated provider;
- where made in writing (including by email) and it is received:
  - before 5pm on a working day, on that day;

– after 5pm on a working day or at any time on a day that is not a working day, on the first working day immediately following the day upon which it is received.

A working day is any day other than a Saturday, Sunday, Christmas Day, Good Friday or a bank holiday.[21]

Where a supplier fails to handle complaints properly, Ofgem may investigate and impose penalties.

Suppliers are required to publish details of consumer complaints received in an annual report. This must be displayed on their websites in a prominent position or copies supplied free of charge.[22]

Complaints about National Grid

If your complaint is about any aspect of the operation of National Grid or its employees and agents, you can use its free complaints service. National Grid will investigate your complaint and respond to you within 10 working days. If it is not possible to investigate the complaint within 10 days, it will inform you when a response can be expected. If no response is forthcoming, there may be grounds for compensation under National Grid's standards of service provisions.

3. **Action by Ofgem**

Enforcement matters

Ofgem has powers to order energy suppliers and gas transporters to do anything it considers necessary to ensure they comply with certain provisions of the Acts or any conditions in their licences. The Energy Act 2023 makes provision for the enforcement of conditions of licences and of other requirements imposed on licence holders.

The matters covered by these powers are called '**enforcement matters**' and include:[23]
- giving and continuing to supply electricity;
- connecting premises to a supply of gas;
- paying interest on security deposits;
- keeping meters in proper working order;
- producing codes of practice or other arrangements to deal with customers in default;
- protecting consumers when energy providers cease trading.

The list of enforcement matters seems more limited than it really is. For instance, disputes about responsibility for bills are not specifically mentioned, but may be covered indirectly because one remedy for a supplier in a dispute is to disconnect you and disconnection may be an enforcement matter. Ofgem can intervene in a dispute if it is likely to end up being an enforcement matter, but it cannot intervene in individual billing disputes.

The conditions in suppliers' and transporters' licences are not enforceable by individual consumers because they are obligations arising between the respective supplier and Ofgem. Many disputes arise directly under the relevant Acts, but those that only involve breaches of licence conditions have to be referred to Ofgem. If necessary, Ofgem's exercise of its powers can be judicially reviewed.[24] In certain circumstances, the suppliers themselves may also be judicially reviewed (see p267).

Standards of performance

Failure by suppliers to comply with overall standards of performance can result in regulatory action by Ofgem. Suppliers are regulated through the Standard Licence Conditions (SLCs). If there is widespread evidence of suppliers flouting or avoiding their obligations under the SLCs, Ofgem is expected to act.

There are two kinds of standards of performance – 'overall' and 'individual'. **'Overall standards'** are targets set by Ofgem to measure the supplier's general performance. Failure to comply with overall standards is a matter between the supplier and Ofgem and is unlikely to affect you directly. **'Individual standards'** are rules of performance (ie, the Electricity (Standards of Performance) Regulations 2015 and the Electricity and Gas (Standards of Performance) (Suppliers) Regulations 2015)[25] which, if they are breached, normally entitle you to a small compensation payment. These regulations set out the sums that electricity suppliers and distributors must pay you by way of compensation for failure to meet specified standards of performance, subject to certain exemptions.

The standards of performance covering electricity distributors set out prescribed time frames for supply restoration to premises in normal and severe weather conditions, supply restoration in the case of multiple interruptions or cases where a power cut arises from the operation of the distributor's fuse. The standards also cover estimates for connection and prior notice of planned supply interruptions where power is rationed on a rota to be provided within a prescribed time frame and cover complaints relating to voltage levels.

If you encounter a breach of licence conditions, report the matter to Ofgem for investigation.

Electricity

Standards apply to all electricity suppliers (referred to as 'operators' in the context of the legislation). Some of these standards also overlap with the responsibilities placed upon electricity distributors. Suppliers provide online information and leaflets describing them – some may also include additional standards which the supplier has set for itself. The standards set down by the law cover:

- failure of the distributor's fuse;
- restoring supply where disconnection was the supplier's fault;
- providing a supply;
- providing an estimate of charges for connection of a supply or moving a meter;
- giving notice when the supplier has to interrupt a supply;
- dealing with voltage complaints;
- dealing with meter disputes;
- responding to complaints about prepayment meters not working;
- responding to requests or queries about charges or payments;
- making and keeping appointments;
- giving notice to consumers of their rights under this scheme.

Where there is a dispute over the application of the standards or entitlement to compensation, the regulations set out the procedure to be followed once the matter has been referred to Ofgem.[26]

Minimum periods and compensation

The standards require actions to be carried out within a certain time frame. Failure to do so entitles you to a fixed sum, from £40 for three hours on a working day and four hours at a weekend (for most matters) up to £95 and with payments in respect of each 12 hours.[27]

The payment from suppliers is limited to one payment per household and not linked to the number of customers affected where less than 5,000 customers are affected, and a power cut arises as a result of a fault or failure in ordinary conditions.[28]

Where more than 5,000 customers are affected, and the supply is interrupted as a result of a failure of, fault in or damage to the distribution system, the maximum compensation is £360.[29]

Standard payments are normally maximum payments, though they may be increased at the discretion of the energy supplier.

If failure to meet the standards causes you to lose more than £40 or £80, you can still claim the larger amount. If necessary, you can go to court. If there is any dispute between you and the supplier over these standards or the payments, contact Citizens Advice consumer service or Consumer Scotland for advice. A dispute resolution process is set out in the Regulations.[30] Your ultimate remedy would be a claim in the civil courts. Documents can be filed electronically.[31]

Severe weather

When there are severe weather conditions, electricity distribution companies have 24 hours to restore the electricity supply if it fails due to a storm.[32]

- For 'Category 1' storms, you are entitled to £80 if the supply is not restored after 24 hours. After the initial 24 hours, you are entitled to a further £40 for every six hours you are without power.

- For 'Category 2' storms, you are entitled to £80 if the supply is not restored after 48 hours. After the initial 48 hours, you are entitled to a further £40 for every six hours you are without power.

There is a cap of £2,000 maximum compensation per household for a single power cut.

Compensation during severe weather conditions is sometimes different to the standard payment scheme. For example, following Storm Arwen in November 2021, one network operator increased statutory payments by 20 per cent and removed the cap. Another paid £150 per household on top of the statutory payment for customers without supply for over 48 hours. Electricity network operators also offered to compensate reasonable expenses for accommodation costs.

If you are cut off more than four times in a year for at least three hours each time, you can claim an extra £90.[33]

However, it is important to note that payments made by a supplier are only made in respect of a premises, not the number of customers within those premises, who may be adversely affected or who may be named on the bill. Where a supplier has made the necessary payment or payments (in the case of an additional standard payment), it is taken as having discharged its obligations to all customers.[34] The customer who receives the payment may request payment to be made in a particular way, including by direct transfer or cheque. Although the supplier is not obliged to make payment in the way requested, the supplier must not unreasonably withhold payment in that way.[35]

These provisions may not apply to customers living on islands where the supply is provided on or under the sea bed and no alternative means is available to the distributor.[36]

Gas

Minimum standards are laid down in regulations for gas.[37] As with electricity, there are some automatic levels of compensation for which standard payments and additional standard payments may be made. Gas companies may also have their own settlement schemes. The customer relations manager in each British Gas region has the authority to settle claims for breach of these standards, up to £5,000.

Getting an order from Ofgem

If you think a supplier or transporter may be in breach of an enforcement matter, contact Citizens Advice consumer service or Consumer Scotland in the first instance. Ofgem may investigate a breach and has a duty to consider information supplied by consumer advocacy bodies.[38] If satisfied that there has been a breach, and that supplier should have co-operated, Ofgem (supporting the Gas and Electricity Markets Authority (GEMA)) may make either a 'provisional order' or 'final order'. Making a provisional order is quicker than a final order, so you should press for the former.[39]

Ofgem has powers to obtain compensation on your behalf and must consider this when making a final order. In deciding the form of final order and compensation available, Ofgem is required to consider whether you are likely to sustain loss or damage while waiting for the order to be made.[40]

Ofgem cannot make an order if:

- it thinks that its general duties laid down by the Acts do not allow it; *or*
- the breaches in question are trivial; *or*
- it is satisfied that the supplier or transporter has agreed to, and is taking all steps necessary to, comply with its obligations.

Ofgem possesses powers to extend the range of energy industry functions and activities that it may regulate and licence, including the activities of third parties (eg, consumer switching sites) subject to approval by the Secretary of State and a resolution of the House of Commons.[41]

Ofgem must tell you if it decides not to make an order. In deciding whether to make an order, Ofgem must take into account, in particular, your lack of other remedies and the loss or damage which you might suffer during the consultation period, which has to take place before a final order is made. If you would otherwise be without a supply, a provisional order will normally be appropriate.

If a provisional order is made and complied with, Ofgem only confirms it as a final order if further breaches are likely to occur.

Before making a final order or confirming a provisional order, Ofgem must serve you and the supplier/transporter with a copy of the proposed order and allow 28 days for representations. If it wants to modify the original proposal, Ofgem must either get the consent of the supplier/transporter or serve copies and allow a further 28 days. A similar procedure must be followed to revoke a final order.

Ofgem must also comply with the ordinary legal rules about natural justice which govern public or government organisations (see p267). In one case, a decision by Ofgas, a former gas regulator, was quashed by the High Court because it did not tell a consumer that it had interviewed an important witness, nor did it give the consumer a chance to reply to what the witness had said.[42]

You are entitled to a copy of any order when it is made.

A supplier/transporter can appeal to the High Court (Court of Session in Scotland) against the making of an order. Although you would not necessarily be directly involved, you can be added as a third party – this is a technical procedure for which you need to get legal advice.

The supplier has a duty to obey any order. This means you can sue for a breach of statutory duty if Ofgem does not enforce its own order. Ofgem can also enforce its orders by ordinary civil action against the supplier/transporter, which would be easier and cheaper for you, if you cannot obtain legal aid funding to do this yourself (see p258).

Each case is decided on its merits. Cases rarely, if ever, reach this stage because suppliers want to avoid formal (and public) action.

Determinations by Ofgem are final, and once a determination has been made you cannot sue a supplier or transporter over the same matters.

Breach of conditions relating to payment difficulties

All suppliers' licences require them to compile methods to deal with customers in arrears. These matters are dealt with elsewhere in this book, but it is worth pointing out that a supplier's failure to comply with these 'methods' is an enforcement matter because it is a breach of the relevant condition.

Consumer redress orders

Ofgem is empowered to make consumer redress orders, which may be used to provide an alternative to lengthy and expensive litigation and benefit all consumers, whether they are aware they have suffered loss or not.[43] An order may require a supplier to provide redress to you directly, compensating you directly where possible or putting you back into the position you were in before the breach.

Ofgem may make a consumer redress order where it is satisfied that a supplier is contravening any condition or requirement and one or more consumers have suffered loss, damage or been caused inconvenience.[44] A loss need not be financial to qualify, so inconvenience or nuisance may be a possible ground.

Under a consumer redress order, a supplier may be ordered to:[45]
- pay compensation to each affected consumer for the loss, damage or contravention;
- issue a written statement setting out the contravention and its consequences;
- terminate or vary any contracts entered into with affected consumers. This can only happen with your consent.

If compensation is part of the order, the amount must be specified.

Ofgem does not have a prescribed set of penalties; it approaches each complaint on a case-by-case basis to retain the widest discretion.[46] The amount of compensation must be reasonable. The maximum penalty that may be imposed on a regulated supplier may not exceed 10 per cent of its annual turnover. The powers are designed to be proportionate and build upon the power to impose penalties and the role of the Ombudsman. Consumer redress orders may be used together with, or separately from, penalties.[47]

Suppliers which cease trading

Where a supplier ceases to trade, Ofgem has the authority to protect the interests of consumers facing a loss of supply. Ofgem will appoint a new supplier – known as the supplier of last resort – for the affected customers as quickly as possible to ensure minimum disruption.[48]

Ofgem has issued guidance on the manner and circumstances in which it expects to exercise these powers.[49] Ofgem arranges the maintenance of supply until new arrangements with an alternative energy supplier are put in place.

Only when the power to appoint a supplier of last resort is not feasible will Ofgem seek the consent of the Secretary of State to make an application for an Energy Supply Company Administrator to be appointed.[50]

In taking over from a failed supplier, the new supplier should honour existing contracts and debts. In September 2021, Ofgem stated in the case of failed supplier Avro Energy that the substitute supplier, Octopus Energy, would honour domestic credit balances for both current and past customers after reviewing accounts and deducting any unbilled charges for supply by Avro Energy.[51]

Can a supplier voluntarily wind up?

A supplier cannot voluntarily wind up without the court's permission.[52] Permission is only granted if the Secretary of State and Ofgem have been given at least 14 days' notice.[53] Ofgem can then revoke the company's licences and appoint a supplier of last resort.

4. Unfair terms

Consumer Rights Act 2015

As your fuel supply is provided under a contract with the supplier, the law relating to contracts, including regulations covering unfair terms, applies.

The relevant law is found in the Consumer Rights Act 2015[54] and in decisions by the higher courts. The Act supersedes much of the earlier law,[55] but decisions under previous regulations and caselaw continue to be relevant.

An unfair term of a consumer contract is not binding on you.[56] A term qualifies as 'unfair if, contrary to the requirement of good faith, it causes a significant imbalance in the parties' rights and obligations which operate to the detriment of the consumer'.[57] Whether or not a term is unfair is determined by looking at the nature of the contract and all the circumstances existing when the term was agreed, together with all the other terms of the contract.[58]

Rights and remedies under the Consumer Rights Act 2015 are available to individuals (but not small businesses or companies). Gas and electricity are treated as 'goods' under the Act if supplied and sold in limited volumes or set quantities.[59]

Transparency – that contract terms can be readily understood – is fundamental to fairness. Written terms of a consumer contract and any written notices to consumers must be transparent.[60] They must be expressed in plain and intelligible language and be legible. This specific requirement operates alongside the requirement of good faith and open and fair dealing (see p19). All obligations and rights should be set out fully, and in a way that the average consumer can understand their practical significance.

If a term could have different meanings, the meaning which is most favourable to you is taken.

Enforcement action for unfair terms may be taken by one of a number of bodies in the UK, including the Competition and Markets Authority, the Secretary of State, a district council in England and Ofgem.[61]

Examples of terms which may be considered unfair[62]

Terms limiting or excluding legal liability for death or personal injury as a result of an act or omission.

Terms which exclude or limit your legal rights in relation to the supplier or another party in the event of total or partial non-performance or inadequate performance by the supplier of any of the contractual obligations.

Any terms limiting the option of offsetting a debt owed to a supplier against any claim which you may have against the supplier.

Terms which allow the supplier to retain money you have paid where you decide not to finish the contract, but do not allow you to receive compensation or a refund where the supplier is the party cancelling the contract.

A term that requires you to pay a disproportionately high sum or penalty clause if you decide to opt out of an agreement.

Clauses which seek to limit when you can begin legal proceedings.

Disproportionate penalties and compensation which may be payable if you end the contract.

Provisions that may allow a supplier to unilaterally dissolve or alter a contract without notice or where no such right is given to you.

Clauses which you do not know about when the contract is formed.

Clauses allowing the supplier to increase prices without giving you the right to cancel the contract if the final price is too high in relation to the price agreed.

Consumer Protection from Unfair Trading Regulations 2008

Action may also be taken against a supplier which engages in an unfair trading practice as defined under the Consumer Protection from Unfair Trading Regulations 2008. These cover unfair commercial practices which affect the operation of consumer choice, referred to as a 'transactional decision' in the regulations. A transactional decision has a broad meaning covering any decision taken by a consumer, whether it is to act or to refrain from acting, concerning whether, how and on what terms:

- to purchase, make payment in whole or in part for, retain or dispose of a product; *or*
- to exercise a contractual right in relation to a product.

A 'product' includes a service and rights and obligations on a trader.[63] 'Commercial practice' is also given a wide meaning and includes a trader's act, omission, course of conduct, representation or commercial communication (eg, advertising and marketing) which is directly connected with the promotion, sale or supply of a product to or from you.[64] The unfair practice can occur before, during or after the transaction, whether or not the transaction ultimately takes place. Thus, unfair attempts to influence you through marketing and cold-calling and steps that might be taken to stop you exercising your rights can be caught by the regulations.

The test of whether a commercial practice is misleading includes whether it contains false information and whether it deceives you into a transaction you would not have otherwise taken.[65] This includes the marketing of a product (including comparative advertising), which creates confusion about any products, trademarks, trade names or other distinguishing marks of a competitor. A commercial practice can also be misleading by way of omission if, in its factual context, it omits or hides the commercial practice, omits material information, provides material information in a manner which is unclear, unintelligible, ambiguous or untimely, or fails to identify its commercial intent, unless this is already apparent from the context.[66]

Importantly, it may also cover the failure by a fuel supplier to comply with a code of conduct if it has indicated that it is bound by the code of conduct, and the breach causes you to enter into a transaction that you otherwise would not have done.

If a trader engages in a misleading commercial practice, it is guilty of an offence and may be prosecuted by a local authority's trading standards department.

In 2012, the Court of Appeal upheld the conviction for an offence under these regulations by SSE.[67] The company was held liable for misleading statements made by a trainee salesperson working for a linked company, Southern Electric Gas Ltd, operating in an area with a considerable population of elderly consumers and which had been designated by the local council as a 'no cold-calling zone'. The Court of Appeal ruled that both companies could potentially have been prosecuted and that SSE fell within the definition of a 'trader' under the regulations as Southern Electric Gas Ltd was held by it as a subsidiary company.[68]

Digital Markets, Competition and Consumers Act 2024
The Digital Markets, Competition and Consumers Act 2024 aims to improve information transparency for consumers. Areas covered by the Act include the following.

- The display of pricing information, including the consistent use of unit pricing to allow for easy price comparison between products.
- Restricting hidden fees and drip-pricing practices, whereby consumers are initially enticed with low prices, but fees are increased as they progress through the purchasing process.
- New standards requiring online platforms to act with professional diligence in their dealings with consumers, particularly with e-commerce material on social media.
- Private rights of redress against traders will be extended to cover unfair commercial practices such as misleading omissions or breaches of professional diligence by traders but these will apply to situations 'involving gas and electricity only if they are put up for sale in a limited volume or set quantity'.[69]
- Provisions for alternative dispute resolution to court will be available to consumers.

Many details will be filled by way of regulation. An additional development is that the Competition and Markets Authority is given powers to enforce provisions which may, in some instances, be additional or beyond the scope of actions available through Ofgem.

5. Using the civil courts

There are two types of civil court action in the field of fuel rights – ordinary court action and judicial review through the High Court. In England and Wales, the relationship between the consumer and the supplier is based on contract law or the law of tort, with remedies available through the civil courts depending on the amount of harm or damage involved. Judicial review is used for actions against state bodies and regulatory authorities and bodies which may be exercising statutory functions. While a supplier can be fined for breaches of its obligations by Ofgem, as well as sued for breach of contract or in tort by you, there is not necessarily any separate claim for compensation available simply for breach of a supplier's obligations at law.[70]

In Scotland, a consumer's relationship with a public electricity supplier/ regional electricity company or transporter is statutory, and so any claim is based on a breach of a statutory duty. This may mean that you have to pursue your remedies through Ofgem.[71] On the other hand, Ofgem is also subject to judicial review.[72]

Legal funding

Before April 2013, Community Legal Service funding was available for taking court action if you had a strong enough case and qualified on financial grounds. However, there are now major restrictions on these cases and realistically legal aid is only likely if a consumer matter also involves a matter of serious personal injury, a threat of loss of home or a discrimination issue. Check gov.uk/legal-aid/ eligibility to see if you are likely to qualify.

In Scotland, the Scottish Legal Aid Board provides civil assistance. Eligibility is based on disposable income after essential expenses have been paid. For more details, see slab.org.uk.

In practice, it may be very hard to find a solicitor or advice and assistance funded by legal aid in many areas. It may also take time for an application for legal aid assistance to be processed.

Emergency legal representation

Assuming a legal aid provider can be found, it may be necessary to apply for emergency legal representation in many cases involving energy problems. An emergency certificate will only be granted if:

- there is a risk to your physical safety or that of any family member or your home;
- there is a significant risk of a miscarriage of justice, unreasonable hardship or irretrievable problems in handling the case;
- there are no other appropriate options available to deal with the risk.

An emergency legal aid certificate lasts for four weeks, but it may be difficult to find a legal aid practice that will undertake such a case.

As an alternative, it may be simpler, and more appropriate, for you to begin a claim in the county court using the arbitration or small claims process. Most civil claims are unlikely to qualify for legal assistance if the amount claimed falls below £10,000. This means that you may have to act for yourself.

Using the small claims procedure in the county court

England and Wales

Every year thousands of people represent themselves in small claims hearings, though until recently they have not often been used by energy consumers. In England and Wales, small claims are heard in the county court which deals with civil cases where up to £100,000 is involved (claims of £100,000 or more are heard in the High Court). See CPAG's *Debt Advice Handbook* for detailed information. It is available free at cpag.org.uk/handbooks.

Where a dispute involves less than £10,000 – as with many consumer matters – it is dealt with under a simplified procedure known as 'arbitration', 'the small claims track' or 'a small claims hearing', normally taking the form of a hearing in private in chambers – ie, the judge's private room.

All designated money claims in civil cases in England and Wales are issued in the Civil National Business Centre in Northampton. The centre is supported by a dedicated contact team that deals with all telephone queries relating to claims. You are encouraged to begin your claim online, although forms may be downloaded or are available from local county courts which are designated as hearing centres.

Proceedings may be brought against a supplier which is in breach of contract (eg, overcharging or wrongly withholding a refund) and for any harm or damage it may cause, either by itself or through its employees or subcontractors.

The small claims court is a relatively informal procedure, suitable for people who are not represented by a solicitor. This might be appropriate if an unlawful disconnection has caused you a relatively small loss or your landlord has been charging more than the maximum resale price for gas or electricity.

Other claims might include where you have a dispute with an energy company about the amount you have paid or where there has been a failure of supply which has resulted in damage such as loss of frozen food. Or you may have a dispute about the amount of fuel consumed at your home which you cannot resolve with the supplier.

Neither side can claim legal costs beyond the court fees involved and, as a result, suppliers tend to settle these cases rather than spend money on contesting them which will not be recoverable.

When the claim form is issued, a court fee is normally payable. However, if you are on universal credit (UC), income support (IS), income-based jobseeker's allowance (JSA), income-related employment and support allowance (ESA) or pension credit (PC), you may be exempt from paying any fee on application to the court (see p269). If you are not receiving any of these benefits, you can apply for remission or reduction of a fee if you would otherwise suffer undue financial hardship because of the exceptional circumstances in your case.

If you succeed in your claim, the court fee is added to the amount which the other side has to pay you. Unlike other court proceedings, only limited costs can be reclaimed. This means that, even if you lose, you will not have to pay the other side's own legal representation costs – ie, each side is responsible for its own costs. If the case is settled or discontinued, there may be a full refund of the hearing fee if you notify the court in writing, at least seven days (excluding the date of receipt and date of hearing) before the trial date or start of the trial week.

The claim form requires you to set down the details of your legal claim. Copies of the form are then lodged in court on payment of the fee (unless this is waived) and a copy is sent to the other side (known as the 'defendant'). The issue of the form requires the defendant to either admit the claim or defend it. In either case, the defendant must reply to the issue of the proceedings. If the defendant does nothing, after 21 days you may be entitled to claim judgment in default. This means you can obtain your judgment without having to argue the case in court, simply because the defendant has failed to reply.

Experience suggests that fuel suppliers rarely contest proceedings in the small claims court, especially in cases involving relatively small sums (eg, less than £500), as the cost of sending someone to attend the hearing often exceeds the amount of money concerned. This factor encourages the settlement of a dispute. Small claims may be particularly suited to the recovery of deposits.

The court will issue a set of directions which should be followed.

In any case, it is important to exchange copies of all documents which you seek to rely upon with the other party before the hearing. This gives the other party the opportunity to settle the case ahead of any hearing.

Under the rules of civil procedure, each side is entitled to see the written evidence and documents used in a claim before the hearing according to the timetable. Each side is expected to list its documents and make copies available. Neither side should be taken by surprise by written evidence at the hearing.

In bringing a claim relating to overcharging or a failure to supply for which you have been charged, you should gather together all your energy bills. If you no longer have them, request them in writing from your supplier. Also bring a copy of all correspondence and the contract with the energy company. These documents should be organised in date order.

Look at the agreed price for supply and work out whether the company has charged the correct rate for units over 12 months. Check whether it has charged more. Use April 1 to March 31 as the start and finish dates. Look especially at any periods where there may have been overcharging. You must produce these documents if a case goes as far as court; before any hearing, you should also send the other side copies of all documentary evidence on which you intend to rely.

For each year, work out how many units over the limit you have been charged and multiply them first by the higher rate and then by the lower rate. The difference is the amount that you should claim for overcharging.

Check whether the supplier has ever given you an explanation of its charging methods. If not, state that you believe you have been wrongly charged from when you became a customer, to the present day. Calculate your entire usage over the period and work out how much it would have cost when your supply started. Then work out how much you have actually paid. The difference between the two figures is what you should claim. Such cases may also arise from undercharging, leading to the supplier suddenly trying to recover money with a demand for a lump sum.

The rules of court encourage parties to try to settle their cases without recourse to court proceedings – at any stage parties can negotiate and make settlement proposals to each other to avoid litigation.

If the matter goes as far as a small claims court hearing, each side can present their case. Any written evidence which is presented should normally be served on the other side well before this final hearing takes place.

Transfer of proceedings

If you become involved with litigation with an energy supplier, it may be important to ensure a transfer of proceedings to your nearest county court (your 'home court') or the High Court if the claim exceeds £100,000. An application may be necessary to the court.[73]

When considering whether to grant a transfer, the court must consider:[74]

- the financial value of the claim and the amount in dispute (if different);
- the convenience of moving to another court;
- the availability of a judge specialising in the type of claim in question;
- whether the facts, legal issues, remedies or procedures involved are simple or complex;
- the importance of the outcome of the claim to the public in general.

Methods of service

The Civil Procedure Rules set out the various methods of service that can be used. The usual method of service is by first class post, with the documents deemed served two days after posting. Service may also be by email, fax or through a document exchange.

Witness statements and all documentary evidence should also be sent to the other side before the hearing. For example, you might wish to call an electrician or meter reader as a witness in a case, in which case it will be necessary to submit a written witness statement of what they will say first. Documentary evidence should normally be exchanged between both sides in a case before the hearing, subject to directions by the court. Each side gives its evidence to the court and has an opportunity to question the other (a process known as cross-examination). The judge may also ask questions of the parties at the hearing.

Representation

You are entitled to 'quiet assistance' from a friend to help present your case. The friend can take notes, suggest questions and give you advice and moral support. The friend may be legally qualified, but this is not essential. Such assistance is known as having a 'McKenzie friend'[75] (or 'courtroom supporter' or a 'lay supporter' in Scotland), and courts are generally familiar with the concept. McKenzie friends often assist debtors in debt recovery proceedings in certain courts. The McKenzie friend has no right to address the court but, in practice, the courts may allow a McKenzie friend to address the court if you have difficulties. The right to speak is discretionary, and anyone granted the right to speak must not abuse the privilege. In particular, it is crucial that any statements made to the court relate to the facts and points of law in the case and are not directed as a general attack on the energy company and its policies. If the right to a McKenzie friend is abused (eg, by making political or personalised attacks), it may be withdrawn. It is important to be polite at all times.

The judgment

A small claims court judgment takes effect like any other county court judgment. Enforcement action can be taken if the party does not follow the terms of the judgment – eg, in a claim for compensation by paying the money owed or awarded.

Scotland

Scotland has an equivalent small claims procedure using the sheriff court for sums up to £5,000 – known as the 'simple claims procedure'. This is governed by the simple claims rules with standard forms – known as summonses – to be completed. The forms can be obtained from the sheriff court clerk or downloaded from the Scottish Courts Service website (scotcourts.gov.uk). The person bringing the action is known as the 'pursuer' and the person being taken to court is known as the 'defender'. The details can be amended before a hearing takes place. It is also possible to apply for time to try to settle the case. Bringing the case to a temporary halt in this way is known as 'sisting' the case.

If the defender does not respond to proceedings, Form 3A should be completed setting out the order you wish to obtain. If a party fails to appear at a small claims hearing, the sheriff can grant an order, known as a 'decree'. No costs are payable if the claim is under £200, but costs can be awarded up to £150 if the claim is over £200.

See scotcourts.gov.uk/taking-action/simple-procedure for a useful guide to making a claim.

Disputes over £10,000 (£5,000 in Scotland)

In county court proceedings involving more than £10,000, each party has to pay its own costs, and the unsuccessful party must also pay the other party's costs. These may be substantial and while individuals can represent themselves, it is advisable to instruct a solicitor. Note that even if you are successful, not every cost incurred is recoverable.

As with small claims, the rules of court encourage parties to settle their cases out of court. The Civil Procedure Rules provide an opportunity for both claimants and defendants to inform the other side what will be acceptable to settle a dispute without recourse to a trial. If a party does not accept an offer made under Part 36, it risks being made liable to pay more in interest and/or costs on a judgment than if no offer had been made.[76] Parties to litigation involving larger sums must ensure that they comply with the Civil Procedure Rules and directions and orders from the court in terms of supplying and filing documents to the other party and the court. Both claims and defences may be struck out by the court or parties subject to sanctions from the court where procedural rules are not followed.[77] Decisions to strike out cases or apply sanctions may be appealed where there is a reason for failure to comply. The Court of Appeal gives an example: 'If the reason why a document was not filed with the court was that the party or his solicitor suffered from a debilitating illness or was involved in an accident, then, depending on the circumstances, that may constitute a good reason.'[78]

In Scotland, a claim over £5,000 goes through the ordinary cause procedure. See CPAG's *Debt Advice Handbook Scotland* for more about ordinary cause.

Claims for harassment and damages

In an important case which indicates that the courts will not tolerate heavy-handed and intimidating actions by energy suppliers, the Court of Appeal ruled that legal threats issued by British Gas could constitute harassment and could be subject to both civil proceedings and a crime under the Protection from Harassment Act 1997.[79]

Over a period of months, British Gas sent bills and threatening letters to the claimant who was a former British Gas customer who had switched to npower. The letters demanded money she did not owe. The threats included to disconnect her gas supply, to start legal proceedings and to report her to credit reference agencies. Despite repeatedly contacting British Gas the threats continued, including after she complained to Energywatch and twice to the chairman of British Gas. As a result, she wasted many hours, and, more importantly, was brought to a state of considerable anxiety. She instructed a solicitor but still received no response. As a consequence, she began legal proceedings claiming £5,000 for distress and anxiety and £5,000 for financial loss due to time lost and expenses in dealing with British Gas and that the course of conduct amounted to unlawful harassment contrary to the Protection from Harassment Act 1997.

Excuses raised by British Gas that it could not be blamed for letters issued by a computer, or that it was a company and should be treated as different to an individual who issued threatening letters, were rejected by the court.

The court ruled that a company such as British Gas could be held responsible for mistakes made by its computerised debt recovery system and the personnel responsible for programming and operating it. The company could be held liable in the same way that a human being could be.

The court also indicated that harassment could be a crime as well as a tort or civil wrong and that in 'any well-documented case, what is sufficient for the one purpose is likely to be sufficient for the other'. This ruling opens the way for energy companies to be prosecuted under the Protection from Harassment Act 1997. It was further observed that the 'primary responsibility should rest upon local public authorities which possess the means and the statutory powers to bring alleged harassers, however impersonal and powerful, before the local justices'. This means that trading standards departments could prosecute where wrongful debt collection turns into harassment. The question will be whether the course of conduct goes beyond annoyance and irritation and has become 'oppressive and unacceptable' or 'fairly severe' so that the law should intervene.[80]

A wrongful attempt at debt enforcement by an energy supplier can also result in damages for slander or libel if statements are made by a supplier that are untrue and may damage your reputation.[81]

Injunctions/interdicts

An 'injunction' ('interdict' in Scotland) is an order made by a court which either prohibits someone from doing something (a 'prohibitory' injunction) or instructs someone to do something (a 'mandatory' injunction). For example, if a supplier or landlord illegally cuts off your supply, you could ask for an injunction to get it reconnected.[82] Failure to obey an injunction is contempt of court, punishable by fines, or even imprisonment in extreme cases.

In urgent cases, you can get an injunction in the absence of the other side (what is known as an *ex parte* injunction) – eg, where locks have been changed without permission or a meter has been unlawfully removed. The injunction is obtained by going to court and making an appointment for an urgent hearing. A standard form (N244 – Notice of Application) is provided, and you are asked to provide evidence in the form of a statement of truth. Normally, the claim for an injunction is part of an action for damages. The application is made before a judge who makes a decision as to whether the injunction should be granted and gives directions about how the other side (known as the defendant) is to be notified of their decision. **Note:** applying for an injunction can be costly. You will need to pay a court fee of at least £155[83] and should also seek advice from a solicitor before using this remedy. The legal help scheme is no longer available for advice about this type of debt, so you would need to meet the cost of instructing a solicitor yourself. Check if you qualify for a fee exemption.

Although there are some situations in which an injunction is granted almost as a matter of course (eg, illegal eviction), you have no 'right' to an injunction. Injunctions are within a court's discretion and whether or not they are granted depends on the overall circumstances of the case.

The most common situation in a dispute with a supplier is where you ask for an 'interim' injunction (or 'interim' interdict in Scotland). This is when you need a temporary court order quickly, usually valid until the whole case can be put properly before the court.

An example where it might be necessary to threaten or seek an injunction is where a supplier starts action to disconnect a supply by mistake – eg, where action is taken against the wrong address. Normally, you will have had a warning but the situation can arise where a supplier or its agent has obtained a warrant against the wrong address and begins steps to disconnect or install a prepayment meter. Or you come home from a holiday to find you have been disconnected in error by a warrant concerning another customer.

In England and Wales, the court applies a balancing act, and it is necessary to show a *prima facie* case and that the harm to yourself is of such a nature that damages alone would not amount to a sufficient remedy if action is not taken immediately.[84] In Scotland, an interim order for specific implement should ordinarily only be granted if there is a *prima facie* case of a breach of a legal obligation, and the balance of convenience favours grant of the order.[85]

During normal court opening hours, a hearing can usually be obtained very quickly. You should try to give as much notice as possible to the energy company. Email or fax a letter to the supplier where circumstances allow, addressing it to the legal department. The threat of applying for an injunction may be sufficient to obtain a suitable response from the supplier and make applying for the injunction unnecessary.

In this situation, neither you nor the supplier/transporter has time to present your case fully, and the court has to decide without hearing the evidence in full. The court will consider the 'balance of convenience' – ie, whether you or the supplier/transporter has more to lose or gain from the refusal or granting of an interim injunction, including whether a later award of damages will make up for any such loss.[86] For example, where a supplier threatens disconnection, the court will balance the inconvenience to you of being disconnected against the inconvenience to the supplier of having to continue to supply someone regarded as a bad customer. A court almost always considers the balance to be in your favour if you are prepared to agree to a prepayment meter at least until your dispute is resolved.[87] If an immediate injunction is granted you will be asked to serve the supplier with notice of the order immediately by phoning them or faxing a letter; a copy of the order will also be drawn up by the court. Failure to obey an injunction puts the supplier at risk of contempt proceedings, for which it may be fined or individuals may be jailed as a punishment. In emergencies, injunctions can be obtained outside normal court hours. The court will have a telephone number to contact in such cases and injunctions can be granted by a judge over the phone.

Can you get an injunction for repairs or to restore your supply?
A court might grant an order for a mandatory injunction or appoint an expert, manager or receiver to carry out repairs to a property to restore a power supply. Such an order may only be made 'in the most exceptional circumstances' where it is clear that a breach has occurred which is causing actual and immediate major discomfort, inconvenience and is a real health risk.[88]

Damages

As well as, or instead of, an injunction, you can claim damages (ie, monetary compensation) for a supplier or transporter's abuse of its powers or failure to comply with its statutory or contractual duties.[89] If your supply is accidentally cut off, you may be able to claim damages for negligence and damage which has come directly from the interruption of electricity or gas supply (but not for the pure supply interruptions themselves). A claim for damages for breach of contract must be based on the amount necessary to put you in the position you would have enjoyed had the contract been performed. Losses that are reasonably foreseeable at the time the contract was made as being a likely outcome of the breach of contract may also be recoverable. In a case of negligence and a claim in tort arising from a harmful act, the measure of damages is the sum necessary.

In a case of failure to supply, damages would cover compensation, not only for the distress and discomfort of being without a supply, but also for additional expenses (eg, takeaway meals) and the loss of specific items (eg, fridge/freezer contents). Interest can also be claimed on any sum awarded in damages. In other cases, the failure of a supplier to disconnect a supply may amount to breach of a duty of care where harm results – eg, a fire which arises in circumstances where electricity should have been cut off.[90] All such losses arising from the breach of contract or duty of care by a supplier need to be specifically set out and pleaded in any claim. Claims for death and personal injury may also be brought in a case of electrocution arising from faulty equipment or supply.[91]

A claim for negligence may also arise where a supplier has caused damage or breached safety rules and damage to a person or property has resulted. What is safe is judged as an objective question by reference to what may be reasonably foreseen by a reasonable and prudent employer. It is also crucial that any breach of duty, including breaches of codes of practice or duties imposed by statute, can be shown to be responsible for causing the damage for which compensation is sought.[92] In cases of personal injury and loss, it is necessary to be able to prove negligence and the mere fact of a gas explosion cannot be relied upon to show negligence on the part of a distributor.[93]

The Economic and Corporate Transparency Act 2023 creates a new offence of fraud whereby an organisation, such as an energy company, is criminally liable where a person associated with it (eg, employees, agents, subsidiaries and others performing services for or on its behalf) commits fraud. The offence occurs where the fraud was intended to benefit the organisation and the organisation did not have reasonable procedures in place to prevent the fraud. The offence is one of strict liability for the organisation; prosecutors will not need to show that the organisation's leaders authorised or had knowledge of the fraud. If convicted, the organisation is liable to an unlimited fine.

Judicial review

Public bodies, such as Ofgem, have both statutory duties which must be performed and powers which allow for a large element of discretion. Similarly, the Secretary of State for Energy Security and Net Zero has wide powers to make decisions about energy policy in the UK. There is usually no right of appeal against a failure to perform a 'power', or as to how that discretion is exercised. However, this does not mean that nothing can be done. Such administrative matters are subject to control by judicial review[94] on the grounds of illegality, irrationality or procedural impropriety (see p268).

The exercise of any 'public' powers by any of the principal bodies discussed in this book and by the Secretary of State can be subject to judicial review.

An **'illegal decision'** is one where the decision-making body has not been given the legal power to do what it has done – ie, if it has gone outside its remit or what it was set up to do.

An **'unlawful decision'** is where a public body or the Secretary of State exceeds the powers available to them in law and the decision may be challenged in the courts. For example, the Secretary of State was ruled to have no power in law to alter tariffs affecting solar panels retrospectively.[95]

An **'unreasonable decision'** may arise where a public body has made a decision which is flawed in some way. In legal jargon, this is 'Wednesbury' unreasonableness, named after the court case in which the principle was established.[96] This principle requires a decision-making body to:

- consider all relevant factors;
- disregard irrelevant factors;
- not act perversely or irrationally.

An **'irrational decision'** is one which is so unreasonable that no reasonable authority could make it if it had properly considered the matter.

Public bodies (including Ofgem) are expected to follow their own rules and guidance and behave in a procedurally fair way.[97] Challenges may be brought on grounds of **'procedural impropriety'** where a public body fails to follows its own rules.[98] This can include breaches of 'natural justice', making decisions which are biased or unfair or which have the appearance of unfairness and prejudice to any impartial observer. If a decision-making body fails to adhere to the requirements of natural justice or the 'Wednesbury principles', then its decisions may be challenged in the High Court by way of judicial review. Any expert evidence submitted is expected to comply with the civil procedure rules.[99] In Scotland, an application is made to the Court of Session. In addition, breaches of the Equality Act 2010 may also be challenged in the High Court.[100]

Breach of one or more of these principles gives the court the power to overturn an authority's decision. It is important to realise that a court cannot overturn a decision simply because it thinks it would have come to a different decision. The court does not put itself in the place of the decision maker, but merely ensures they have kept within the boundaries of the law and have reasonably interpreted guidance and policies.[101] It is possible for two different, even contradictory, decisions to lie within those boundaries so that it would be equally lawful for the decision maker to choose either. It should also be remembered that judicial review is viewed as a remedy of last resort, and you should normally exhaust all other available remedies before embarking upon it. For example, judicial review may not be commenced if the matter in question is still awaiting the result of an appeal or a decision by Ofgem.[102]

Applying for judicial review is a three-stage procedure.[103] You must serve a letter on the public body or minister setting out the claim and giving notice of intention to seek judicial review. You must first apply for leave (ie, permission for judicial review) by lodging an application with supporting documents and written evidence. A judge then considers the papers and decides whether leave should be granted – ie, permission to take the case on to a full judicial review hearing. In Scotland, the application is made to the Court of Session.

In England and Wales, the court can make an order overturning a decision ('quashing' order) or requiring the body which is being judicially reviewed to do or not to do something ('mandatory' or 'prohibitory' order) in the same way as an injunction (see p265). In Scotland, a decision can be quashed by 'reduction', and a 'declarator' ('declaration' in England and Wales) can be issued establishing the legal position. From February 2022, claims involving public bodies in Wales are required to be issued and heard in Wales.[104]

An E-Working Pilot Scheme PD510 has been introduced with the intention to increase the ability of the Administrative Court to work electronically with effect until 1 November 2024.[105] It is important to realise that judicial review is a discretionary remedy and that different courts may or may not grant a remedy.

Applications for judicial review in England and Wales must be made promptly to the High Court and, in any event, within three months of the relevant decision. The three-month period can be extended, but only where there are strong mitigating circumstances. Even if leave is granted, the court may still refuse relief at the full judicial review hearing. In Scotland, applications must be made to the Court of Session; there is no specific time limit, but applications must not be unduly delayed.

HM Courts and Tribunals Service has published a guide on bringing a judicial review case in the Administrative Court.[106]

Human Rights Act 1998

The Human Rights Act 1998 applies to public authorities whose functions are of a public nature – such as regulators and suppliers. The Public Law Project may be able to comment and advise on the Act. Rights protected under the Human Rights Act are those contained in the European Convention on Human Rights. These include the right to property (Article 1), the right to a fair hearing (Article 6) and the right to privacy and family life (Article 8). Legal measures adopted by any state body that affect protected categories of human rights must be proportional to the aims to be achieved.[107] **Note:** human rights legislation is not affected by Brexit.

Remission of court fees

If you get UC, IS, income-based JSA, income-related ESA, PC or working tax credit (but not getting child tax credit), you are entitled to apply for a fee remission when beginning county court proceedings. Proof of entitlement may be established by producing a current benefit letter. If you are turned down on an application for remission of fees, there is usually a right of appeal. An application for a remission is made on Form EX160, which can be downloaded from gov.uk. You apply for help with fees at the same time as you are making your court or tribunal application and would otherwise be paying the fee. Staff will process your applications at the same time and inform you if you need to pay towards the fee or if more information is needed.[108]

If there is an emergency matter that needs an urgent decision of the court, the court manager can grant a remission without supporting evidence, though you are likely to be required to provide evidence within five days of the remission being given.

6. **The Energy Ombudsman**

The Energy Ombudsman is an independent body approved by Ofgem. The Ombudsman resolves disputes and complaints after negotiations have failed. It operates across the UK and its schemes offer members of the public a relatively informal and cheap alternative to civil litigation.[109]

The Ombudsman covers problems related to:
- energy bills;
- sales activity;
- switching gas or electricity supplier;
- the supply of energy to a home, such as power cuts and connections;
- micro generation and feed-in tariffs.

So far in 2024, the main complaint categories are billing, smart meters and customer service.[110] This reflects the same pattern as 2023.

You can only refer your complaint to the Ombudsman if you have tried to resolve it with your energy provider but have received a 'deadlock letter' (see p248) or eight weeks have passed since you first made your complaint to your provider. The Energy Ombudsman expects you to have fully exhausted the supplier's complaints process first.

If you have been unable to resolve your complaint with your supplier within eight weeks, you can escalate your complaint to the Energy Ombudsman. You can use the online complaints service at ombudsman-services.org. Be clear what you are complaining about and what you would like the outcome to be. It is useful to include a chronology of events, listing key events in date order. This provides a summary of what happened and when. If you have incurred financial losses, submit copies of receipts, bills and invoices you have had to pay to corroborate what you claim.

If the Ombudsman decides to make an award, and you accept it, your supplier must abide by the decision. The Ombudsman can ask your supplier to provide any or all of the following:

- a service or some practical action that will benefit you;
- an apology or explanation;
- a financial award up to £10,000 (£10,000 is only payable in exceptional cases; normally awards are much lower).

All of the UK's major energy providers are members of the Ombudsman scheme, which means they must abide by any decision that it makes about your complaint. If, however, the supplier does not follow the Ombudsman's recommendations, it may be reported to Ofgem for action. In 2019, Ofgem ordered Scottish Energy to repay £1.97 million to 157,236 customers after overcharging.

It is possible to ask for the Ombudsman's decision to be reviewed if you are unhappy with any aspect of it. The Ombudsman is required to meet the requirements laid down in the Alternative Dispute Resolution for Consumer Disputes (Competent Authorities and Information) Regulations 2015.

There is a limit to the legal issues which the Ombudsman can consider – eg, if an examination of the application of common law contractual concepts or the interpretation of contractual terms is involved. The Ombudsman cannot investigate complaints that have already been to court or are due to go to court. If you have started court proceedings, the Ombudsman may be able to help if you abandon, stay or suspend the court proceedings. You cannot seek compensation under the Ombudsman scheme and continue to take civil proceedings.[111]

For more information, visit ombudsman-services.org.

Notes

1. Available remedies
1 EU Reg 1227/2011 (REMIT)
2 SI 2018 No.1326
3 ss2-4 European Union (Withdrawal) Act 2018; *The Status of Retained UK Law*, House of Commons Briefing Paper No.85375, 30 July 2018

2. Negotiations
4 Reg 10 GE(CCHS) Regs
5 Ofgem press release, '*EDF Energy to pay £3 million following Ofgem investigation into the company's complaints handling arrangements*', 22 August 2014
6 Conditions 27 and 39 SLC
7 *Smith and Others v South Eastern Power Networks plc and Other Cases* [2012] EWHC 2541 QBD(TCC); *Thompson v Smiths Shiprepairers (North Shields) Ltd* [1984] QB 405

8 Reg 10(3) GE(CCHS) Regs as amended by The Gas and Electricity (Consumer Complaints Handling Standards) (Amendment) Regulations 2017 No.428
9 Reg 10(3) as amended by SI 2017 No.428 from 14 April 2017
10 Part II & III GE(CCHS) Regs
11 Reg 2 GE(CCHS) Regs
12 Reg 3(1) GE(CCHS) Regs
13 Reg 3(3) GE(CCHS) Regs
14 Ofgem, Supplier Performance on Consumer Complaints
15 Reg 6(1) GE(CCHS) Regs
16 Reg 4(1) GE(CCHS) Regs
17 Reg 3(3) GE(CCHS) Regs
18 Reg 4(5) GE(CCHS) Regs
19 Reg 4(6) GE(CCHS) Regs
20 Reg 4(4) GE(CCHS) Regs
21 Reg 2 GE(CCHS) Regs
22 Reg 11 GE(CCHS) Regs

3. Action by Ofgem
23 Condition 2 SLC
24 See *R v Director General of Gas Supply ex parte Smith* CO/1398/88 31 July 1989, unreported (QBD) citing *Lloyd and Others v McMahon* [1987] AC 625; [1987] 1 All 1118 Lord Bridge at pp702H to 703A
25 E(SP) Regs as amended by the Electricity and Gas (Standards of Performance) (Suppliers) (Amendment) Regulations 2020 No.116; EG(SP)S Regs
26 ss39, 39A and 39B EA 1989; Sch 3 E(SP) Regs
27 Reg 11(3) and Sch 2 EG(SP)S Regs; ofgem.gov.uk/information-consumers/energy-advice-households/check-compensation-rules-power-cut-or-supply-problem
28 Reg 5 E(SP) Regs
29 Reg 6(2) E(SP) Regs
30 Reg 11 EG(SP)S Regs
31 Practice Direction 7C CPR Part 7 and PD 5B
32 Reg 7 E(SP) Regs
33 Reg 8(2) EG(SP)S Regs
34 Reg 8(5) EG(SP)S Regs
35 Reg 8(7) EG(SP)S Regs
36 Reg 9(3) EG(SP)S Regs
37 EG(SP)S Regs amended by the Gas (Standards of Performance) (Amendment) Regulations 2021 No.257
38 s25 CEARA 2007
39 Sch 3 EA 2023
40 s25(3) EA 1989

41 s143 EA 2013
42 *R v Director-General of Gas Supply ex parte Smith* CO/1398/88, 31 July 1989, unreported (QBD)
43 s144 and Sch 14 EA 2013
44 s27G(1)(b) EA 2013
45 s27H(1)(a)-(c) EA 2013
46 Ofgem, *Financial Penalties and Consumer Redress Policy Statement,* 6 November 2014
47 Ofgem, *The Gas and Electricity Markets Authority's Statement of Policy with Respect to Financial Penalties and Consumer Redress Under the Gas Act and the Electricity Act,* para 1.4, 31 March 2014
48 Condition 8 SLC
49 Ofgem, *Supplier of Last Resort: revised guidance,* 21 October 2016
50 *Gas and Electricity Markets Authority v GB Energy Supply Ltd* [2016] EWHC 3341
51 Ofgem, *Avro Energy Customers: your questions on new supplier Octopus Energy,* 26 September 2021
52 s161 EA 2004; s96 EA 2011
53 s161(3)(b) EA 2004

4. Unfair terms
54 As amended by Part 7 The Consumer Protection (Amendment etc.) (EU Exit) Regulations 2018 No.1326
55 s75 and Sch 4 para 34 CRA 2015
56 s62(1) CRA 2015
57 s62(4) CRA 2015
58 s62(5) CRA 2015
59 *Tamarind and Others v Eastern Natural Gas and Eastern Energy* [2000] QBD 27
60 s68 CRA 2015
61 Sch 5 CRA 2015
62 Sch 2 CRA 2015
63 Reg 2(1) CPUT Regs
64 Reg 2(1) CPUT Regs
65 Reg 5 CPUT Regs
66 Reg 6 CPUT Regs
67 *R (Surrey Trading Standards) v Scottish and Southern Energy plc* [2012] EWCA Crim 539
68 *R (Surrey Trading Standards) v Scottish and Southern Energy plc* [2012] EWCA Crim 539
69 Cl 247 Digital Markets, Competition and Consumers Bill, February 2024

5. Using the civil courts
70 *Morrisons Sports Ltd v Scottish Power UK plc* [2011] UKSC 1
71 *Morrisons Sports Ltd v Scottish Power UK plc* [2011] UKSC 1

72 *R v Electricity Commissioners ex parte London Electricity Joint Committee Co* [1923] All ER Rep 150; *Npower Direct Ltd and Other Companies v Gas and Electricity Markets Authority (Competition and Markets Authority intervening)* [2018] EWHC 3576 (Admin)

73 s42 County Courts Act 1984

74 CPR Part 30.3

75 *McKenzie v McKenzie* [1970] 3 WLR 472

76 Part 36 CPR

77 *Oak Cash and Carry Ltd v British Gas Trading Ltd* [2016] EWCA Civ 153

78 *Mitchell v News Group Newspapers Ltd* [2013] EWCA Civ 1537

79 *Ferguson v British Gas* [2009] EWCA Civ 46

80 *Ferguson v British Gas* [2009] EWCA Civ 46 per Nicholls LJ and Jacobs LJ; *Shakil-Ur-Rahman v ARY Network Ltd and Ghafoor* [2016] EWHC 3110

81 *Say v British Gas Services Ltd* [2011] All ER (D) 216

82 *Gwenter v Eastern Electricity plc* [1994] August 1995 *Legal Action* 19

83 HCTS, *Court Fees for the High Court, County Court and Family Court,* 2 August 2016

84 *American Cyanamid Co v Ethicon Ltd* [1975] AC 396

85 *Massie v McCaig* [2013] SC 343; *British Gas Trading Ltd and Centrica PLC (Pursuers) against Derek McPherson (Defender)* [2020] CSOH A106/62

86 The principles are set out in *American Cyanamid v Ethicon Ltd* [1975] AC 396

87 *Gwenter v Eastern Electricity plc* [1994] August 1995 *Legal Action* 19

88 *Parker v Camden LBC; Newman and another v Camden LBC* [1985] 2 All ER 141

89 *Faulkner v Yorkshire Electricity plc* [1994] February 1995 *Legal Action* 23; *Gwenter v Eastern Electricity plc* [1994] August 1995 *Legal Action* 19

90 See *Red Star Pub Company (WRII) Ltd and Others v Scottish Power Ltd* [2016] CSOH 100

91 *Hartley v Mayoh & Co* [1953] 2 All ER 525; *Sellars v Best* [1954] 2 All ER 389

92 *Smith and Others v South Eastern Power Networks plc and Other Cases* [2012] EWHC 2541 QBD(TCC)

93 *Shepherd v Northern Gas Networks Ltd* [2022] (HC) Newcastle Upon Tyne District Registry, 14 April

94 Part 54 CPR

95 *Secretary of State for Energy and Climate Change v Friends of the Earth and Others* [2012] EWCA Civ 28

96 *Associated Provincial Picture Houses v Wednesbury Corporation* [1948] 1 KB 223

97 *British Oxygen Co Ltd v Minister for Technology* [1971] AC 610

98 *R v Director General of Gas Supply ex parte Smith* 1989, unreported and CO/1398/88, 31 July (QBD)

99 *R (Jeremy Cox) v (1)The Oil and Gas Authority Office (2) Secretary of State for Business and Energy and Industrial Strategy* [2022] EWHC 75 (Admin)

100 Ofgem, *Consumer Vulnerability Strategy,* 4 July 2013

101 *May-Lean & Co Ltd v Gas and Electricity Markets Authority* [2017] All ER (D) 78

102 *R (on the application of Summerleaze Ltd) v Secretary of State for Energy and Climate Change* [2015] EWHC 1729 (Admin)

103 Part 54 CPR

104 Practice Direction 54C; r7.1A CPR

105 Practice Direction 510 supplements CPR rr5.5 and 7.12

106 gov.uk/government/publications/administrative-court-judicial-review-guide

107 *R (on the application of Bloomsbury Institute Ltd) v Office for Students* [2020] EWHC 580 (Admin)

108 See *How to Apply for Help with Fees* (EX160A), at gov.uk/government/publications/apply-for-help-with-court-and-tribunal-fees/how-to-apply-for-help-with-fees-ex160A

6. The Energy Ombudsman

109 *R (on the application of Thakerar) v Ombudsman Service Energy* [2013] EWHC 2283

110 Energy Ombudsman, *Energy Ombudsman releases updated complaints data for 2024,* 5 September 2024

111 *R (on the application of Thakerar) v Ombudsman Service Energy* [2013] EWHC 2283

Appendix 1

Useful addresses

Fuel and energy industry bodies

Ofgem
10 South Colonnade
London E14 4PU
ofgem.gov.uk
Tel: 020 7901 7000

Ofgem Scotland
Commonwealth House
32 Albion Street
Glasgow G1 1LH
Tel: 0141 331 2678

Ofgem Wales
The Maltings
East Tyndall Street
Cardiff CF24 5EA

Gas Safe Register
PO Box 6804
Basingstoke RG24 4NB
Tel: 0800 408 5500
gassaferegister.co.uk

Energy UK
26 Finsbury Square
London EC2A 1DS
Tel: 020 7930 9390
energy-uk.org.uk

Consumer advice and information

Citizens Advice consumer service
Helpline: 0808 223 1133 (Relay UK service available)
Welsh speaking line: 0808 223 1144
Online chat: citizensadvice.org.uk/about-us/contact-us/contact-us/
consumer-service

Consumer Scotland
Email: info@consumer.scot
Advice Direct Scotland: 0808 800 9060
consumer.sco
Online chat: energyadvice.scot/#contact-us

Competition and Markets Authority
Victoria House
37 Southampton Row
London WC1B 4AD
Tel: 020 3738 6000
gov.uk/government/organisations/competition-and-markets-authority

Fuel campaigning and information organisations

Energy Action Scotland
eas.org.uk
Tel: 0141 226 3064

Energy Saving Trust (EST)
energysavingtrust.org.uk
EST England tel: 020 7222 0101
EST Wales tel: 0800 512 012
Home Energy Scotland tel: 0808 808 2282

Fuel Poverty Action
fuelpovertyaction.org.uk

National Energy Action
nea.org.uk
Tel: 0191 261 5677

National Energy Foundation
nef.org.uk
Tel: 01908 665 555

Appendix 2

Reading your meter

Electricity

There are four types of electricity meter in common use.

Standard credit meter

A standard meter measures electricity consumption in kilowatt hours (kWh) – the number of units of energy used in an hour. With this type of meter, all electricity units are charged at the same rate 24 hours a day. Most standard meters have an electronic or digital display showing a row of numbers. Older meters may have a dial display with four or more dials, each with a pointer.

Variable rate credit meter

A variable rate meter operates on the same principle as a standard meter but gives more than one reading display – ie, to show daytime, normal or peak electricity use, overnight or low off-peak use and (if appropriate) controlled circuit use. Customers with a variable rate credit meter will have either one or two meters showing up to three sets of numbers. The majority of these meters will have electronic or digital displays showing rows of numbers. A few customers may still have two dial display meters installed – one each for peak and off-peak consumption.

Prepayment meter

A prepayment meter measures electricity use in exactly the same way as a credit meter. A prepayment meter has a digital display screen which can show a range of information.

Smart meter

A smart meter is an electronic meter. It operates in the same way as a credit meter in terms of registering electricity consumption. Many smart meters have visual displays to highlight energy consumption levels. Most have a digital display which can show a range of information.

Reading your meter

The numbers on electronic and digital displays should always be read from left to right. Write down the first five numbers shown. Red numbers, or numbers after a decimal point, should be ignored.

If you want to work out how much electricity you use, write down the numbers and take a note of the date. The next time you take a reading subtract the second reading from the first and you will know how many units (kilowatt hours) you have used in the period since you took your first reading.

The same principle applies for reading dial meters. These should also be read from left to right, ignoring the final (usually red) dial. Write down the number closest to each pointer. If the pointer is between two numbers, write down the lower number, but if the pointer is between 9 and 0, write down 9.

If there are two rows of numbers, the top row is usually for off-peak and may be marked 'low' or 'night'. The bottom row is usually for peak and may be marked 'normal' or 'standard'.

Some variable rate meters have only one digital display. This type of meter will usually show the charging rate that's currently in use. These meters should have a button that will cycle through the readings for the different rates.

If you are working out how much electricity you have used, make sure you note clearly which reading is which.

Prepayment meters normally display the amount of credit remaining for use. To obtain a reading from a prepayment meter, you will have to press a button on the meter to change the digital display. Pressing the button repeatedly will allow you to cycle through the display screens (to return to the original screen, stop pressing the button). Every prepayment meter provides a range of information but all are configured slightly differently. However, most use letters to count the display screens and include displays for:

- current credit;
- total credit accepted – ie, amount topped up onto meter;
- reading for rate 1;
- price per unit for rate 1;
- reading for rate 2 (if appropriate);
- price per unit for rate 2;
- standing charge;
- amount available for emergency credit;
- debt repayment level (if appropriate).

Note: you may have to insert your key/card/token to view all the displays.

Gas

There are three types of gas meter in common use.

Standard credit meter

The majority of gas customers have a credit meter which records the amount of gas used. Gas consumption is measured in units. For many older meters – imperial meters – gas usage is measured in cubic feet. For newer metric meters, gas usage is measured in cubic metres.

Most standard meters have an electronic or digital display showing a row of four or five numbers. Older meters may have a dial display with four or more dials, each with a pointer.

Prepayment meter

A prepayment meter measures gas use in exactly the same way as a credit meter. A prepayment meter has a digital display screen which can show a range of information.

Smart meter

A smart meter is an electronic meter. It operates in the same way as a credit meter in terms of registering gas consumption. Many smart meters have visual displays to highlight energy consumption levels. Most have a digital display which can show a range of information.

Reading your meter

The numbers on electronic and digital displays should always be read from left to right. Red numbers, or numbers after a decimal point, should be ignored.

If you want to work out how much gas you use, write down the numbers and take a note of the date. The next time you take a reading, subtract the second reading from the first and you will know how many units you have used in the period since you took your first reading.

The same principle applies for reading dial meters. These should also be read from left to right, ignoring the final (usually red) dial. Write down the number closest to each pointer. If the pointer is between two numbers, write down the lower number, but if the pointer is between 9 and 0, write down 9.

Prepayment meters normally display the amount of credit remaining for use. To obtain a reading from a prepayment meter, you will have to press a button (this may be marked 'A') on the meter to change the digital display. Pressing the button repeatedly will allow you to cycle through the display screens. Every prepayment meter provides a range of information but all are configured slightly differently. However, most use letters to count the display screens and include displays for:

- current credit;
- last credit (most recent amount topped up. Displays on some meters may also show how much was paid towards gas consumption, emergency credit repayment and debt repayment);
- total credit accepted – ie, amount topped up onto meter;

- reading;
- price per unit;
- standing charge;
- amount available for emergency credit;
- debt repayment level (if appropriate);
- debt remaining.

Note: you may have to insert your key/card/token to view all the displays.

Submitting meter readings

If you want to provide meter readings to your supplier, you can do this online or over the phone. This will help ensure that any bills you receive are accurate, that weekly/monthly payment amounts are appropriate and it will help prevent debt building up on your account.

Calculating your costs

Before you can calculate the cost of your electricity and gas consumption, you will need to know what your tariff (the amount you pay for every kilowatt hour) is. You will find the specific name for your tariff on your fuel bill or your annual statement. Alternatively, you can phone your supplier to ask. Depending on the type of tariff you have, you will usually have a standing charge to pay along with the cost of your ongoing fuel use. This will also be shown on your bill and annual statement as a daily charge.

For gas consumption, you need to check your meter to see whether you have an old imperial meter or a newer metric meter. If it is an imperial meter measuring gas in cubic feet, it will usually have the words 'cubic feet' or 'Ft³' shown somewhere on the front of the meter. If it is a metric meter measuring gas in cubic metres it will usually show the words 'cubic metres' or 'M³'.

Your tariff for gas will be in kilowatt hours (kWh), so the readings from your gas meter need to be converted into kWh, so that you can then work out how much the fuel you use is costing. You can do this by:

- multiplying units used by 2.83 to give the number of cubic metres of gas used (if the meter is a newer metric one measuring gas in cubic metres this part of the calculation is not needed);
- multiplying by the temperature and pressure figure (1.02264);
- multiplying by calorific value (approximately 39.5, though the exact calorific value can be found on a gas bill);
- dividing by 3.6 to get the number of kWh.

Appendix 3
Vulnerable situations

From *Taking Control of Goods: National Standards* issued by the Ministry of Justice on 6 April 2014. The full document is available at gov.uk/government/publications/bailiffs-and-enforcement-agents-national-standards.

70. Enforcement agents/agencies and creditors must recognise that they each have a role in ensuring that the vulnerable and socially excluded are protected and that the recovery process includes procedures agreed between the agent/agency and creditor about how such situations should be dealt with. The appropriate use of discretion is essential in every case and no amount of guidance could cover every situation. Therefore the agent has a duty to contact the creditor and report the circumstances in situations where there is evidence of a potential cause for concern.

71. If necessary, the enforcement agent will advise the creditor if further action is appropriate. The exercise of appropriate discretion is needed, not only to protect the debtor, but also the enforcement agent who should avoid taking action which could lead to accusations of inappropriate behaviour.

72. Enforcement agents must withdraw from domestic premises if the only person present is, or appears to be, under the age of 16 or is deemed to be vulnerable by the enforcement agent; they can ask when the debtor will be home – if appropriate.

73. Enforcement agents must withdraw without making enquiries if the only persons present are children who appear to be under the age of 12.

74. A debtor may be considered vulnerable if, for reasons of age, health or disability they are unable to safeguard their personal welfare or the personal welfare of other members of the household.

75. The enforcement agent must be sure that the debtor or the person to whom they are entering into a controlled goods agreement understands the agreement and the consequences if the agreement is not complied with.

76. Enforcement agents should be aware that vulnerability may not be immediately obvious.

77. Some groups who might be vulnerable are listed below. However, this list is not exhaustive. Care should be taken to assess each situation on a case by case basis.

- the elderly;
- people with a disability;
- the seriously ill;
- the recently bereaved;
- single parent families;
- pregnant women;
- unemployed people; and,
- those who have obvious difficulty in understanding, speaking or reading English.

78. Wherever possible, enforcement agents should have arrangements in place for rapidly accessing interpretation services (including British Sign Language), when these are needed, and provide on request information in large print or in Braille for debtors with impaired sight.

Appendix 4

Abbreviations used in the notes

AC	Appeal Cases
All ER	All England Reports
Art(s)	Article(s)
CA	Court of Appeal
CPR	Civil Procedure Rules
Crim LR	Criminal Law Reports
EWCA Civ	England and Wales Court of Appeal (Civil Division)
EWHC	England and Wales High Court
LC	Lands Chamber
Para	paragraph
QB	Queen's Bench Reports
r(r)	rule(s)
Reg(s)	Regulation(s)
s(s)	section(s)
Sch(s)	Schedule(s)
ScotCS	Scottish Court of Session
SLC	Standard Licence Conditions 2021
UKSC	United Kingdom Supreme Court
UKUT	United Kingdom Upper Tribunal
WLR	Weekly Law Reports

Acts of Parliament

CEARA 2007	The Consumers, Estate Agents and Redress Act 2007
CRA 2015	Consumer Rights Act 2015
DA 2015	Deregulation Act 2015
DPA 1972	The Defective Premises Act 1972
EA 1989	The Electricity Act 1989
EA 2013	Energy Act 2013

EA 2023	Energy Act 2023
EPA 2022	Energy Prices Act 2022
GA 1986	The Gas Act 1986
GA 1995	The Gas Act 1995
HA 1980	The Housing Act 1980
HA 1985	The Housing Act 1985
H(S)A 1987	The Housing (Scotland) Act 1987
H(S)A 2006	The Housing (Scotland) Act 2006
IA 1986	The Insolvency Act 1986
LG(MP)A 1976	The Local Government (Miscellaneous Provisions) Act 1976
LTA 1985	The Landlord and Tenant Act 1985
RE(GEB)A 1954	Rights of Entry (Gas and Electricity Boards) Act 1954
R(S)A 1984	The Rent (Scotland) Act 1984
TA 1968	Theft Act 1968
UA 2000	The Utilities Act 2000

Regulations and other statutory instruments

CPUT Regs	The Consumer Protection From Unfair Trading Regulations 2008 No.1277
DRS Regs	The Debt Respite Scheme (Breathing Space Moratorium and Mental Health Crisis Moratorium) (England and Wales) Regulations 2020 No.1311
E(CSP) Regs	The Electricity (Connection Standards of Performance) Regulations 2015 No.698
E(PM) Regs	The Electricity (Prepayment Meter) Regulations 2006 No.2010
E(SP) Regs	The Electricity (Standards of Performance) Regulations 2015 No.699
EE(PRP)(EW) Regs	The Energy Efficiency (Private Rented Property) (England and Wales) Regulations 2015 No.962
EG(SP)S Regs	The Electricity and Gas (Standards of Performance) (Suppliers) Regulations 2015 No.1544
EPB(EW) Regs	The Energy Performance of Buildings (England and Wales) Regulations 2012 No.3118
EPB(S) Regs	The Energy Performance of Buildings (Scotland) Regulations 2008 No.309
ESQC Regs	The Electricity Safety, Quality and Continuity Regulations 2002 No.2665
G(PM) Regs	The Gas (Prepayment Meter) Regulations 2006 No.2011

G(SP) Regs	The Gas (Standards of Performance) Regulations 2005 No.1135
GE(CCHS) Regs	The Gas and Electricity (Consumer Complaints Handling Standards) Regulations 2008 No.1898
GS(IU) Regs	The Gas Safety (Installation and Use) Regulations 1998 No.2451
GS(RE) Regs	The Gas Safety (Rights of Entry) Regulations 1996 No.2535
HB Regs	The Housing Benefit Regulations 2006 No.213
HB(SPC) Regs	The Housing Benefit (Persons who have attained the qualifying age for State Pension Credit) Regulations 2006 No.214
SFCWP Regs	The Social Fund Cold Weather Payments (General) Regulations 1988 No.1724
SFWFP Regs	The Social Fund Winter Fuel Payments Regulations 2024 No.869
SS(C&P) Regs	The Social Security (Claims and Payments) Regulations 1987 No.1968
UC Regs	The Universal Credit Regulations 2013 No.376
UC,PIP, JSA&ESA(CP) Regs	The Universal Credit, Personal Independence Payment, Jobseeker's Allowance and Employment and Support Allowance (Claims and Payments) Regulations 2013 No.380
WHD Regs	The Warm Home Discount (England and Wales) Regulations 2022 No.722
WND(EW) Regs	The Warm Home Discount (Scotland) Regulations 2022 No.1073

Index

How to use this Index

Entries against the bold headings direct you to the general information on the subject, or where the subject is covered most fully. Sub-entries are listed alphabetically and direct you to specific aspects of the subject.